PRAISE FOR *I'LL TAKE YOU THERE*

"Mavis Staples and the Staple Singers are a mighty river running through more than a half-century of song, connecting Sam Cooke to Prince and Bob Dylan to Wilco. Thoroughly researched and elegantly told, *I'll Take You There* offers powerful and inspiring insight into not only American music but American history."

—Alan Light, author of *The Holy or the Broken: Leonard Cohen, Jeff Buckley, and the Unlikely Ascent of "Hallelujah"*

"Involving from beginning to end . . . [Kot] charts the [Staples] family's origins in gospel music; their gradual drift into folk, soul, and pop; the reverberations of their increasingly political songs during the civil rights era. . . . *I'll Take You There* . . . is rich musical history."

—*The New York Times*

"Emotional honesty resonates throughout *I'll Take You There*. Kot provides an unflinching look into the Stapleses' struggles to maintain their spiritual and artistic integrity. . . . *I'll Take You There* is a biography that's well worth the heavenly journey."

—NPR

"Kot depicts the endurance of Mavis Staples and her family's music as an inspiration, a saga that takes us, like the song that inspired this book's name, to a place where ain't nobody crying."

—*The Washington Post*

"[*I'll Take You There*] takes us deep into the golden age of Mavis and her marvelously talented group."

—*Publishers Weekly*

"A biography that will send readers back to the music of Mavis and the Staple Singers with deepened appreciation and a renewed spirit of discovery. . . . Through it all, the ebullience of Mavis Staples and her music shines through."

—*Kirkus Reviews* (starred review)

"Kot chronicles the amazing story of a family that went from a hardscrabble life in Mississippi to Chicago's church circuit to worldwide fame, merging the genres of roots, gospel, and soul. . . . This is a moving tribute to a very talented family and one gracious woman, in particular."

—*Booklist* (starred review)

"A lively, engaging family biography, written with the Stapleses' cooperation and filled with vivid portraits, celebrity cameos, and descriptions of music so evocative I kept wishing the book had come with a set of CDs."

—*Tampa Bay Times*

"Kot's take on the singer's immense discography is invaluable, and Staples's indomitable spirit shines through."

—*The A. V. Club*

"A thorough and illuminating biography that offers plenty of revealing details about a group the Band's Robbie Robertson once likened to 'a lonely train in the distance.'"

—*Paste Magazine*

"Remarkable . . . With Mavis opening up the Staples archives and providing access to family and friends, Kot . . . [shapes] a story bigger than just that of a singing group."

—*The Commercial Appeal*

"A darn good story . . . Whisking readers over a span of nearly 100 years, author Kot presents a roller-coaster ride of the highs and lows of one of gospel and soul's most iconic families. . . . A great look at history, both musically and culturally . . . If you're a fan of soul, R&B, or gospel, *I'll Take You There* is a book you'll want to corner."

—*The Topeka Capital-Journal*

"That Staples's life story is deeply intertwined with the Rev. Martin Luther King Jr., Sam Cooke, the Band, Bob Dylan, Lou Rawls, Jeff Tweedy, Prince, Aretha Franklin, Mahalia Jackson, Jesse Jackson, Curtis Mayfield, Stax Records, and Jerry Butler is no mean feat. . . . The gems are here in all their richness."

—*Windy City Times*

"Fascinating . . . Musical analysis doesn't get much better."

—*DownBeat*

"A fascinating testimony . . . Kot's portrayal of Mavis is deft and balanced, worthy of a performance that, no matter how often you play it, never fails to live up to the promise of its title."

—*Chicago Tribune*

I'll Take You There

Mavis Staples, the Staple Singers, and the Music That Shaped the Civil Rights Era

Greg Kot

SCRIBNER

New York London Toronto Sydney New Delhi

Scribner
A Division of Simon & Schuster, Inc.
1230 Avenue of the Americas
New York, NY 10020

First Scribner trade paperback edition November 2014

SCRIBNER and design are registered trademarks of The Gale Group, Inc.,
used under license by Simon & Schuster, Inc., the publisher of this work.

For information about special discounts for bulk purchases,
please contact Simon & Schuster Special Sales at 1-866-506-1949 or
business@simonandschuster.com.

The Simon & Schuster Speakers Bureau can bring authors to your
live event. For more information or to book an event contact the
Simon & Schuster Speakers Bureau at 1-866-248-3049 or
visit our website at www.simonspeakers.com.

Book design by Ellen R. Sasahara
Cover design by Jason Heuer
Cover photograph © Jim Marshall Photography LLC
Back cover photographs courtesy of the Staples family

Manufactured in the United States of America

5 7 9 10 8 6

The Library of Congress has cataloged the hardcover edition as follows:

Kot, Greg.
I'll take you there : Mavis Staples, the Staple Singers, and the march up
freedom's highway / Greg Kot.
pages ; cm
1. Staples, Mavis. 2. Staple Singers. 3. Gospel musicians—United States—
Biography. I. Title.
ML400.K873 2014
782.25'40922—dc23 2013032633
[B]

ISBN 978-1-4516-4785-3
ISBN 978-1-4516-4786-0 (pbk)
ISBN 978-1-4516-4787-7 (ebook)

All insert photographs courtesy of the Staples family except where noted.

For Deb, Katie, and Marissa, always

Contents

~

I'll Take
You There

Prologue

"Freedom Highway" in sequined flats

I'm tired and I'm feeble," declares Mavis Staples, with a high-beam smile that says exactly the opposite.

Mavis pretends to shuffle into the room as though a step away from collapse while paraphrasing Thomas Dorsey's "Take My Hand, Precious Lord," a song that has been with her since she started to stir church congregations as an eight-year-old vocalist. Her sister Yvonne rolls her eyes in mock exasperation. A small flock of onlookers starts to laugh, breaks away from their backstage hospitality beers, and surges toward the sisters to clasp hands and offer hugs in a kind of group anointing.

Mavis and Yvonne—cofounders of the Staple Singers with their father, Roebuck "Pops" Staples, and siblings Pervis and Cleotha—have arrived at the Hideout, an unassuming Chicago bar tucked amid West Side warehouses. In a few minutes they will be on a big stage outdoors in front of a hometown festival crowd of eight thousand just as the sun is disappearing on a mid-September day in 2011. Mavis and Yvonne, both in their seventies, have been up since 5 a.m. after playing a show the night before in Michigan. Mavis has been pumping vitamin C to fight off a cold and a scratchy voice. "This is loosening me up, though," she says as laughter and conversation fill the Hideout's back room.

Donny Gerrard, one of her backing vocalists, does not by any stretch consider himself a gospel singer, or even a believer. But Mavis has a way of pulling even skeptics along in her wake. She is an artist who grew up in church and on the civil rights battlefront, but she doesn't fingerpoint, preach, or prod. She leads with her enthusiasm for the day ahead.

"When I was asked to join her group, I was worried about the God stuff, frankly," says Gerrard, adjusting his tortoiseshell glasses as he watches Mavis banter with her well-wishers. "Don't believe in it, myself. But damn, if she doesn't make you feel something else is at work when she's around."

The tall, curly-haired singer takes off the glasses, and his eyes gleam. He's ridden the music industry roller coaster in a career that has had failures, hits (he sang Skylark's huge '70s single "Wildflower"), and a few health problems.

"It doesn't matter how low you feel," he says. "Sometimes I carry it on the stage with me, and then I see Mavis and it's like you can't feel down anymore. She's always up no matter what happened that day."

Mavis looks into her carrying bag and with the drama of a magician makes an announcement: "I know what the stage needs!" She digs out the prize. "It needs glitter! Every singer needs her stage flats, sequined flats!"

A dozen onlookers scramble for their cell phones to take photos of the diva wear. "Y'all are some slow paparazzis." Mavis laughs as the amateur photographers click away and begin texting, tweeting, and Instagramming their friends.

Mavis, her glitter flats and matching sequined black scarf ascend the five steps onto the stage to cheers that stretch across a vast lot. Fans perched in windows and on rooftops of the buildings beyond wave their greetings. Yvonne, just off her sister's right shoulder, is clapping just as boisterously. Nonbeliever Gerrard joins Mavis, Yvonne, and their band in an a cappella version of "Wonderful Savior": "I am His, and He is mine." Within seconds, the audience turns into Mavis's moonlight choir with their rhythmic clapping.

Violin-playing indie-rocker Andrew Bird joins for The Band's "The Weight," which the Staple Singers had performed as part of *The Last Waltz* concert in 1976. Bird and Gerrard each take a verse, and then Mavis "takes it to church," as her old friend Levon Helm used to say, a tambourine accenting every beat. Mavis twirls her hands above her head, and Yvonne is loving it, applauding her sister's feistiness. Bring it on, Mavis roars, as she slaps her chest. "Put the load, put the load, put the load right on me."

When the Staple Singers' civil rights anthem "Freedom Highway" arrives, the band rolls into a marching beat and the call-and-response vocals between Mavis and her backing singers pick up the pace, more urgent with each turn. "March!" "Up freedom's highway!" It is an echo of '60s freedom marches, the sound of citizen soldiers girding for a beatdown, in the name of a cause that they believe is worth their blood and tears, and quite possibly their lives.

"My father, Pop Staples, wrote that song in 1965," Mavis says as the anthem winds down. "Yes, he did, he wrote it for the big march from Selma to Montgomery, Alabama. We marched, we marched, and we marched, and it ain't over yet!"

The band rumbles, voices from the audience shout encouragement. Most of the fans weren't even born when activists, ministers, and everyday citizens locked arms and marched into a gauntlet of police clubs, snarling dogs, and water cannons in the name of racial equality.

"I'm still on that highway," Mavis says. "And I will be there until Dr. Martin Luther King's dream has been realized."

At the side of the stage, the teenage Chicago musician Liam Cunningham is watching with a few members of his band, Kids These Days, who had played earlier in the day. They've read about the freedom marches in school, seen the news footage of the shaking fists and swinging police batons. Now they're standing a few feet from one of the leading messengers of that era. Cunningham is mesmerized. "Her existence brings tears to my eyes," he says softly.

The show doesn't so much conclude as get passed on, one voice to the next. Mavis hands the closing duties to the audience, which embraces a twelve-minute version of the Staple Singers' "I'll Take You There" and sings it back to her. Mavis waves and exits alongside Yvonne, then hugs her brother, Pervis, who is standing in the wings applauding. She and her sister slide into a waiting black limousine behind the stage, roll down a tinted window, and wave to a small group of fans.

"Time to remove the sequined flats," Mavis says with a laugh. "They got more work to do."

1

Voices in the Mississippi night

One gray, cold Mississippi Delta day in 1920, five-year-old Roebuck Staples peered out his window and saw a mule-driven wagon slowly approach his family home to take his mother away. After giving birth to, cooking for, and looking after fourteen children, all the while toiling in the cotton fields, Florence Staples's heart had finally given out.

Rain began to pummel the funeral procession as it marched the Staples family matriarch several miles to her grave in the nearby town of Drew. Young Roebuck was in a daze, miserable in the rain and still trying to come to grips with the tragedy that had suddenly landed on his family. What happened next astonished him. As the procession trudged along the muddy, rain-splattered road, a white man hurried out the front door of his home toward the wagon with a blanket in his arms. He gently draped it over the coffin and ran back.

In Roebuck's world, blacks and whites lived and worked in close proximity but rarely interacted, and then only in matters of business. If a white person ever approached, it was usually from a position of strength, condescension, or hostility. Roebuck had already been warned by his father to keep his distance from their white neighbors on the Dockery Plantation.

The blanket bearer's gesture lingered in Roebuck's mind for decades. "Some human conditions, like death, override adversity or hostility between the races," he mused a few years before his own death in 2000. "Sometimes kindness slips through the cracks of bigotry and racial hatred."

Born December 28, 1914, in Winona, Mississippi, Roebuck was the seventh son of Warren and Florence Staples. When he arrived, his mother broke out in a fever and was bedridden, postponing the wedding of one of Roebuck's older sisters, Rosie. His thirteenth sibling, Flora, was born two years later. As soon as the baby learned to walk, she and Roebuck became playmates, commanding a huge front yard on which they'd make mud pies. Their bubble of not-a-care-in-the-world security burst when Florence died.

A few years after his mother's funeral, Roebuck stood still long enough to have his portrait taken. The boy in the straw hat and overalls looks as if he's sizing up the photographer from behind almond-shaped eyes as much as posing for him. His smooth, unblemished skin makes the hardness all the more unsettling: the determined jaw, an unsmiling mouth, the chest thrust back with hands resting confidently on hips.

Soon after the photo was taken, Roebuck lost his beloved Flora, too. As the youngest, his sister was assigned indoor work such as starting the stove. One day, as she was dousing the wood with kerosene from a five-gallon can, it exploded in her hands. She died from the extensive burns.

By then, Roebuck was already a working man. He carried wood, milked the cows, and eventually joined his older siblings in the cotton fields at Dockery Farms. His days began and ended in darkness, defined from sunup to sundown by an exhausting routine of plowing, planting, chopping, and picking balls of cotton. Thorns split the skin on his hands and tore up his fingernails. The soles of his feet became hard and calloused as he worked barefoot from April to October.

The Southern economy had been built for centuries on the backs of black men and women much like Warren and Florence Staples. Warren's father, William, had been a slave who defied bullets and bullwhips to live to be 103 years old and to see his emancipation—if not true "freedom" in the Jim Crow South.

"Legend has it that [William Staples] was a very good worker . . . but he was a 'crazy Negro' so [the white slave owners] stopped bothering him," Roebuck said. "One day Grandpa got to tangling with the white man. He struck his master and the mistress got to hollering to bring the bullwhip." William ran and was shot by one of the plantation security guards, but he somehow managed to stagger off into the woods and escape.

"Grandpa just flew away. He stayed away until he got so hungry that he had to go back to the old master. They took him back, fixed his wound, fed him, and nursed him back to health until he was well. But Grandpa said that the old master gave his wife hell for having him shot because he was a good worker and was not supposed to be shot up. People always said that if a 'nigger' hit a white man, he was crazy. . . . But Grandpa was respected because he had a good reputation. In those days, a man's reputation was his passport out of trouble."

The tale was passed down the Staples family line as a personal code for coping with racism, a guide for surviving in the world of the white man without groveling. A man or woman's reputation did matter in the divided South. The boss man could insult you, beat you, even try to kill you, but dignity and pride were held sacred in the home of Warren Staples. As a member of his family, you did not buckle.

"My father never did allow a white man to ride over us," Roebuck said. Warren Staples would gather the family and illustrate stories and parables from the Bible. Once, he grabbed a bundle of twigs from the field and tried unsuccessfully to crack them over his knee. Then he took the twigs one at a time and broke each in half. "This," he said, "is what can happen to a family if it doesn't stick together."

Mavis Staples nods when the story is recounted to her years later. "Whenever we'd go into town down South to buy something, Pops would always say don't start nothin' . . . but don't take nothin' either. And he never did take nothin' from anybody as long as he was alive."

Warren Staples tried to make a go of it as a farmer and landowner in the forested hill country near Winona at the turn of the twentieth century. Roebuck was born in Winona, but by the time he was two, Warren had sold the farm and moved the family to the more fertile Mississippi Delta region southwest of Drew. He rented about 150 acres on the northern edge of Dockery Plantation and grew corn, cotton, white potatoes, peaches, peanuts, tomatoes, watermelon, and raised cattle.

The Delta is a 250-mile leaf-shaped plain that stretches from just outside Memphis to Vicksburg, bounded by the Mississippi River on the west and the hill country on the east. The plantations and towns within that region became the center of the cotton industry; at one time Drew was reputed to have more cotton gins than any other town in America.

Will Dockery had established his farm on forty square miles not far from the Sunflower River in 1895, using a $1,000 inheritance from his grandmother as seed money. The swampy land was cleared of trees and a town established with an elementary school, churches, a gin mill, a blacksmith, a doctor's office, and picnic grounds. The Peavine railroad ran through the plantation connecting Cleveland and Rosedale, the largest town on the Mississippi between Memphis and Greenville. The plantation owners hired cheap labor to help them farm the property; they provided seed, tools, livestock, and shelter, and paid a wage of about 50 cents a day per worker. Dockery had a reputation for fairness, but many working-class whites stayed away because the land was infested with malaria-carrying mosquitoes, so blacks tended to make up the vast majority of the four hundred tenant families employed at the farm's peak. When the cotton was sold after harvest, each family of sharecroppers received a share of the proceeds—minus the landowner's costs, which often exceeded the sharecroppers' earnings from the crop.

Little wonder that despite working his family and a team of mules nearly year-round in the fields, Warren Staples could never climb out of debt to his boss, Liston Sage. As far as young Roebuck was concerned, Warren Staples's sharecropping life sure looked like just another version of William Staples's slavery.

"It was just pitiful," Roebuck recalled. "I would be feeling so bad, and after all that work the man would tell us, 'You almost made it, maybe next year you'll do it.' He would give you a rebate and let you borrow on your next crop. We stayed in the cycle of debt."

Whereas on the farm Warren Staples went to great lengths to keep his family out of harm's way—which meant as little contact as possible with white people—the same was not true when his teenage sons ventured into Drew, a town of about eight hundred in which blacks were barely tolerated by the white population. A black man had to scurry to the other side of the street whenever he encountered any whites heading toward him. One time, Roebuck didn't change course as a group of white boys approached and got a lit cigarette shoved down his shirt for his impudence. In another instance, Roebuck's older brother Sears got in an argument with a grocer, and he and Roebuck were chased out of the store by the gun-wielding proprietor. Their father feared they'd be lynched and so stowed his two sons at his married sister's plantation about twenty miles away. After three days, Warren was able to make peace with the store's owner, and the two chastened brothers returned home.

Not all was sweat and grind and worry. Whenever Roebuck got the chance, he joined the other black kids on the plantation for a game of baseball at the park diamond on the north side of Drew. They had to wait till the white kids were through before taking the field, but the games were fiercely contested and Roebuck excelled as a fastball-chucking pitcher. He learned to race his father's horses; twenty-five-pound sacks of pecans helped bolster his weight and kept young Roebuck securely aboard his favorite ride, a blue-blond stallion named Dan. By the time Roebuck grew into a 140-pound teenager, he was fighting barefoot in local competitions at a plantation south of Drew in Ruleville. If nothing else, it brought out the entrepreneur in the young pugilist, who won five fights and went home with his pockets stuffed with cash thrown into the ring by approving gamblers, far more than he could make in the cotton fields.

True solace was found in music—in the churches, where black people could be themselves outside the glare of white scrutiny; in the fields, where songs of faith and fortitude sustained the field hands against the sun's relentless glare; and in the home, as parents and children unwound after supper.

Each night, the Staples family gathered on the long front gallery of their home to sing the hymns that were part of Methodist Sunday service at their rickety wooden church: "Amazing Grace," "Everybody Will Be Happy Over There," "Steal Away Home to Jesus," "Will the Circle Be Unbroken."

The dusk was filled with voices that carried across the fields, calling out to the other black families on the plantation. Couples and their children would stroll onto the Stapleses' wide front yard and join in the four-part harmonies they had honed in church. Shouting and syncopated handclapping would break out, as the singers slipped into a particularly beloved melody and stretched it out, as if to draw out the song's spirit and beckon it to linger awhile longer in the moonlit Mississippi night. The songs often mingled sadness and hope, expressed as yearning: "Is a better home awaiting / In the sky, in the sky?"

"I was kind of ashamed to be black," Roebuck said decades later. "I didn't want to be black. It was because we lived near white people. My little friend next door was having everything so good. I wished I had what he had. The bus would come and take him to school in town. We had our school in a church, two or three grades in one room, all trying to recite at the same time. But like we sing, 'I like the things about me that I once despised.' I woke up one morning to see we had found our natural self and I thought, 'Here it is, we're coming to ourself.'"

For African Americans on the plantation, music spoke to their better selves and comforted them with the possibility of a better life—if not in this world, then in the next one. The music in the Staples home was strictly spiritual. Blues was the music of sinners, boozers, and women chasers, and Roebuck was expressly forbidden to partake. That only served to pique his curiosity, however. His brother David had acquired a guitar and learned to play it proficiently. By age twelve, Roebuck was hooked. A few years later, he spotted two $5 Stellar guitars at a hardware store on the north end of Main Street in Drew and paid the owner 50 cents a week until he acquired one of them. He would run home each day from the fields to be reunited with his new companion, even taking it to bed with him, strumming it quietly beneath the covers until his father would run out of patience and tell him to knock it off.

With fourteen children, Warren Staples couldn't be the gatekeeper for all of them twenty-four hours a day. Roebuck was a hard worker, but as the youngest son he developed a fierce sense not only of competitiveness, never wanting to be outdone by his older siblings, but also of adventure, a desire to see if there was another life available to him beyond the one he and his family already knew. He ventured out whenever possible to explore all the pleasures his corner of Mississippi had to offer. There was music everywhere—not just gospel in the churches and at home, but also the illicit blues in the streets of Dockery Farms and Drew. Dockery and other nearby plantations would become the cradle of much of the blues music that would permeate the twentieth century, and to Roebuck Staples the center of that world was a brick hardware store by the train tracks.

There he encountered Charley Patton, who lived on the lower plantation. He would set up outside the store on Saturday afternoons after most of the workers retired from the fields for the weekend. Patton, born around 1890, was in his prime when young Roebuck first saw him in the late 1920s. The singer was a mere five foot five, but he played with such ferocity and passion that he seemed much larger. Patton was a charismatic entertainer who pounded his feet, rapped on his guitar, and flipped it in the air while performing. He sang with a gravelly howl that made another young Dockery Farms blues upstart, Chester Burnett, later known as Howlin' Wolf, take notice. In the next instance, Patton could deliver a deep blues of harrowing intensity such as "High Water

Everywhere" or sing about plantation life with knowing veracity in "Pea
Vine Blues" and "34 Blues." Besides the allure of his music, there was
the symbolism of what he represented: a free man who didn't have to
sharecrop to eat, who could come and go as he pleased, making records
and playing for people in far-off towns.

After seeing that, even with his hands raw and bleeding beneath the
cotton-picking sun, Roebuck could envision those same hands playing
the guitar and making records. The notion of getting off the farm that
had been bubbling inside Roebuck's head since he was nine now took
human dimension. Patton, Wolf, Willie Brown, Henry Sloan, Tommy
Johnson, and other guitar-playing bluesmen who entertained the plantation workers shouted that there was a better life out there—anywhere
but here.

Roebuck studied the guitar players, how their hands moved up and
down the frets. "They mostly played in the key of E, which is a blues key,
and they'd jump off something fast every once in a while, too," Roebuck
recounted in a 1964 interview. "That sold me on guitar. My greatest
ambition was then to play and record."

By the time he was sixteen, Roebuck had grown proficient enough
on guitar to entertain workers high on booze and eager to grind on the
dance floor with their ladies on the local chitlin circuit. Separate rooms
would be set up at the designated plantation house of the night for dancing, eating, and gambling. Backroom stills would crank out home brew
and white lightning.

"We would sing the blues and gamble while the ladies would be in
the kitchen cooking chitlins and greens," Roebuck said. "Folks would
dance: the slow drag, the black bottom, the Charleston."

And best of all, a blues guitar player could make money—good
money. The house-party landlord would collect cash at the door and
then pay the musicians who helped draw the crowd. Roebuck could
make as much as $5 a night—an extraordinary haul by the lowly wage
standards of a sharecropper.

But Roebuck didn't entirely rebel against the music so dear to his family and especially his father. He also sang with the choir at church and then later with a gospel quartet, the Golden Trumpets.

"I was one of the directors and in the country we'd go to different churches," he said in '64. "We'd have huge crowds, and some beautiful singing, beautiful gospel singing, and I was inspired when I was a little boy from my older sisters and brothers who used to rehearse in our house, and from there I tried to catch on a little bit."

In these settings, his guitar was forbidden, even though in his own head the blues and gospel were like concurrent, even complementary streams. His father looked at the blues with contempt: The "devil's music," he called it. Many of the churchgoing adults "looked down on it, they didn't want you to touch it," Roebuck recalled. But in his own mind, he saw more similarities than differences between the two styles: "A Christian should sing God's praises, but there are some things that some people call a sin that I don't see as such. Singing the blues is telling a story, and it's telling a true story. You take all those [blues] guys, they're talking about a woman. They're talking about experience—that's all it is."

It was a trait Roebuck would demonstrate throughout his life, a balance of practicality and faith. The blues could pay the bills; gospel spoke to his heart. He didn't see any disconnect as long as each was performed with sincerity. At the plantation store, Roebuck heard music that connected blues and spirituality in a way that his strict family upbringing denied. The 78 rpm recordings of Blind Willie Johnson combined deep blues feeling with lyrics steeped in visions of the afterlife. Johnson "was the most moving of all country religious performers," Roebuck said, and "exerted a profound and lasting influence on me." He would stand transfixed by these recordings, goose bumps pimpling his arms, as Johnson moaned over a shivering slide guitar about the crucifixion of Jesus on "Dark Was the Night, Cold Was the Ground." On "Keep Your Light Trimmed and Burning," Johnson's vocals are answered by a female singer, likely Willie B. Harris. The blues man's voice evoked some of the singing Roebuck heard at revival meetings in churches on the farm.

"The old people'd be singing the familiar hymns . . . and some old sister way over in the 'Amen Corner' would begin to moan," Pops recalled. "I didn't understand that language. And I asked my father when I got home. I said, 'What does she mean by moaning?' Old man says, 'Son, when you moan, even the devil don't know what you talking about.'"

Music was Roebuck's greatest passion—with one exception. When he was eleven, he met a nine-year-old beauty named Oceola Ware in his grade school, and the two courted as teenagers. Born in Greenville, Mississippi, Oceola moved as a child with her parents and four siblings nearer to Drew to work the cotton fields. Over both families' objections, she and Pops were married in 1933; she was only sixteen, Roebuck eighteen. A daughter, Cleotha, was born to the young couple in April 1934 and a son, Pervis, followed in November 1935.

By this point, Roebuck had his compass pointed north. To him, the South offered no future, no viable means of supporting his family. As with his marriage to Oceola, Roebuck's family was less than enthused about his plans. "You ain't never been nowhere," his father declared, incredulous that his son would want to leave the only world he had ever known.

"His brothers were all older than him and they were all giving him advice, too," Pervis Staples says. "One time Uncle John told Pops, 'You're a hell of a man, Roebuck, but you'll never be the man I am.' They trained the behavior pattern, you stayed in line and worked for the old man until he died, and then you died."

But Roebuck was listening to a different set of advisers, and they could not be denied. One in particular struck a chord because he laid out a possible future so succinctly: "I'm going to Detroit, get myself a good job."

In 1995 at the Cultural Center in Chicago, Roebuck Staples sat and finger-picked a talking blues on his guitar that invoked the moment when he first heard Blind Blake's "Detroit Bound Blues."

"I said, 'What did that man say?'" Pops gently sang. "The blues man always says what's on his mind twice. He said it again: 'I'm going to Detroit, get myself a good job . . .' I said, 'That's it, that's what I'm gonna do.' I started right then and there saving my money. . . . Down there, I could hardly make it. My clothes had holes in 'em. I was so close to being naked, they called me 'Few Clothes.' I'd be comin' by and they'd say, 'Here comes Few Clothes.' But that's all right, the Lord took care of me."

Except Roebuck had a different destination in mind than Blind Blake, a place where his brother John and Oceola's uncle already had moved. After a year of saving, Roebuck had scrounged together the $12 bus fare to Chicago.

2

Hard time killing floor

When Roebuck Staples stepped off the bus in Chicago in the first weeks of 1936, he immediately felt out of place. His summer clothes and thin jacket were no match for the shock of winter in the shadow of the downtown skyscrapers and the Great Depression. Men stood shivering in breadlines and walked the streets looking for work, food, an extra blanket. Roebuck wondered if he'd be joining them in a couple of months.

But Roebuck was never going back to the cotton fields if he could help it, no matter how out of place he felt in this cold, dirty city. He had left his guitar and his musical aspirations back home in the Delta. Everything was about finding a job, an apartment, and a new start for his family. After three months, he sent for Oceola, who showed up at the 12th Street train station with Pervis bundled in her arms and Cleotha gripping her hand. Roebuck had landed a job in a place called the House of Blood.

In 1931, one of the blues musicians working around the Delta, Skip James, had recorded a song about Roebuck's new place of employment: "Hard Time Killing Floor Blues." "Lord, I'll never get down this low no mo'," he wailed.

The Union Stock Yard & Transit Company was a 475-acre market that had been a central industry for Chicago since the year the Civil War ended. Stretching from Pershing Avenue to 47th Street on the West Side, it was indeed a killing floor, a House of Blood, a place where tens of thousands of workers butchered and shipped millions of hogs and cattle annually.

Roebuck found himself working alongside not only fellow blacks newly arrived from the South but also immigrants from Eastern Europe and Mexico, many of whom could barely speak English. Little skill was involved. Endurance and muscle mattered more. Side by side they worked on blood-soaked floors in the slaughterhouses, where the stench of raw meat, blood, and excrement mingled with the shrieks of the hogs as they were hoisted to the ceiling and dangled by a hind leg to have their throats slit. In summer, temperatures could rise to 100° or more inside the stockyards. But the pay was good, about $25 a week, at a time when streetcar fare was 7 cents.

Oceola also worked, first at a rubber factory on 31st Street and later at the Morrison Hotel downtown, where she served as a maid and laundry supervisor. She also gave birth to two more children: Yvonne in October 1937 and Mavis in July 1939. Pops and Oceola worked different shifts to ensure one of them would always be home with the kids.

After World War II broke out, Roebuck quit the stockyards because shoveling fertilizer for ten to twelve hours a day was making him nauseous. He moved from job to job: building airplane parts, working in a soft-drink factory, laying bricks for a construction company, toiling in the steel mills in nearby Gary, just outside Chicago in northwestern Indiana. Each year, he was able to move the family into a bigger apartment on the South Side. By then his sister Katie had moved in with the family and was helping pay the bills and mind the children. Roebuck, who had dropped out of school in Mississippi in the eighth grade to work the cotton fields, enrolled at Wendell Phillips High School and took enough night classes to eventually earn his diploma.

On weekends, Roebuck treated the children to his homemade peanut brittle and a Saturday matinee. Saturday nights, Roebuck and Oceola pulled out a tin tub and bathed the kids. Relatives would gather later in the evening for drinking, cardplaying, and dancing. Cleotha in particular was right in the middle of it, dancing with her father to the records on the family phonograph.

"The 'sand,' the jitterbug—I loved to dance," Cleedi said. "Pops would throw me up to the ceiling, whirl me around, and I'd end up the next day with lots of money. The adults would give me nickels, dimes, quarters, and half-dollars for putting on a show."

Sunday was for churchgoing, followed by a 2:30 p.m. feast from Mom: red beans and rice, black-eyed peas, hot-water cornbread, biscuits and pigs' feet, a coveted treat from back home that Oceola fried and smothered in gravy. Watermelon, fruit, and vegetable wagons canvassed the streets where the Staples family lived, the South Side's "Dirty Thirties," a blue-collar neighborhood that by the early '50s was almost completely populated by African Americans. Milk shakes drew the kids to the drugstore at 35th and Wentworth; when one of the youngsters got sick, Pops ordered a "castor oil fizz," a mix of soda pop and castor oil.

Pervis made a name for himself in the summers as the "snowball king" by dragging a wagon with a snowball-making ice machine. At 5 cents per fruit-flavored snowball, he cleaned up in the junior police parade of 1949, hauling in $190. He also became adept at pool, running games with his pal (and future jazz saxophonist) Eddie Harris. The young hustler in the Staples family also became personal caretaker of Pops's father, Warren, who came to live in Chicago after cataracts blinded him and prevented him from sharecropping. Warren and Pervis shared a room, and every Sunday the boy dutifully walked his grandfather to church. Pervis also served as bodyguard for his sisters at school. "His job was to make sure no one laid a hand on my daughters," Pops said. Pervis also instructed his sisters in self-defense, and Mavis—the smallest yet toughest of all her female siblings—took his lessons to heart.

"Yvonne was always such a good girl, I had to fight for Yvonne," Mavis says. "I was about eleven when Yvonne got bit in the back by the neighbor downstairs at 506 East 33rd, Mary Jones. Yvonne came home screaming. I jumped in my jeans and my sneakers and I hit the door. I went looking for Mary Jones. And by the time I found her—What do you call that little guy? The Pied Piper?—there were so many people following me: 'Oh, Mavis gonna get Mary Jones.' And when I finally found her—you know, girls talk a lot, they like to talk smack before they swing—so she started talking, 'I didn't do no . . .' She was tall, she was mouthy, but I got her real quick [laughs]. Pervis taught me how to fight the tall girls. He said, 'Mavis, while they talking, go get 'em. Those tall ones, jump up, pull 'em down, and put 'em in a headlock.' This girl screamed, and when I let go I saw my arm was all bloody. I had pulled her earring right through her ear. I ran home, jumped in the laundry bag, and pulled the strings. That was my hiding spot, 'cause Mom would always tell us, 'Wait till your father gets home.' If he couldn't find me, then I got away."

Even though Mavis was small enough to hide in a laundry sack, no one wanted to mess with her. She carried herself with a certain confidence, speaking (or shouting, as necessary) in a rich, low voice that she inherited from her mother and her mother's mother, Mary Ware, a stern, Bible-quoting matriarch who was even stricter than Warren Staples when it came to toeing the line between blues and gospel.

During the school year, Pops and Oceola would send one or two of their children to live with Grandma Ware in Mound Bayou, Mississippi, because they couldn't afford winter shoes for all the kids. Mound Bayou was a largely black community and an early center of the civil rights movement in the '50s. Yvonne thrived in the slower pace of the South: "It was the love of my life living with Grandma Ware. She could cook, and she knew the Bible inside and out. Preachers would come to her for advice and interpretation of the Bible passages, and it was good for my ears to hear them talk. Mavis was well liked down there, too, because she was comical, liked to hang out and talk a lot of trash. That's Mavis.

I'm the quiet one. All business. I stayed, but Mavis got out as fast as she could."

Grandma Ware's house had an outhouse in the backyard, and on one visit little Mavis crashed through the rotten wood into the muck below. Unable to free herself, Mavis yelled until her grandmother came running and took her straight to the bathtub.

Grandma Ware frequently had a chew stick—a twig or matchstick—between her teeth, dipped in the snuffbox she carried with her everywhere she went. One time, as Mavis was walking through a nearby cotton field, she was stung by a wasp. "I ran crying to Grandma. She just took out her chewing tobacco and popped some of it on there, and the pain went away. Then she made my uncle Albert give over his cotton bag so I could lay on it. He was rolling his eyes—he was mad. He had to pull me all over the field while he was picking cotton."

For eight-year-old Mavis it was sweet payback. A few weeks earlier, Albert had turned her first public singing performance into a catastrophe.

"I'm walking down this gravel road every morning to school, and this record would be playing from a jukebox in town," Mavis says. "It was [the swanky Ella and Buddy Johnson blues lament] 'Since I Fell for You,' and I started singing it outside school. We had a variety show, and the other kids pushed me out there because they knew I could sing. I started in on 'Since I Fell for You,' and it felt good. People applauded. I saw my uncle Ham [Albert] there, and I'm thinking he's coming over to tell me I'm singing good. Well, he snatched me off the stage without saying a word. He marched me all the way to my grandma's house, threw me through the door, and told her I was singing the blues.

"And Grandma says, 'Oh, you singin' the blues, huh? You go out there and get me some switches.' I didn't understand. Nobody told me what I could and could not sing. I came back with a handful of these switches, and she whipped me pretty good. Tore my legs up. Each time she whipped me she said, 'You . . . don't . . . sing . . . no . . . blues! In this family you sing church songs.' Grandma Ware sent me back to school with a short dress on that showed my legs. My legs were all torn up and I was ashamed."

After that day, Mavis's stay in the South was short-lived. Yvonne came back to Mississippi every year until she graduated from high school, but Mavis wrote her mother begging to come home. Like Mary Jones, Grandma Ware was on the hook until Mavis could get some payback.

The matriarch maintained her distaste for the blues, but when Mavis matured as a singer and woman, she no longer had to fear her grandmother's wrath or her switches. "When I was thirty, I recorded 'Since I Fell for You' for Stax while my grandma was living with us in Chicago," Mavis says with a laugh. "I came in one day and said, 'Grandma, come here, I want you to hear something.' I played it for her and she smiled. 'You didn't forget that?' I said, 'I sure didn't. I won't forget that the rest of my life.'"

3

"If I Could Hear My Mother Pray Again"

The Dirty Thirties teemed with music. The Staples kids were among a generation of future musical prodigies from the neighborhood that included Lou Rawls, Sam Cooke, John Carter (who would join doo-wop giants the Flamingos and Dells) and, later, Johnnie Taylor.

Leroy Crume, who would go on to sing and play guitar with Cooke and others, was particularly close to Pervis and Cleotha Staples at Doolittle Elementary School on 35th Street. "I was just a kid playing in the yard when I first heard Sam's name during recess," Crume says. "I didn't know he was just three blocks down the street from me. Everywhere you looked there was someone who could sing or play an instrument."

"Eddie Harris was the horn, he lived on 69th Street," Pervis Staples says. "Mahalia Jackson lived in Chatham around 83rd. It seemed like everybody lived right around the corner from us. We were in a neighborhood where you couldn't do too much wrong because your daddy would beat your ass if you did. We would walk everywhere, but you stayed away from the streets where the kids had their caps on backwards. We'd go around those streets. You couldn't walk around the Midway because the white boys would run your ass back down to 39th Street. There were some places you just didn't visit, because your parents let you know. They had a way of keeping you out without making you a hateful individual. The gangbanging stuff, we just couldn't be a part of that.

"The neighborhood was full of older sisters and aunts—my mom's big sister Billie, Pops's older sisters Katie, Rosie, Maddie—and they wouldn't mind speaking their minds. My mother was nice and polite, but not her sister Billie. She'd walk up to those little tough guys and say, 'That's my nephew, and your ass don't need to talk to him.' The broads were tougher than the dudes. And the little gangbangers respected them. All these families were looking out for each other, and for their kids to do something besides hanging out in the street. So some of us learned an instrument and the rest of us sang. We saw it as our way of getting out of there, otherwise you'd be folding laundry at the Morrison Hotel the rest of your life."

The music seeped across genre lines: gospel, R&B, blues, bebop. Neighborhood kids soaked up the sounds pouring from the blues joints on or near 12th Street (now known as Roosevelt Road), the churches that arched heavenward every few blocks, and venerated theaters such as the Regal on 47th Street that regularly brought national talent to the South Side: Nat "King" Cole, Ella Fitzgerald, Sarah Vaughan, Redd Foxx, Duke Ellington, Moms Mabley, Dinah Washington, Lionel Hampton.

Future blues giants Muddy Waters, Otis Rush, Little Walter, Magic Sam, and Pop Staples's old Dockery Farms neighbor Howlin' Wolf all migrated from the South to Chicago in the '40s and early '50s, electrifying the music that they had learned in the Delta. Gospel, too, was in its golden era. Gospel was first recorded at the start of the twentieth century and soon spread into various streams and styles, but it hit a new level of sophistication in the 1940s with songs that combined swinging rhythms, blues inflections, and sacred lyrics. Electric guitars and organs were commonplace in gospel, giving the music a drive and toughness lacking in the more subdued orchestrated arrangements of white pop.

Songwriters such as Georgia-born Chicago preacher Thomas A. Dorsey, Lucie Campbell, R. H. Harris, Roberta Martin, and W. H.

Brewster fed a rising tide of quartets (usually four male singers with guitar) and gospel groups (mostly female vocalists accompanied by piano and organ). A national circuit of churches and auditoriums evolved where gospel singers could perform, and records such as Mahalia Jackson's "Move on Up a Little Higher" and the Five Blind Boys' "Our Father" were known and embraced in virtually every black community in America.

For young black men and women growing up on the increasingly segregated streets of Chicago, gospel music was as much a sound track of their lives as the blues and R&B hits of the day.

"Lou Rawls, Sam Cooke, his brother L.C. . . . all of us went to Doolittle, the same grammar school," Pervis Staples says. "After school, we'd go to Sam's house and sing under the streetlights. But a big, old fat lady by the name of Mrs. Sherrod would come out and be all annoyed with us after a while: 'Take your asses outta here.' And we'd be gone. So we found a place in Sam Cooke's basement to practice. Lou Rawls would be there in his flannel shirt with the pin, and he'd tell Sam to sing the high parts because he couldn't go that high. Sam and Johnny Carter—they had voices that were so sweet, they could make the mice come down the pole and watch. Sam would sing, 'Come down,' and out they'd come, then Johnny would say, 'Go back up,' and there they'd go. That's true stuff."

For Pervis Staples, master of tall tales, the curious mice might've been a metaphor for the females he and his barely teenage pals aimed to attract. Pervis always made sure to have his nose in a book when he had a free moment, in hope of picking up a 25-cent word that he could drop to impress a prospective girlfriend. But it was the weekend afternoon church performances by the fledgling groups, such as the Highway Q.C.'s—whose members included Cooke, Rawls, and Johnnie Taylor at various times—that put the neighborhood's teen hormones in overdrive. They would gather at Hopewell Missionary Baptist Church, across the street from Doolittle.

"That's where we'd always go, because they had a piano there," Pervis says. "All the singers would come, and where the singers went, all the girls would follow. We sang gospel songs. But if Sam Cooke's father wasn't there, if Pops wasn't there, we sang anything. We sang everything. Sam could sing anybody. Lou couldn't—he had that raunchy, growly voice. Sam was more genuine. He could sing and lift burdens."

Mavis Staples and her girlfriends from the Thirties would gather at Hopewell, mostly to swoon over the suave, fourteen-year-old Sam Cooke. "They would have a battle of the singers," she says. "Hopewell was down from the school, so all week ahead of time everybody let it be known there was going to be a battle. Pervis and Sam had these long bangs and they wouldn't keep 'em back. Pops would say, 'If y'all don't keep those bangs back, I'll cut them off.' And he meant it, too. That's when Pervis and Sam started using Murray's [hair gel] and wearing a stocking cap, to hide the bangs from the adults. They would sing, and there'd be no one in the church but us children, so they'd let their hair down [laughs]. The pastor would let us use the church, because it kept us off the street. We'd be sitting there in the pews eating potato chips, french fries, and peppermint sticks. Cleedi always had her butter-pecan ice cream. Sam could sing. Pervis could sing, too. I don't remember how the battles turned out, who won or what. But I do remember Sam Cooke—he had the most beautiful voice, and when he would do that 'Whoah-oh-whoah-oh,' the girls would lose their minds."

The girls weren't screaming about salvation in the afterlife—unless it was the kind of salvation that only Sam Cooke's embrace could bring. Long before soul music had a name, Cooke, Rawls, Pervis Staples, and the other young crooners from the Dirty Thirties were jumbling the sacred with the secular—so long as the grown-ups weren't listening. When the adults were in charge at Sunday service and the more formal gospel programs, the hymns and spirituals invariably turned heavenward, but with little loss of feeling. The goal was always to "shout" the congregation, to get people out of their seats as the spirit came over them, with the singer serving as a heavenly transmitter.

Pop Staples never left that world, even though he put down his guitar for twelve years after he came to Chicago while juggling a succession of

jobs, high school classes, and child rearing. On the side, he managed
to squeeze in some gospel singing at the Progressive Baptist Church on
37th Street, and played local programs with a six-member male gospel
group calling themselves the Trumpet Jubilees. Pops was third lead,
singing mostly in a falsetto voice, and managed the group, booking their
appearances and scheduling the rehearsals. He was a stickler for punc-
tuality and precision, for looking and sounding sharp, for taking the
job seriously. But not everyone in the group shared his commitment;
his exasperation mounted until one day he quit. Pops decided to devote
his time to a singing group that he could run from top to bottom, that
would show up on time at every rehearsal, no questions asked. Mostly,
he wanted to sing because it was a crucial part of his identity; since boy-
hood all he could remember was the pleasure singing brought him and
his older brothers and sisters. When singing in the Trumpet Jubilees
became a chore, he turned to his family.

"One night he came home early because the guys in the Trumpet
Jubilees didn't show up for rehearsal," Mavis says. "He was disgusted.
He went into the closet in the living room and got a little guitar he had
brought home from the pawnshop. It didn't have more than three or
four strings on it, but it was enough to get us started."

Mavis, Pervis, Cleotha, and Yvonne sat in a semicircle in front of their
father on the beige carpet in their living room at 506 East 33rd Street.
Pops hunched over his $7 guitar and plucked a series of notes, assigning
one to each of his children.

"People always ask, 'How do we get the sound we have?' And that
came from my father—the sound he had with his family in Mississippi
when they sang on the gallery after dinner. He gave us [an E chord] and
the parts his brothers and sisters would sing. He would hit a note on
his guitar and would say, 'Now, Mavis go here,' a baritone part, because
even then I had the deepest voice. Pervis was second lead behind Pops
because he had the most experience, and he could hit those high notes
like Michael Jackson later could. Cleedi had the high harmony. The first
song he taught us was 'Will the Circle Be Unbroken.' Every now and

then he'd have to stop and get us back in line. Pervis would be all the way up there—'By and by, Lord, by and by.' We sang that over and over until we got it good. Aunt Katie was living with us and was listening each night as we got better and better. She came over to Pops and said, 'Shucks, you sound good. I want y'all to sing at my church.' We had no idea what we were being asked to do; we were just so glad to sing somewhere else other than the living room floor."

Mavis was all of eight years old in early 1948. Other than her ill-fated public debut in Mississippi, which won her only the strong disapproval of Grandma Ware, her singing had been limited to children's songs at school.

"Mavis was headstrong and stubborn," Pops recalled. "What a time I had getting her to learn her part. When she was seven, Mavis could not hold a tune. It took her almost two years before she could catch on to her part. Finally, the little skinny girl with the heavy voice learned a song from her Aunt Katie, 'If I Could Hear My Mother Pray Again.'"

Yvonne detested having to sing at all; she was a quiet kid who hated to be the center of attention. Pervis would've much rather been out carousing and chasing girls with Sam Cooke and Lou Rawls, but singing came naturally to him. Cleotha, the oldest, approached her assignment with dutiful sincerity—her fondest wish was to make her father happy. With the call to sing in church, their rehearsals took on a new urgency. All that fuss Pop always made about the family sticking together and the power of the group versus the relative weakness of the individual started to ring true. Together they had something; they were young city folk, yet they somehow sounded at least twice their age, throwbacks to sharecropper country.

Aunt Katie bought Mavis, Cleotha, and Yvonne outfits for their debut: off-white quilted skirts and blue nylon blouses. Pops and Pervis wore their Sunday best dark suits and ties. Pops tried to shield his secondhand guitar from the rain as he and the children hopped a red streetcar to Holy Trinity Baptist Church on 33rd Street, where Pops's brother the Reverend Chester Staples was pastor. The church was only about half full, but nerves nearly got the better of Mavis when the family was called up to sing. She couldn't even look at the congregation. A chair boosted her tiny frame closer to the microphone, and she cast her eyes on the ceiling, a picture of sanctified innocence that belied the mischief maker she would've been in most any other circumstance. The family looked handsome, pristine, impossibly young—charming, to be sure, but likely a novelty at best to a congregation of seasoned gospel appreciators. The group had prepared only two songs, assuming their stay in front of the congregation would be a brief one. But they sailed through "If I Could Hear My Mother Pray Again" with such feeling, the unpolished mix of voices so redolent of the South with its Mississippi twang and bluesy undercurrent, that the congregation clapped uproariously, insisting on multiple encores. With each pass through its tiny repertoire, the group shook off its anxiety and sang with greater confidence.

An offering brought the family the princely sum of $7. What's more, the congregation included a minister from Mt. Zion Baptist Church on 46th Street. "I never will forget," Pops said years later, "there was an old minister there named Lathrop, and he said, 'I want you children at my church next Sunday.'" When the family got home, Pops turned to his protégés and smiled. What had started out as a way to pass the time in their apartment had taken a turn.

"Children," he declared, "we gon' learn some more songs."

4

"This May Be the Last Time"

Mavis Staples was a pocket-size dynamo; she wasn't just the tiniest of gospel singers, she also was dwarfed by most of her schoolmates. Worshipers were astonished to see this skinny little girl climb atop a chair in the middle of church service to reach the microphone and then sing the Lord's praises with a grown woman's voice.

"People would come up crying and put money in my hand, and I didn't understand. I thought I was hurting them," Mavis says. "So I asked Mama, 'Why are people crying?' She said, 'Mavis, they're happy. Your singing makes them cry happy tears.' When I sang, I looked straight up at the ceiling. I couldn't look at the people because I was so shy. Sometimes I would close my eyes, and I'd feel someone tugging my hand. They would get out of their seats and come up to where we were singing to give me money, and I'd put it on the piano. And I'd look back later and it would be gone. Stealing in church! Thieves in the temple! [laughs] That's when my mama started sewing pockets in my dresses so I'd have somewhere to put the money."

The Staples family's second weekend appearance, at Mt. Zion Baptist Church, went even better than the first. The collection brought $35, and Pops and the family went home with $17.50. Soon they were

making double that amount as word spread on the South Side and congregations swelled to glimpse the family that harmonized with such old-
school fervor.

Pops bought fifteen minutes of airtime Sunday mornings on WTAQ,
an AM radio station that broadcast out of Wedgewood Towers, a flat-
iron high-rise hotel on 64th Street that was a center of African-American
life in Chicago. The Staples sang two gospel tunes and Cleotha would
announce where the family would be singing next, usually performing
two programs every Sunday at 3 and 8 p.m. They began getting invita-
tions from churches in Milwaukee; suburban Evanston; Joliet, Illinois;
and Gary, Indiana.

Pops bought his first electric guitar in 1950 with a tremolo unit that
gave him a dark, reverberating tone that sounded as swampy and humid
as a Delta summer night. When Pervis's voice dropped an octave once he
reached puberty, Pop shifted Mavis to lead vocals. As with many family
decisions imposed on her, Mavis did not comply quietly.

"I thought my voice belonged in the background, I didn't want to be
out front, even though I had the range to cover the highs and the lows,"
Mavis says. "I was stubborn. 'Nah, Daddy, nah, Daddy.' I was a little
you-know-what [laughs]. Daddy had a little leather strap and he'd get
my legs with it if I got out of line. He reached for that strap, and suddenly the idea of singing lead didn't seem so bad, after all."

It was around this time that Pops experienced not so much a religious
conversion—because he was already a churchgoing believer—as a deep-
ening of his commitment to a Christian way of life. "I guess the best way
to describe it is that he was 'born again,'" Mavis recalls.

Pops grew up in a strict Christian household in Mississippi under
Warren Staples. But he was also a regular at house parties in and around
the plantation where nobody was playing gospel music or strictly adher-
ing to Christian values. Blues was the sound track, white lightning was
swilled, guys and gals went grinding on the dance floor, and cards and
cash flew in the back room. These house parties are where all the local

teens took their girls, and it was where young Roebuck Staples courted Oceola Ware, who was pregnant by the time she was sixteen.

But after coming to Chicago, Pops "changed over," Mavis says. "He was playing in those juke joints as a kid, but he never told us much about that. We knew they used to gamble and drink the moonshine and play the blues. But I never saw my father drunk—he'd have a hot toddy with Old Grand Dad and tea when he had a cold, but that was about it. I think they would have money on the table on Saturday nights at our house. They would set up a card table and play. But once Pops got born again, he wouldn't let us have cards in the house. We couldn't listen to anything but gospel music in the house. I would listen to R&B at school, play the jukebox, but never at home."

Her father's shift in attitude began after the family joined Mt. Eagle Baptist Church at 45th and Lawrence, where C. J. Rodgers was the minister. "Reverend Rodgers was such a powerful minister, and he got to Pops," Mavis says. "He had to be baptized. From that, he turned his life over to God. He started to play strictly Christian music. I never knew he even played blues on his guitar, even though later on I learned that's what it was. My granddaddy, Pops's dad, was staying with us by then. He was blind, and he'd sit in a chair in the living room and sing, 'You must be born, you must be born, you must be born again.' "

Pops was a music man, and gospel songs filled the apartment. Local favorites the Soul Stirrers, especially the incarnation led by the great R. H. Harris, and the Highway Q.C.'s, the Dixie Hummingbirds, the Five Blind Boys, the Pilgrim Travelers—Pops was an avid and studious listener, and his music was a sound track to family activities whenever he wasn't leading the kids in another rehearsal. One singer in particular stood out for Mavis just when she started to perform with her family.

"I was playing with my dolls in the play area when I was about eight years old, and I could hear a lady's voice," she says. "That was the first time I remember hearing a lady singer, because my dad played a lot of male gospel quartets. I moved to the living room and sat on the floor in front of the

record player and watched that big 78 record. Pops later told me I was just
sitting there rocking back and forth listening to Sister Mahalia."

Mahalia Jackson arrived in Chicago from New Orleans in the 1920s
and became a protégé of Thomas Dorsey's—a power couple if there ever
was one in gospel music. She was known nearly as much for her towering beehives and gowns as her staggering voice. Mavis absorbed the
influence of other gospel greats, especially Dorothy Love Coates of the
Gospel Harmonettes and Ruth Davis of the Davis Sisters. But she credits Jackson as the woman who "taught me my voice." Beyond that, she
had a personal connection with Mahalia that blurred the lines between
the artistic and the familial.

When Mavis was eleven, Pops came home on a Friday night and
informed the family that they had been offered an opening slot for Jackson the next Monday at Tabernacle Baptist Church.

"I walked around all that weekend singing her songs, thinking about
what I was going to say to her—my heart felt like it was going to burst
right out of my chest, I was so excited, " she says. "Then Monday night
finally came, and we were in the same dressing room. My sisters were
watching me, because they didn't want me to get on Sister Mahalia's
nerves. But I was watching the door, and when she came in I made a bee-
line for her. No way they were stopping me."

Jackson "looked like a giant princess to me," Mavis says. "She had on
this brocade, cream-colored gown. I walked up to her and introduced
myself, told her that I sing and that I sing loud, that she'd be sure to hear
me."

After her family's performance, Mavis and her friends grabbed their
jump ropes and started to sneak out during the minister's sermon. Jackson "saw us starting to leave and said, 'You take that coat back off and
sit your little butt down and let me tell you somethin'. Do you want to
be like me and sing a long time? Don't you know all your pores are open
and you'll catch cold? You need to put on some dry clothes. Take that
wet bra off and put on one of your brother's T-shirts.' Then she called
my mother the next day to make sure I got the message."

Jackson could be aloof or even hostile when mingling with other gospel singers. The gospel circuit could be cutthroat, rife with gossip and competitive attitudes worthy of the most diva-like pop stars. But Mavis was young and deferential enough that Mahalia never perceived her young protégé as a threat, and their relationship remained a fond one right up until Jackson's death in 1972.

Mavis's charmed life hit a bump on January 4, 1952, when a fifth Staples sibling was born. Baby Cynthia's arrival was not met favorably by Mavis, who as the youngest was used to being indulged. But after some initial misgivings, she and Cynthia developed a close relationship.

"Cynthia, when she was a baby, I was so mad at her," Mavis says. "She took my position. I was the baby for twelve years. Pops used to come home and throw me up in the air and blow on my stomach and make me laugh. And when that baby came, he'd head straight for that cradle. I would get mad. See, I didn't know Mama was expecting a baby. Mama was heavyset, so nothing really changed. I didn't know where babies came from anyway—I was twelve years old. Pops told me, 'Mavis, I want you to go with me to get the baby.' I said, 'What baby?' He said, 'Mom is in the hospital, you got a new sister.' They asked me to name her—that was their way of trying to pacify me. I came up with Cynthia Marie. Then when I got to the hospital, Cynthia was so big—she was ten pounds eleven ounces—that I nearly dropped her.

"But Cynthia and I later became the best of friends. I called her 'Blessed.' We just connected. I would be the only one at home after school, because everyone else was at work, so I would have to take her to the babysitter in the morning and pick her up in the afternoon. She was in my care, and we just fell in love."

But the age difference meant that Cynthia would never fully participate in the family's career. Soon after she was born, the group began to call itself the Staple Singers. In 1953, Pops had Pervis, Cleotha, and Mavis join him around a single microphone on a two-track recorder to cut crude, homemade versions of "These Are They," which had been popularized by Dorothy Love Coates and the Gospel Harmonettes, and

"Faith and Grace," a Pops original. (By now Yvonne, the reluctant singer, was spending most of the school year in Mississippi with Grandma Ware and no longer regularly participating in the group.) Pops pressed five hundred copies of the 78 rpm single on his vanity label, Royal, which the group hawked at shows.

Evelyn Gay heard the Staples on their WTAQ broadcasts and didn't know quite what to make of the family's sound, but she was impressed. "Y'all sound country," she told Pops, as if she were seeing something out of a rural hillbilly church in the 1920s or '30s. In a way she was, because that dark, mystical sense of yearning was ingrained in Pops every day at Dockery Farms, in the fields under the hot sun and on the gallery at dusk. Evelyn Gay meant her "country" remark as a compliment, for she and her group, the Gay Sisters, were hardly wedded to convention, preferring to put their own spin on decades-old tradition. The Gay Sisters were established stars on the gospel circuit, and Evelyn put her clout to work on Pops's behalf.

"Evelyn Gay is the cause of us being on record," Mavis says. "She talked to Daddy, she said, 'Staples, I don't know what you got your kids singing, but it's some different stuff and you should be making records.' "

She introduced Pops to a Chicago businessman, Leonard Allen, who invited the family to cut some tracks for his United Records label. United, born in 1951, recorded artists from a cross-section of genres, including jazz (Gene Ammons, Della Reese), blues (Big Walter Horton, Memphis Slim), and gospel (Robert Anderson, the Caravans). The Staples' first session, in September 1953, produced a slow, spooky reading of "Won't You Sit Down (Sit Down Servant)," released in December as a single. Pops's guitar is relatively muted underneath the call-and-response vocals between the chorus (Pops, Cleotha, Pervis) and Mavis's impassioned lead contralto. More prominent in the mix is a piano—played by Evelyn Gay, according to Mavis. The single flopped, selling only a few hundred copies.

Several more recording sessions followed, including an early run-through of "This May Be the Last Time." Gay's dazzling right-hand lead lines on piano provide counterpoint to the Staples' vocals, especially the increasingly agitated interplay between Mavis and Pops, who pushes his voice to the top of its range.

"This may be the last time, may be the last time I don't know," they sing with a rising sense of urgency, as if they knew they were running out of opportunities to impress Leonard Allen. It's a terrific performance, but wasn't released until years later on the New Jersey–based Sharp label, a subsidiary of Savoy, which had bought some of United's masters after its 1957 demise. United was looking for hits and encouraged the Staples to move in a more rock 'n' roll direction, according to Pops, but he would have none of it.

"We stayed with him for two years," Pops said in a 1964 interview with Chris Strachwitz. "He wanted us to sing blues. He said Mavis could make a lot of money singing blues. I didn't want her singing blues."

Mavis, as she always had in public, followed her father's lead in the same interview: "I didn't want to sing any blues. I didn't know anything about singing the blues. I had been brought up in the church and been singing church songs around the house and I didn't know anything about any blues. I wouldn't have known what to do if Daddy had said, 'Yes, she can do it.' I would have been lost. I just enjoy singing spirituals."

Decades later, Pops looked at the old wound from a different angle: "The man at United said to us: 'How many Mahalias y'all gonna find singing not to make money but to be Christian?'" He was bitterly disappointed. When the Staples' contract expired in 1955, Pops returned to his job at the steel mill, in no hurry to jump back into the music business.

5

"Gospel in a blues key"

M avis Staples's voice teacher at Parker High School on Chicago's South Side didn't get her.

"My voice was heavy, I used to fight in grammar school down south because my voice was so low and kids would tease me about it," she says. "But I was a tomboy who loved to fight. They used to tell me, 'You sound like a boy.' 'Okay, I'll show you how a boy fights.' My mother's voice was strong, and my grandmother's, too. Only difference was, my mother couldn't sing. Whenever she started to sing around the house, we'd beg her to stop [laughs]. In my a cappella choir in high school, I tried to sing with the girls but I couldn't. 'Mavis, Mavis, you're singing in the basement again,' my teacher, Mr. Finch, would say. 'You're singing with the boys.' I was so embarrassed. I quit the choir because I couldn't sing like Mr. Finch wanted."

Fast-forward a few decades, and Mr. Finch would likely still be exasperated by his former student's lack of training. "One time I was supposed to sing the national anthem for the Lakers" before an NBA game, Mavis says. "The organist asked me what key I would like to sing it in, and I said, 'Good question' [laughs]. I had to call Pops. Pops got his guitar and said, 'Show me the highest point of your vocals.' I was singing where I was comfortable, and he said, 'Go back and tell the organist you're singing in A.' I had no idea."

From the start, the Staple Singers weren't easy to peg. They were a charming, handsome family, easy to look at, easy to root for. The gospel music circuit could be unforgiving, though, and there were traditions to be observed, rules that needed to be followed, lines that couldn't be crossed without consequences. The Staple Singers evoked a tradition—several traditions, really—in a most untraditional way.

"That old man should just take them kids home—those kids ought to be in school," some put-out worshipers would mutter when the Staples first started appearing at South Side churches.

"The regular gospel singers laughed at us," Pops told *Goldmine* in 1996. "They'd sing loud and then we'd get up there with our little, soft singing."

Who were these amateurs? The ages of the singers—two teenagers and a conspicuous preteen flanked by a dapper, guitar-playing gentleman with a caramel complexion and close-cropped salt-and-pepper hair—didn't quite match up with the sound. One might've expected something adolescent and exuberant. Instead, the Staples delivered music amid the concrete and steel of Chicago that was solemn, Southern, and rural—"hillbilly," as gospel singer Donald Gay described it. To worshipers who still had the South in their DNA and their accents, this music was deeply nostalgic. Just one of Mavis's long moans, Cleotha's swoops into a minor key, or a trembling chord on Pops's guitar could instantly evoke the world they'd left behind.

"The Staple Singers had a different sound from any other group at the time," Leroy Crume says. "Pop is from down home, and he sounded like it. When Pop came on the scene, he brought this little gadget you put on an amplifier—at the time they weren't making amps with tremolos. Pop was the first one to have that little contraption on his guitar. People used to call it 'Pop Staples and his nervous guitar.' That set him apart from everybody."

The Staples' vocal style also struck Crume as odd, if in a pleasing way. "They weren't superpolished. That country-type singing just came naturally out of them. It was a heck of an identity for them, but they didn't know any better. Mavis had that big voice coming out of that little body—that just blew people away. A girl bass singer! She was different. The entire group was different, the way they harmonized, it wasn't 'correct.' Other groups had instructors. Somebody from a name group would come in and help out the younger guys, like my older brother A.C. was instructing the Crume Brothers, and one of the guys from the Flamingos started to teach us how to read music. He had us sounding like the Mills Brothers. The Staples really didn't sound like anyone else you knew."

When R&B singer Jerry Butler was still a kid in the years before he joined the Impressions with his friend Curtis Mayfield, he remembers hearing an early recording by the Staple Singers and being struck by "the girl with the low voice—at first, I thought it was a man.

"Someone said, 'No, that's a girl, and she's about twelve, thirteen.' I couldn't believe it. As I listened more, I realized how beautiful, organic, and unique it all felt, the way the vibrato of Mavis's voice matched the vibrato of Pops's guitar amplifier."

Mavis generously deflects some of the attention heaped on her whenever the Staples sound is parsed for originality. "I credit Pops's guitar and Cleedi's voice as making our sound. She hit those high harmonies, and Pops would take her to a minor key a lot. When we first sang 'Will the Circle Be Unbroken,' Cleedi had a way of turning that song in a way that would just ring in your ear—it wasn't harsh or hitting you too hard; it was soothing. Cleedi gave us that country sound."

Jon Shields, an ardent gospel fan who was two years younger than Mavis when both attended Francis Parker, calls the family vocal blend "a fine whine."

"What was unique to them—and it's true about many family groups like the Barrett Sisters, the Pointer Sisters—there is a blend that only their family has," Shields says. "Cleo is the one who really had that distinct sound. When they would bend a note to end a song, it goes into a whine. If you listen to the Staples' voices individually, you can hear that whine in each, they pitch down at the end of a line. That's very country, very Southern, very much their trademark."

Crume hears it, too, and suggests that such trademarks owed everything to their insularity. "It was probably good they didn't have any formal instruction," Crume says. "When you learn music you can get mighty picky trying to sing it 'correctly.' When I came to the Soul Stirrers, Sam [Cooke] had three different keys he'd like to sing in, depending on whether he was rehearsing, singing for the radio, or singing in concert. He knew what effect it would have on an audience; he knew his voice hadn't woken up in the morning, so he'd have a lower, 'broadcast' key. To save his voice during rehearsal, he'd sing in a middle key. And then he'd have his program key, where he'd sing in his highest voice to be heard over the screaming in the audiences at auditoriums and gyms. With Mavis and them, they didn't know what key they sang in. Pops played in but one key, E, and that's all they needed."

Gospel critic Anthony Heilbut says that lack of formality made the group more accessible to people. "Their voices are all in a very singable range," he says. "With other gospel acts, it was very hard for the congregation to identify with the singing range, it just seemed beyond them. But the Staples very much felt like one of them, and that made them very appealing. In that way they were like a folk act from the very beginning."

Just how innovative were the Staple Singers? Pops would often repeat the story that he was gospel-guitar pioneer. "We were the first gospel group to be allowed to bring a guitar into church," he claimed in his unpublished memoir. Indeed, there is some evidence that ministers in the Methodist churches didn't look kindly upon guitar playing at their services, though guitars and tambourines were commonplace in Baptist, Pentecostal, and more sanctified church settings.

Crume agrees with Pops to an extent: "The Crume Brothers and the Staples were the only groups in Chicago with a guitar-based gospel sound. There were no other local groups with the guitar when we came on the scene. I was the first guitar player on the radio with a gospel group, and Roebuck was next."

But the guitar already had a long tradition in gospel music. Sister Rosetta Tharpe rocked a guitar on gospel-swing hits in the 1930s and '40s, prompting even a young Mavis Staples to request a few guitar lessons from Pops. The bluesy guitar evangelism of Blind Willie Johnson—Pops's old Mississippi favorite—inspired modern proponents besides the Staple Singers, most significantly the Florida-based Consolers. Singer Iola Pugh and her guitar-playing husband, Sullivan Pugh, favored a "down-home" approach that was even rougher and cruder than the Staples sound. Sullivan's guitar—which he positioned sideways to his stomach, almost like a lap steel—rang out with country-blues reverb that Staples fans surely would recognize.

Some of the gospel greats could be condescending about the Staples sound. R. H. Harris, formerly of the Soul Stirrers, once commented to Heilbut: "That relaxing style, I hates it."

"But the black gospel audience did understand the Staples had a special sound, and Pops was very good at coming up with hooks," Heilbut says.

"Pops's guitar was not busy or active or fancy or in front—it's an environmental sound," says Ry Cooder, a master guitarist and student of the early Staple Singers albums and later a collaborator with both Pops and Mavis. "What Pops was giving was a tone behind the voices. They didn't have bass, drums, all those silly things they didn't need and shouldn't have. What he did have was these spooky chords that made it sound like you're in a cave, or you're in some dark place, and then out of that darkness would come these wailing four-part harmonies. I assume that came from the black shape-note churches, which don't exist anymore down south. Pops adapted that sound from his youth for his family. It was the four voices—the three kids and him—and he combined that old, country, black-church harmony with this spooky guitar. It must've been incredible for all these transplanted people who made their way up north to Detroit or Chicago or Gary to hear this, because they're all homesick. They've all left their hamlets and towns in this tremendous upheaval of northern migration, and here come the Staple Singers singing just like they remembered."

The census bureau reported that between 1940 and 1960, the black population in Chicago nearly tripled to 813,000 from 278,000, most from the South. Blacks accounted for nearly one-quarter of the city's population in 1960, up from barely 8 percent two decades earlier. The city was in many ways as segregated as the South, however, with blacks largely confined to increasingly congested housing on the South Side and facing blatant hiring discrimination in the retail and construction industries. City jobs for black police, firefighters, and bus drivers were largely limited to black neighborhoods, with little opportunity for advancement into management positions.

For this marginalized community, the black church provided sanctuary, solace, and a place to vent. Just as the slaves and then the sharecroppers found respite in church songs after long days in the fields, the black migrants—factory workers, stockyard laborers, nannies, maids—in the northern cities went to church to lift their voices and spirits.

Singers and preachers were the leaders and celebrities of this community; gospel programs often blended songs and sermon in a synergy of salvation. The word of the most revered performers and ministers carried enormous weight. Mahalia Jackson, the reigning queen of gospel, refused to sing the blues, even though she had borrowed certain vocal mannerisms from blues singers. "I sing God's music because it makes me feel free," she said. "It gives me hope. With the blues, when you finish, you still have the blues."

That was the hard line the Staples were up against, and Pops preached a similar stance to his kids. But his music was far less rigid; the Staples essentially made up their own rules, established their own vocabulary, one that borrowed from several genres without really embodying any of them. There were the four-part harmonies that Pops sang with his family on their Dockery Farms porch; the blues he heard and played at

the Saturday-night house parties on the plantations; the handclapping
and foot stomping that Mavis and Yvonne witnessed at Grandma Ware's
little wooden church on the hill in Mound Bayou; the doo-woppers and
street serenaders that Pervis emulated during the Sunday battle of the
bands on the South Side.

Duke Ellington understood what Mavis's high school voice teacher
did not. What seemed like "mistakes" to certain purists were turned into
strengths by the Staples. "You play gospel in a blues key," Ellington told
Pops. It was as apt a description as any for what came next.

6

"Uncloudy Day"

The Staple Singers became free agents at a time when black music was flourishing on the South Side, with gospel, blues, and doowop on the ascent and soul rumbling to life. Pops and the family were coveted by the largest black-owned record company in the country, Vee-Jay, the core of Chicago's "Record Row" on South Michigan Avenue along with Chess Records. The label, which opened in 1953, was run by Vivian Carter and Jimmy Bracken, husband-and-wife R&B and gospel connoisseurs. Bracken had initially approached Pops about recording for Vee-Jay shortly after establishing the label in 1953, but the Staples had already struck their deal with United.

"Jimmy told us to come and see him when the contract expired with United," Pops recalled, but he was in no hurry to make a deal with another label, given the dispiriting experience at United. Instead he went back to his factory job and borrowed some books from the library about the music business. After six months of studying, he touched base with Bracken again, and the label owner assured Pops that he wanted to cut gospel records with the Staple Singers.

Carter and Bracken were black cultural evangelists, part of a flourishing network of South Side labels, clubs, newspapers, barbershops, banks, and saloons that catered to the African-American community. By the time the Staples joined, the label had already broken through with Jimmy Reed, the Spaniels, John Lee Hooker, and Pervis Staples's old battle-of-the-bands rival, the Highway Q.C.'s, led by Johnnie Taylor.

Yet at first, it was more of the same. The initial Vee-Jay session in November 1955 produced three tracks. The Staples had been performing "If I could Hear My Mother Pray Again" since their very first live appearance in the late '40s, and it featured some of the key elements in their sound: Pops's skeletal, shimmering guitar chords and group harmonies underpinning his twangy vocal with a brief leap into falsetto, finally resolving in a long, downward swoop. The sixteen-year-old Mavis's vibrato-tinged contralto anchored "God's Wonderful Love" and "Calling Me." The songs went nowhere commercially, and Pops again expected to get axed. But Bracken promised him a second chance.

"I asked the man at Vee-Jay when we signed the contract, 'What would you be happy with? How many would you be happy selling?'" Pops told *Goldmine* in 1996. "And he said, 'If it makes a thousand, I'll be happy.' I think we sold about 200. So after about two, three months I went back and said, 'I guess we'll let it go since we ain't come up near to your expectations.' And he said, 'You let me be the judge. Now when you ready to go back in again?'"

The label's brilliant talent scout, A&R man Ewart Abner, in particular sensed something that United Records had not. He encouraged the Staples to stay the course, to hew to its "down-home" approach instead of trying to keep up with trends by adding heavier rhythmic accents or making a sharp turn toward a more easily marketed dance-oriented sound.

The family reentered Universal Recording studio on the near North Side on September 11, 1956. As was typical of Vee-Jay recording sessions, the Staples split time with two other acts on the label, organist Maceo Woods and the doo-wop group the Spaniels. A drummer, Paul Gusman, also was on hand, but the focus remained on the family's voices and Pops's guitar.

The session began inauspiciously. Mavis was feeling ill and sat through the three hours in the studio to conserve energy as she sang. But she sounds in superb voice, nonetheless. Pops takes the lead on his "I Know I Got Religion," turning the invocation "dipped in the water" into an incantatory call-and-response with his children. He lays down a percussive guitar line on "Swing Down, Chariot (Let Me Ride)," with brushed drums pushing the brisk tempo.

"Uncloudy Day" trumps them all. The Staples had rearranged the traditional hymn to suit their strengths and had been performing it for nearly a decade. The song was known to almost anyone who had attended a Christian church service. It was written in 1879 by Josiah K. Alwood, an itinerant preacher from the Midwest, after riding through a midnight rainstorm and catching a glimpse of what he said was a rainbow. The vision prompted a reverie about the afterlife: "O they tell me of a home where no storm clouds rise / O they tell me of an unclouded day."

It has remained in the gospel repertoire ever since, recorded and performed by countless artists, ranging from gospel royalty to pop and country performers including the Eagles' Don Henley and Willie Nelson. Johnny Cash said it was the first song he ever performed in public, at the age of twelve in 1944 while growing up in Arkansas. Most versions have a stately, quaint feel.

In the Staples' telling, the song enters like a mirage or a hallucination, evoking a cotton field on a summer afternoon. Each guitar note seems to wobble in the heat as the group harmonizes on the first verse. Halfway through the song, Mavis enters, her voice in its lowest register: "Well, well, well . . ." A call to attention, not unlike something John Lee Hooker or Muddy Waters might say before starting to strut. But Mavis is talking about a different place, a glimpse from a dream. She stretches out the first verse for a minute and a half; the chorus meditates on the words, "They tell me," in the manner of a preacher who returns to the same phrase over and over again for rhythmic emphasis. Mavis lets her

voice sail, enraptured by "a home far away." The song couldn't be simpler or more stark, yet it carries weight: the dark gravity of Mavis's voice, the heavy drapery of Pops's guitar. It's a masterpiece of concision, and yet it feels wide-open, a vast space that included the long-ago South and the wished-upon afterlife.

"Three groups went down at once and, believe it or not, we cut our record before twelve o'clock that night," Pops said. "And those boys, the Spaniels, were blasting away playing back from the speakers and our little record seemed so weak and pitiful. I said, 'Well, we ain't doing nothing with this.' They released all of them at the same time and . . . our record it took off like a greyhound running!" [laughs]

The record was a huge hit, especially by gospel standards. Precise numbers were impossible to ascertain given the impenetrable maze of record-company accounting in that era, but estimates range from tens of thousands to as many as a million. With Vee-Jay's name behind it, "Uncloudy Day" got pushed at radio stations around the country and enabled the Staple Singers to tour nationally for the first time.

"They were with the premier black label of the '50s," says gospel journalist Bill Carpenter. "If anyone was going to put out your record to the black market and do it service, that was the one. And 'Uncloudy Day' in particular really captured the moment. It reminded a lot of people of home, those people who had migrated from the South after World War II to work in Chicago, Michigan, Ohio, Indiana. Those bluesy chords reminded people of the South the way Motown reminds baby boomers of their teenage years. The song had been around for a while, but to give it that down-home, bluesy feel was all Pops's doing. Most gospel during that time wasn't like that."

Pops was merely doing what came naturally. "That sound came from 90, 100 years ago," he told *Goldmine* in 1996. "My grandfather lived to be over 100 years old and I saw him before he passed—that was the kind of song that he used to sing."

"Daddy's daddy [Warren Staples] used to sing these songs to me," Mavis recalled. "It's the same sound Grandpa was singing, and Pops passed it down to us. . . . When 'Uncloudy Day' came out, they thought we were old people singing that kind of down-home stuff."

With a hit record raising their profile and boosting their credibility, the Staples found themselves transformed from a novelty to hometown stars who still carried themselves like everybody's next-door neighbor.

"The first time I saw them was Greater Mount Sinai Baptist Church on the West Side in the mid-'50s, and the girls were in white dresses, no lipstick, a little powder—they looked like angels and they sounded like angels," Jerry Butler says. "I was about fifteen, and Mavis was in the same range. They were in attendance and they were called up by the minister to sing. By then, 'Uncloudy Day' was on the radio; it wasn't R&B, it wasn't spiritual, it was the Staples being themselves. And the response when people heard Mavis's voice was ecstatic: 'Bless you, child,' 'Yes, Lord!' People were out of their seats. It was the full coat of armor."

As with everything he did, Pops proceeded with careful deliberation. The group's live performances were gimmick-free. "He made sure the family was never under-rehearsed, underprepared, underdressed," Butler says. "Their show was not about a whole lot of dancing or twisting. There was clapping of hands, stomping of feet, Pops's guitar—that was their show. And it worked because of the feeling they put into it."

The family members were already seasoned entertainers. "By the time we got out of high school, I'd been to Atlanta; Jackson, Mississippi; North Carolina; all over the South," Mavis says. "We'd go out on the weekends, start back home at 3 p.m. Sunday after our afternoon program, and not get home till Monday. So I'd do my homework and get back to school Tuesday."

When "Uncloudy Day" took off, the tours got longer and the money got better. After one weekend and two shows down south—a Friday carnival in Jackson and a Saturday-night gospel program in New Orleans—Pops came home with nearly $800 in his pocket.

"I had to make a career choice," Pops said with a laugh. "I was making $65 a week at the steel mill in Gary, and I felt I couldn't afford to quit. But we got down to Jackson, and the Masonic Temple was packed. We tore the house down in New Orleans, I could hardly get in the place. They gave us $300, plus a $50 bonus. When we got home, I told my wife I made more in a weekend than in a month on the job in the steel mill. She said, 'Pop, it's time to go sing with your family.'"

7

A guitar, an amplifier, and a gun .

The success of "Uncloudy Day" enabled the Staples to expand outside of church programs to play larger auditoriums and gymnasiums, eventually playing to as many as a thousand people. Here, the performers—and the promoters—could feel even less constrained.

A flyer advertising a gospel revue headlined by "the Famous Staple Singers of Chicago, Illinois" for a $1.75 ticket at the Trade Technical School auditorium at 400 West Washington Boulevard, shouted: "$35 to the best dressed stout lady (170 lbs. and up!). So Girls bring the pounds."

Gospel wasn't immune to old-fashioned hucksterism, especially because there was money to be made. Stars came and went, often based on the whims of the marketplace. "Everything depended on your last record," critic Anthony Heilbut says. "If you had a hit, you got a crowd. In that respect, the gospel circuit was no different from R&B."

In June 1957, Mavis graduated from Francis Parker High School, Pops quit his job at the steel mill, and the family started to tour for weeks at a time, instead of restricting themselves to weekends to work around Mavis's school schedule. "Pops turned this into a full-time thing," Mavis says. "Cleedi and Pervis quit their jobs. But I told him I wasn't sure. I wanted to go to college, I wanted to go down to Nashville to study nursing. I loved those outfits they wore back then, the white cap and stockings and shoes—a crisp uniform. I could see myself in one of those. But Daddy said, 'Mavis, listen, you're already a nurse. You're healing people when you sing. You're making people feel better.' He just ran it on me. He could tell me anything and I'd believe him. So I decided to go with it for a little while and see how things turned out."

The Staples' new fans weren't quite prepared for what they saw. "Uncloudy Day" suggested the work of a much older group, with a male baritone or possibly a heavyset matron as a lead vocalist, not a slender teenager.

"We'd trick 'em," Pervis says. "The audience would be looking for me to come up with the low part—this was for the people who heard the record but had never seen us before. I'd come up to the mike and switch over at the last second where Cleotha was, then Mavis would step up. That messed them up, but it woke up the crowd. When you wake up the crowd in church, the spirit starts hitting 'em. It goes through them. Even the ones who want you to think they're already sanctified were going at it. It's like they couldn't believe what they were seeing, like a little miracle or the hand of God or some shit like that."

A national hit changed the way audiences anticipated the family's performances. "When it was our turn to sing," Mavis says, "people would be sitting on the edge of their seats, especially when it came to 'Uncloudy Day.' People would bet that it wasn't a girl singing my part. One man was so mad at me afterward. He said, 'Little girl, I bet my whole paycheck that it wasn't you.'"

In the summer of 1957, the Staple Singers landed a major tour of the South with the Dixie Hummingbirds, the Soul Stirrers, and the Spirit of Memphis. "We didn't know nothing about the other gospel singers not wanting you to outdo them," Mavis says. "We'd just sing. After we'd do 'Uncloudy Day,' everybody would be on their feet, and the other singers thought we were through. But we had another song, 'Tell Heaven.' Pops would call, and I'd answer him. I would get down. People were shouting. Each verse as powerful as the last, and it would go on and on."

"Two women were hanging on to Mavis," Pervis recalls with a laugh. "I'd have to go into the crowd and pull her out."

Mavis shakes her head with mock outrage. "Pervis was supposed to be watching out for me and these two women were tossing me back and forth like a beach ball. Pervis is in his new Italian cream-colored suit, looking cool as can be, walking over to get me. I told Daddy in the dressing room afterward, 'Pervis has got to walk faster!' "

The response made the family more conscious of putting on a "show," instead of just standing rigidly on stage and singing their parts. They sensed the imperative not just to sing but to entertain. "Well, you had to have a little production," Pervis says. "All of it was entertainment, but you had production. Some people didn't want to come to church. You know the story: The boy who's only there because his momma made him come, because he didn't want to listen to no preacher, no singers praising the Almighty. But now, you give him something that makes him want to move, that's a different story. Mavis used to get through with the people in Atlanta, and the acts on after us, they'd have to call an intermission. No way they were going on right after that. Mavis and Cleo would put on robes that look like dresses, because they liked to jump and they'd shake, and the young guys in the audience enjoyed that [laughs]. Couldn't hold things down. Mavis would do that low voice, and Pops would come up with 'I'm Coming Home' and 'Help Me, Jesus'—you could not sit still."

The group jumped on a gospel circuit that already included many of their friends from Chicago. Sam Cooke was in the Soul Stirrers but making a transition to R&B, soon to be replaced by Johnnie Taylor. Lou Rawls led the Pilgrim Travelers. Out of Detroit, Reverend C. L. Franklin was making the rounds with his daughter Aretha, who would usually play a song a night as prelude to one of her father's sermons.

"Unlike many of them," *Goldmine*'s Bill Carpenter asserts, "the Staples got paid."

Pops and the family traveled light: his guitar and amplifier, and the family's clothes stuffed into the trunk of a 1954 Bel Air. Pops later moved up to Cadillacs, which he continued to drive until the group started flying to shows in the '70s. He also carried a gun, which he frequently kept in an attaché case with the family's road earnings. The money was usually split five ways, with the four traveling family members each getting 20 percent and the remainder going home to Oceola, Yvonne, and Cynthia.

For Pops, getting paid was more than just a matter of pride or fairness. It was about feeding his children. He brought righteous indignation—and occasionally his handgun—whenever settling up with promoters, some of whom had a reputation for shortchanging performers if the attendance didn't meet expectations.

"I remember Roebuck talking family with these promoters—he was notorious for striking a hard bargain," Heilbut says. "The first time I saw the Staples in New York—at Mount Moriah Baptist Church in January 1958—it was a big bill, and there were hardly any people there. It was embarrassing for all involved, but the Staples gave it their all. The promoter was the famous crook Ronnie Williams, and afterward all the managers would have to bitch about getting their money. I'm sure no one got full pay that day. But Pops let him know about it. Ronnie Williams would not, not pay him again."

"Uncloudy Day" struck a deeper chord in the South. The Staples were called on to play concerts not only in major cities but also in towns and churches throughout Tennessee, Georgia, Louisiana, Alabama, and Mississippi.

"The Soul Stirrers didn't fool around in the Deep South, we only played Jackson [Mississippi] and Memphis with any regularity," Leroy Crume says. "But that was Staple Singers territory and they played everywhere down south, not just Jackson and Memphis but all points in between. They cleaned up down there. Mississippi was probably the worst state in America for black people, especially black musicians traveling on their own, but Pops and his family were pretty fearless, and they felt comfortable down there."

Many hotels, diners, and bathrooms were off-limits to blacks in the segregation era. The Staples may have been stars for the one hour they were onstage every day, but they couldn't risk stopping between towns trying to find a place to sit down and enjoy a meal. So they'd stock up on groceries, make sandwiches, and eat in the car or by the side of the road. At night, they found shelter in boardinghouses, black-run motels, the backseat of their car—and they couldn't be particularly choosy about the accommodations. Some businesses were almost like safe houses for blacks, including the Riverside Hotel on the banks of the Sunflower River in Clarksdale, Mississippi. It was a former eight-room hospital converted in 1944 by Mrs. Z. L. Hill into a sprawling, thirty-room sanctuary for traveling musicians, including guests such as the young Ike Turner, Howlin' Wolf, and the Staples. There was a piano in the parlor, on which Turner and Jackie Brenston rehearsed their era-defining single "Rocket 88" in 1951, and a best-behavior attitude enforced by the no-nonsense Hill. "We never had a killing, and we never had a robbery," Hill said proudly.

Other overnight stays were a bit more adventuresome. "On one of our first trips, we met a preacher who wanted us to go down to Houston," Pops recalls. "We stayed in a house where his mother lived. She had just died, and Mavis and Cleo had to stay in the room with her casket" while Pops and Pervis slept in the car.

Pops was good for about twelve hours of driving during the day, with Pervis filling in. Mavis frequently took the night shift while the rest of the family burrowed beneath its coats and fell asleep.

Mavis's loyal late-night companion was *Randy*, the nightly *Randy's Record Hi-Lights* program on fifty-thousand-watt WLAC out of Nashville, which could be heard all over the South and into the Midwest. The show was named after Randy's Record Shop in Gallatin, Tennessee, and hosted by Gene Nobles, a DJ who blasted cutting-edge R&B, blues, rock 'n' roll, and gospel by the likes of Chuck Berry, the Spaniels, Etta James, Sonny Boy Williamson, and the emerging Staple Singers, with comedy interludes from salty black entertainers such as Moms Mabley, Redd Foxx, and Dewey "Pigmeat" Markham.

"One time I was driving at night through Lookout Mountain [outside Chattanooga] and everyone else was asleep," Mavis says. "I was cracking up listening to Moms Mabley on *Randy* and speeding. A policeman pulled me over. I told him, 'Officer, sorry I was laughing so hard listening to Moms Mabley I wasn't paying attention.' I cracked him up, and the officer let me off with a warning. I guess he was listening to *Randy*, too [laughs]. Later I pull in to a service station to get gas, and Pops woke up. 'Mavis, you be careful now, I dreamed the police stopped you.'"

Pops also would park a little battery-powered phonograph between the driver's and passenger's seats underneath the dashboard, and play DJ with a steady stream of his favorite gospel 45s.

"There was a gospel record that Cleedi loved, 'Standing at the Judgment' by the Sensational Nightingales," Mavis recalls. "We stopped at a service station in the South, and we all got out to go to the bathroom. We got back in, and Pops started driving. A little while later, Pops says, 'I'm going to wake up Boo'—he always called Cleedi Boo—'and put on her favorite record.' He put on 'Standing at the Judgment' and turned it up loud. 'Boo, you don't hear your record?' We thought she was asleep under a pile of sweaters and coats in the back, but she wasn't in the car. We went back to the service station sixty miles, speeding all the way, and there she was—Cleedi with pink rollers, no shoes on, summertime. 'I figured y'all would miss me eventually.'"

8

"That's the guy who sings 'Blue Suede Shoes'"

Pops Staples had a marvelous head for music, but he was new to the game of routing tours and scheduling live appearances. One time he drove the family two thousand miles straight out to California from Chicago to play a couple of shows, with no stops in between. "We didn't know any better," Mavis says. "But we got to see some great scenery on the way out there. And we learned."

Eventually, the Staples would base themselves for a week in bigger cities such as Memphis, Jackson, Shreveport, Savannah, and Little Rock, where it was easier to find lodging and play a series of shows in nearby towns.

"Gospel was so big down south they could play towns a hundred miles apart and draw an audience," Jerry Butler says. "When Curtis [Mayfield] and I were first doing the Impressions, we moved into R&B, and you didn't have that advantage. Because they were dealing with the Lord, so to speak, they could perform two, three times a day—a morning church service, afternoon worship, and then an evening gospel program."

A seventeen-year-old DJ named Al Bell began playing "Uncloudy Day" in 1957 on the Sunday-morning gospel program at KOKY in Little Rock and began a lifelong relationship with the Staples family.

"As I started going through gospel music, I came across 'Uncloudy Day' and that got my undivided attention," Bell says. "R. L. Weaver, the gospel jock during the week, was playing it, too, and several other Staple Singers records. He and I started talking about promoting shows and we brought in the Staple Singers for one concert, then brought them back in 1958 and did five dates in Arkansas with Reverend C. L. Franklin, Aretha Franklin, the Swanee Quintet, and Sammie Bryant."

Bell had the entire family on his Sunday-morning radio show to promote the upcoming concerts. "With some artists it's not easy to interview or talk to them, but our interview was more like a conversation. Pervis, Pops, Cleotha, and Mavis were all in the studio, and we talked for a while more afterward, too. I thought these are beautiful, sincere, genuine people. There was no uppityness. Many artists onstage and off-stage are two different stories in the way they relate to people, but not them. We talked like we knew each other all our lives."

An imposing six foot four, Bell speaks with the cadence and authority of a preacher. "Rare," he says of the Staples sound, turning the word into an extended exclamation. "Then and now, I've never heard any gospel group that sounds quite like them, harmonized like them, with Pops playing the blues in his gospel way. You talk about rare."

He is still moved when he recalls how Mavis Staples could inhabit a song. "It affected me in a way I never shall forget," he says. "We had them in state for a few concerts, the last one in Pine Bluff, Arkansas, at a school auditorium. I made sure to collect the money in time to watch the entire Staple Singers show. Generally speaking, Mavis never sang a song alone, but 'On My Way to Heaven,' she did it alone, and she cried as she sang, and pretty soon I was crying, too.

"I asked her what was going through her mind at the time, and she said, 'We had been on the road a long time, and as I sang I started thinking about my mother, and missing my mother, and realizing that

I would perhaps get home soon and see her, and I just started crying.' Something happened between the two of us that night, a bond occurred that night that I don't have the words to describe."

As the family came back on subsequent visits, Bell saw Pops refine the group's presentation and marketing. "I would watch how he would set shows up, very organized to the letter," Bell says. "He would have them perform so many songs, make sure he got the audience to a certain point of emotional investment. He wanted to make sure the audience felt what they were about. Then they would take a break just as things were peaking, and not a moment later. There would be an intermission, then they would play their latest album over the PA, and the girls and Pervis would take the albums out to the audience and he would be onstage asking people to buy them, or take a picture with the family. He did it in such a way that you didn't feel offended. It was very casual and good-natured. 'You see my son, Pervis, over there? He's a good-looking fella. Why don't you take a picture with him?' Then they'd get back onstage, and they were back into it. He was just masterful at keeping that vibe, pushing out this powerful, moving music, but selling it, too."

Pops, the all-business businessman, got along well with Bell. "I never saw the gun," Bell says with a laugh, "and fortunately never had to encounter anything like that with him. When I was paying Pops, he said, 'Young man, you're a good businessman. This is the first time I ever made $1,000 in one night. You can book me anytime.' C. L. Franklin said the same thing. One thing about Pops, he was an expert at human relations. You were crystal clear on what was going on in his mind and what he would take and not take. He was as soulful in his communication as he was singing and playing that guitar."

The Staples were getting plenty of airplay on WDIA in Memphis as well. The station, which hit the airwaves in the 1940s, had become a fifty-thousand-watt African-American tastemaker that had launched the careers of Rufus Thomas and B. B. King, among others. Each Christmas, the station staged a Goodwill Revue charity concert that brought a who's who of gospel, blues, R&B, and soul to town. In 1957, the Staples performed on a Goodwill bill that included a young Memphis gospel group, the Dixie Nightingales, with sixteen-year-old David Ruffin, future vocalist in the Temptations.

"He was a little skinny guy—even I was taller than him," Mavis recalls of watching Ruffin perform at Mason Temple, a Pentecostal church with more than thirty-five hundred celebrating fans in attendance. "But he sang with so much feeling, he'd go all through you. You'd just have to sit there and hold yourself to keep from exploding. Cleedi couldn't keep herself from shouting, she just had to let herself go. But I'd fight it. You see, he was bad."

Ruffin's cool was pierced by Rufus Thomas, ever the practical joker. "Rufus jumped down off the stage into the audience with this can, opened up the can right in David's face, and out popped a three-foot [fake] green snake, and David's eyes got as big as . . . he thought it was a real snake!" Mavis says. "He shot down the aisle. He eventually came back to his seat still shaking."

While the Staples performed, three leather-jacketed figures appeared in the wings just offstage. Mavis noticed them because they happened to be just about the only white guys in the room, and they were carrying motorcycle helmets. After she got offstage, one of the bikers struck up a conversation.

"He told me his name but it didn't register," Mavis says. "He knew our music real well, though, and he told me he loved the way Pops played his guitar. 'I like the way your daddy plays that nervous guitar.' David Ruffin comes up to me afterward and is all excited. 'Do you know who that was?' I just shook my head. 'That's the guy who sings "Blue Suede Shoes"!'"

9

"God was in the room"

Elvis Presley wasn't the only one who loved Pops Staples's guitar playing. His style created an atmosphere that was immediately distinctive, a hypnotic swirl of reverberation, repetition, and riff. Chords were implied as much as articulated, notes were blurred, tones and overtones were carefully layered like the bricks Pops used to cement into place at his construction jobs.

That guitar is a cornerstone of the thirty-nine tracks the Staple Singers cut for Vee-Jay between November 1955 and January 1961.

"I'm Coming Home," recorded in 1957, was another masterstroke in the aftermath of "Uncloudy Day," a blues in everything but name, with call-and-response vocals straight off the plantation gallery. Pops plays guitar "as if he's tuning it rather than playing," critic Bill Carpenter wrote. The performance radiates desperation, with Pops's high-pitched vocal give-and-take with Mavis congealing into screams. It's almost a shock hearing the typically cool patriarch sounding so unhinged.

"Home" is once again about a place somewhere beyond the horizon, a destination in the imagination, a sanctuary from the harshness of the present. More showstoppers followed in 1958, with the incantatory momentum of "Help Me, Jesus" and the troubled "This May Be the Last Time," slower and more foreboding than the 1954 version the Staples cut for United. "I've Been Scorned," a 1961 classic, is as doomy and mystical as anything cut by Robert Johnson. Over a brooding guitar riff, Pops sings in a tremulous voice about the trouble he's known and how it's driving him to ride into the afterlife with "two white horses, running side by side."

The Staples' repertoire mixed gospel evergreens that were frequently reconfigured to fit their style, and Pops originals that smudged the line between the spiritual and the practical, a kind of commonsense guide to living not just righteously but with humility and restraint.

"Our father and mother kept their role as parents while we were singing," Mavis told *Pitchfork* in 2010. "We would first go on the road, they would let us know, you stay humble. These people running up to you telling you how great you are, don't let that go to your head. Low is the way. Pops even wrote a song called 'Low Is the Way.' You stay low, not high and mighty. You don't forget this is a gift from God. If you abuse it, it'll be taken away from you."

Jerry Butler recalls that when he and Curtis Mayfield signed with Vee-Jay in the late '50s, they looked up to the Staple Singers as established stars. But the family always treated them as equals. "We were Pops's children, too," Butler recalls. "He looked after us, treated us with respect. He never acted like he was better or knew more. He would talk to us about business, asking us for advice, and he and Curtis would always trade notes about guitar playing."

Butler says Mayfield and Pops may have been the most distinctive guitarists he has ever known, both self-taught, both "untrained," yet both so distinctive you could identify them within two notes. "He and Curtis did as much for the sound of guitar playing in gospel, folk, and R&B as Wes Montgomery did in jazz. I would be in studio sessions where musicians would be told to 'play it like Pops,' 'play it like Curtis,' because in a way they had invented their own style."

Mayfield and Staples both had highly individual perspectives on harmonics, defined by gentleness and subtlety, distinguished by sparseness and concision. Butler has suggested that Mayfield was in part influenced by Pops, most notably in the sense that individuality mattered more than virtuosity. For Pops, his style was something he never thought much about until later:

"My best playing on the guitar is on 'Uncloudy Day,' 'I've Been Scorned,' 'Swing Low, Sweet Chariot.' That sound I was getting out of my amplifier then [at Vee-Jay], I cannot get now. There is tremolo on it, but they do not make the tremolos like they did. My old twin amp is worn-out. It was a Fender Twin, a ten- or twelve-speaker with a foot tremolo. I had a stomp box, too, but I cannot remember what kind. Lord knows, if I had known this day was coming, I would have kept all that stuff. I did not understand the value of some of my guitars, like the Stellar and the Les Paul."

His one-of-a-kind sound, he teased, came from "arranging the buttons [a certain way] on the amplifier." That Pops was a seasoned showman by the time the Staples became national figures is abundantly evident in "Too Close"; a live version recorded in a Chicago church captures the Staples at the height of their powers during the Vee-Jay years.

It starts off with Pops's solo, sinking into Charley Patton mode, sing-speaking the lyrics, then wailing about trying to extricate himself from "a world of sin." When he swoops into a lower register, the congregation begins to laugh appreciatively and applaud. The rest of the family sings in close harmony, then Pops starts to rap. He addresses the congregation, the minister, even the opening group, the Spirit of Memphis: "I'm too close to turn around. Keep on, Brother Wright! 'Cause the Lord has a crown waiting for ya. I tell ya I feel all right, now. The Spirit of Memphis has got me feelin' good. And I want you to know I'm not ashamed knowin' 'em either. And I want you to know tonight that no matter how heavy my burden may get or how harsh the way may be, I'm on my way to heaven, and I don't intend to turn around."

The music drops to near silence, and Mavis enters, moaning over the gorgeous wordless harmonies of her family and taking the song out. "I'm on my way, I'm on my way," they harmonize, and Mavis begins to let loose.

"That's all right!" a voice from the congregation exults. "Don't stop!"

The Staples' ability to move a crowd had been honed for nearly a decade. In gospel, precise performance and brilliant singing weren't enough. This business of singing about God and salvation could be fiercely competitive.

"If you happen to be on a church program, if you didn't 'shout' the people, your peers would be tough," Anthony Heilbut says. "The singers were very aware of this. Mahalia Jackson may have been the queen of the gospel singers, but in the Chicago circuit, they let it be known if other singers were outdoing her. I've seldom seen such a viciously competitive world. In gospel, there was no money, but if someone outshouted you, got people shouting, dancing, that was the real tale of your value."

As a teenager in the '50s, Heilbut closely followed gospel and attended performances in Harlem. He first saw the Staples in 1958 play to a small crowd at a Baptist church, and the performance was somewhat underwhelming.

"The Staples were still very much youngsters and they got to New York on the strength of those hits, 'Uncloudy Day' and later 'Will the Circle Be Unbroken,' but they were working with people who were very much more experienced and professional," Heilbut says. "One of the greatest assets the Staples had was that all the members were beautiful. Roebuck looked like a ladies' man. People were charmed by them, but to the big guys in gospel, the legends, the Staples weren't significant. They would acknowledge the Staples had hit records, but that's it."

Later that same year, Heilbut again saw the Staples at the Apollo Theater on a bill with the Swan Silvertones and Maceo Woods.

"Roebuck sang 'Too Close,' and it was among the best performances I'd ever seen," Heilbut says. "He went up in falsetto—'I can feel Jesus as he breathes on me'—and it was just stunning. It was an old R. H. Harris trick from the Soul Stirrers, but the audience loved it. The Staples got a tremendous reception and they were happy afterward, as if they had finally demonstrated they were worthy of being up there with these heavies."

The Staples got name-checked in the Dixie Hummingbirds' "Let's Go Out to the Programs Number 2," the second of two singles in which the famed gospel quartet imitated some of their peers and rivals, this time focusing on mostly female vocalists. Howard Carroll channels Pops's guitar sound, and Ira Tucker credibly approximates Mavis's contralto. "It's not a particularly strong record," Heilbut says, "but the big point is that after two years on the road, the Staples' sound had become that recognizable."

Mavis also was starting to emerge as not just a potent singer but also a more confident and charismatic performer. Pops was the emcee, a mix of preacher, guitar player, musical director, and soothing voice of wisdom. Mavis would play his foil, sanctified emotion personified. She had been watching and learning from performers such as Ruth Davis of the Davis Sisters and Dorothy Love Coates, who would wade into the audience while performing to clasp hands and march down the aisles. It was a type of choreographed spontaneity that brought a physical dimension to what was being sung, and audiences responded in kind—leaping out of their seats, shouting encouragement to the performers, raising their arms in ecstatic celebration.

"They were with C. L. Franklin and Aretha at Mount Moriah Baptist Church again in 1960, and it was a huge difference from the previous time two years before," Heilbut says. "This time it was a full house, and Mavis had learned a few tricks. She came down into the crowd and was working them. Aretha, for all her talent, could be a cold, somewhat remote and erratic performer. Mavis doesn't do what Aretha does, but she has more charm. Mavis knows how to sell a crowd. If the Staples were just Roebuck and the group, they couldn't have held their own against the powerhouse gospel singers, but with Mavis they could. She always works from her heart."

Jon Shields saw a similar transformation. He went to the Staples' home at 649 East 89th Street to buy six tickets, at $5 each, for a concert at DuSable High School in the fall of 1960. Oceola and Yvonne were at the high school entrance checking people in and selling tickets. Hundreds were in attendance, and the show was blatantly oversold—fans not only filled the seats but packed the aisles and sat on the floor in front of the stage. The South Side was out in force and in its Sunday best: fedoras, mink stoles, heels, suits, and ties.

"I had spectator's pumps and brown slacks—we were dressed to the nines," Shields recalls. "This was a family outing that people took pride in. But people burst out of that finery when the spirit took over."

Shields was already a veteran gospel watcher; he once attended a Dorothy Love Coates and Davis Sisters gospel program where the emotions ran so high that "a woman in a mink stole threw a baby up in the air and someone else in the audience caught the baby." But even against those memories, this Staple Singers performance stood out.

The performers matched their audience in style and fervor. Pops and Pervis as always wore identical dark two-piece suits, shirts, ties, and leather shoes that gleamed in the spotlights. Mavis and Cleotha wore pumps and matching long-sleeved robes that reached the floor.

"The Staples were the first gospel group that I saw where Mavis and Cleo put a belt around their robes and the back of the robe hung loose," Shields says. "They were being creative to change the look of the 'gospel uniform.' At that time, most of the female gospel singers wore loose-fitting choir robes. Mavis and Cleo, being young women, wanted to look a little more stylish. The belt gave the robe a form, and you could more clearly see the shape of their bodies."

Cleotha had studied dressmaking at Dunbar High School and worked as a seamstress at Hart Schaffner & Marx, a business that specialized in tailored menswear.

"Cleedi was an innovator in giving us our look; we'd go to bridal shops and buy dresses that bridesmaids would wear," Mavis says. "The sheikh dress was in style—a straight, loose dress that set us apart on the gospel programs. Pops and Pervis would wear Italian silk suits, alligator shoes. We wanted to look sharp."

But it was the group's investment in its songs that moved the audience and burned itself into Shields's memory, in particular the fierce exchange between Pops and Mavis on "Tell Heaven."

"It just tore the auditorium up, and people went into hysterics with the call-and-response between Pops and Mavis," Shields says. "Mavis had tears running down her face. Everybody in the auditorium could feel what she was feeling inside. I have asked Mavis from time to time to sing that song again, and she says, 'You're trying to put me to work.' She won't do it anymore. That was really her and Pops singing back and forth to each other, and then Pervis and Cleo would hit a background note between the interacting leads. Mavis didn't miss a note, break a note, but the tears were flowing as this tune was coming out of her mouth. The tears reflected the emotion in her voice. It gives me chills just to think about it. I was twenty. I had a friend who lived in Pine Bluff, Arkansas, and he told me when they came there, he said the same thing happened when they sang 'Tell Heaven.' He said he had never heard an anointed voice the way her voice was anointed during that song. Everybody had lost control. It was an out-of-body experience. No question about it, God was in the room."

10

Sam Cooke and Aretha

The Staple Singers were a gospel group as far as Pop Staples was concerned, but his definition of "gospel" had some play in it. His own record label said as much in an advertisement for the *Uncloudy Day* album that ran in the August 31, 1959, issue of *Billboard:* "A family fivesome, dad harmonizing with four children, aged 7 to 25, in stirring spiritual Americana."

The factual error aside (seven-year-old Cynthia really wasn't part of the group), Vee-Jay saw the group more clearly than perhaps even Pops would allow himself to do. His guitar playing evoked the blues he first heard at Dockery Farms, and the group's arrangements borrowed heavily from other genres. Evelyn Gay heard them as "country" or "hillbilly," a down-home group that evoked a melting pot of early twentieth-century Mississippi styles. Pop may have had his head in the gospel world, but his kids were soaking up everything else; Mavis was tuning in WLAC out of Nashville on her late-night drives to hear not just "Uncloudy Day" but also the latest from Jimmy Reed, Muddy Waters, Sam Cooke, Ray Charles, and the Flamingos.

"Good News," a 1959 Staples recording for Vee-Jay, copped Charles's opening riff for his huge R&B hit that year, "What'd I Say," just as the

Staples' version of the gospel standard "Stand by Me" was reconfigured by Ben E. King, Jerry Leiber, and Mike Stoller into an R&B classic. The soulful pop music Charles and King forged in the '50s and '60s was based on Southern church singing, so the affinity between the two camps was hardly unexpected.

"I once ran into Pervis in a dressing room at a gospel show, and he was talking about how the vamp for their 'Sit Down Servant' was based on a Ray Charles song," Anthony Heilbut says. "Pops was the real genius, the smarts of the group, the vision was his. But his family were all savvy kids. It was very clear to me that there was almost a tug-of-war within the group. The kids were totally of their generation, hanging out with Carla Thomas and the R&B talent, and Pops was very much of his generation, commiserating with the preachers and older gospel singers. Mavis was schooled by Pops, but she's very much a modern singer—that means that everyone from James Brown to Aretha to countless others would have been absorbed."

On the road, the family witnessed the tug-of-war between gospel and the artistic and commercial lure of secular music play out in front of them. Their first major tour after Mavis graduated from high school in 1957 was with the Soul Stirrers, whose lead vocalist was their old Dirty Thirties friend Sam Cooke.

Cooke's father, Charles, was a Baptist minister, and Sam grew up singing gospel, eventually becoming lead vocalist in the Highway Q.C.'s and then, at the age of nineteen in 1950, replacing the great R. H. Harris in the Soul Stirrers.

Even then, Cooke's charisma brought a level of hysteria to gospel programs that was as much erotic as spiritual. "He was king in the gospel field," Mavis says. "S. R. Crane was the Soul Stirrers' manager, and if some group like the Pilgrim Travelers was up there tearing it up, getting the ladies shouting, Crane wasn't having it. He would send Sam strolling up the middle aisle [while the rival group was still performing], and it would be over when the ladies saw Sam Cooke in his suit looking fine, with that cool, confident strut. Crane would do it on purpose. Daddy would warn him, 'Crane, you better not do that to us.' Crane would say, 'You got to learn to take care of your own business.' "

In 1956, Cooke cut the song "Lovable," essentially a secular remake of the Soul Stirrers' gospel hit "Wonderful." Fearing the repercussions of singing the "devil's music," Cooke had the single released under the transparent alias "Dale Cooke." Hardly anyone was fooled, and subsequent Soul Stirrers concerts became forums for gospel purists and Cooke's most ardent fans to loudly express their clashing views. The Staples' 1957 tour with the Soul Stirrers was Cooke's last as a gospel singer, Mavis says.

"Sam got up with the Soul Stirrers and sang 'Lovable,' and those sisters [in the audience] at Mason Temple in Memphis, a huge place, stood up and shouted at him. 'You sit down! We don't want you singing the blues.' They kept on and Sam just threw his hands up and walked off-stage. I didn't see him that night when we went back to the hotel. I knew he felt bad, because he loved gospel just as much as the love songs. But the next thing we heard from him was 'You Send Me,' and that was the end of his gospel days."

Pervis and Cleotha were the Staples family members who were closest to Cooke, because they had been classmates at Dunbar High School. "We were strictly gospel, and I was strictly into it," Pervis says. "But I would go to see Sam and Lou [Rawls] perform after they crossed over. I'd argue with Pop about it. 'Do you think religion was designed to make pleasures less?' If he didn't have an answer, he'd walk away from me, and I'd go to the concert. When he was thinking about switching over, Sam would visit. He'd say, 'Pops, what do you think my dad will say to me?' We got on the middle of the fence, but he switched right over. [Crossing over to pop music] kept you alive, too, kept you having gigs. But Pops wasn't having it, at first."

Cooke was among the first major performers to cross over from gospel to pop, and "the gospel singers couldn't talk about nothing else,"

Aretha Franklin recalled. Soon enough, Franklin would make her own transition into secular music, with the blessing of her father, the revered preacher C. L. Franklin.

Franklin signed in 1960 with Columbia Records, and her first single for the label, "Today I Sing the Blues," announced her career change. It was released only weeks after she and her father had gotten off the road with the Staple Singers, playing for $1 admission at gospel programs in the South. Now she entered a different world, playing venues such as the tiki bar and restaurant Tradewinds on Chicago's Rush Street and incongruously opening for the likes of comedian Buddy Hackett. Whenever she showed up in Chicago, she'd often stay at the Staples family home, where Oceola kept her door and kitchen open twenty-four hours a day for visiting friends. Mavis, Yvonne, and Cleotha in turn would vacation together and visit the Franklins—Aretha, her sisters, Erma and Carolyn, and brother, Cecil, and stepbrother, Vaughn—at their home in Detroit.

"Reverend Franklin would call the house looking for Aretha, and Pops would say, 'Yeah, she's in the basement with Yvonne,'" Pervis recalls. "'Send her home, she has a show tonight,' he says, and Pops was like, 'Man, she's sick.' And I'll never forget how Reverend Franklin would respond: 'What does she have that $10,000 tonight won't cure?'"

Mavis laughs when the story is recounted. "Aretha didn't care—$10,000 didn't make her move. She stayed right there."

For a time in the '60s, Mavis, Yvonne, and Aretha were confidantes and girlfriends; Mavis occasionally fixed Aretha's hair for her gigs and album covers (notably the 1965 *Yeah!!!* release on Columbia with Aretha peering over a pair of sunglasses perched on her nose). They also fought like sisters.

At age nineteen, Franklin married thirty-one-year-old Ted White over her father's objections. White would later become her manager, but the relationship was troubled from the start. The tensions spilled over one day in the Franklins' kitchen in Detroit, while Mavis and Yvonne were visiting on vacation.

"Me and Yvonne were staying at Aretha's when Ted White came in," Mavis says. "We were like one big family. But Aretha is out of sorts. She tells [her sister] Carolyn to change clothes, because she had on Bermuda shorts and didn't want her looking like that in front of her husband. Then she came after me, 'Mavis, everybody loves you, so why don't you go after my husband?' I said, 'I'm not like that.' Then she pushed me and I grabbed her collar. I had her up against the sink. Erma [Franklin] and Yvonne had to pull me off. Erma was saying, 'She doesn't mean it, she's drunk.' But when she pushed me, that was it. Yvonne and I got out of there."

Yet Aretha relied on the Staples family for advice and support, often using their home on 89th Street as something of a chill-out space apart from her increasingly hectic life and career.

"Aretha was crazy about Mama," Mavis says. "She was going through some changes with her marriage to Ted. One time, she was supposed to catch a plane to Vegas, but instead she came to see Mama. She stayed for three weeks, telling Mama all her problems, what was going on with her and Ted. Mama said, 'Baby, you have to pray.' And Aretha said, 'I try to pray, but I can't finish the prayer.' And Mama just said, 'Wherever you stop, that'll be your prayer.'"

Bobby Womack was a teenager singing in a gospel group with his brothers out of Cleveland when first Cooke and then the Staple Singers took him under their guidance. Womack's preacher father, Friendly Womack, finagled an opening slot for his boys at a Soul Stirrers concert in 1956 in Cleveland, and twelve-year-old Bobby and his brothers wowed the audience.

"Sam led the ovation, called my mother onstage and put $10 in her purse," Womack says. "Then he had her stand by the door to collect more—we made about $73 that night." Soon after, the Womack Brothers hit the gospel circuit with the Staple Singers, playing to as many as three thousand people a night.

"The Staples were the first ones who took us out on tour," Womack says. "They introduced us to people in the music business. Pops was like my dad. Mavis, Cleotha, and Yvonne are like my sisters. We grew up together on the road and, being older, they taught us a lot."

When Cooke signed the Womacks to his SAR label, he followed a familiar strategy: He changed their name to the Valentinos and then had them record "Lookin' for a Love," a pop version of Bobby's gospel song "Couldn't Hear Nobody Pray." The song was a hit and set the stage for a long and highly successful career in R&B for Womack, who would also play guitar in Cooke's band. But it incensed Friendly Womack, who kicked his boys out of the house for abandoning gospel.

"My father was more strict than Pops was," Womack says. "Pops was telling my dad, 'You got to let these boys sing. As long as they sing good lyrics it's not a problem. Don't separate gospel from secular.' He had a different outlook than a lot of gospel people. He would try things. He was a Christian, but he was also a music man. My father would listen to him because he respected Pops. He was our second dad. He would talk to us, very cool and calm, never raised his voice. That got our attention."

Even after Cooke and Franklin switched over to pop, the Staples would continue to run into them on the road, often returning to the common ground they found in childhood.

"We'd go to different cities, meet in different places, Sam would be appearing someplace in a show, we might be on a gospel program, and we would get in the hotel room and sit there almost all night singing gospel songs," Cleotha said. "Everybody would come to our hotel room because we had church going on in there, sure did. Sam would go in Reverend Franklin's room and they'd have conversations with our father and Reverend Franklin. We were just tight, because all of us grew up in the slums together. Sam came from a religious family, and I don't think he ever forgot it, even in his work. 'Cause although he didn't sing gospel, he acted the part. He was still a religious person 'cause of the way he acted toward his fellow man. See, when you start making money, a lot of people don't know how to accept it. They get a grand and won't speak to you 'cause they look down on you. Sam never did that. His friends were always the same."

Cooke played the suave, unflappable crooner on stage and in public life. But behind the scenes with the Staples, he could be himself, often behaving like a kid. He'd enter their motel room in the morning and pull Mavis, still in her pajamas, out of bed feet first.

The sisters were chaste compared to the trouble Pervis and Sam Cooke's guitar player, Leroy Crume, frequently found. When the Staple Singers first went on the road with the Soul Stirrers in the '50s, Pervis, Crume, and Cooke went out marauding. They were into the usual road silliness involving women and liquor, though the tales might seem tame to later generations of pillaging rock stars. Cooke was a silky celebrity who had girls chasing him in every town, and Pervis and Crume weren't shy about joining the party. "We were some wild kids," Crume says with a laugh. "If we weren't with the Staple Singers, me and Sam would be crazy. We would act double stupid with Pervis, though. Pervis and I called each other 'Blab' because we both talked so much. We didn't pay any attention to the business stuff. We wanted to sing, get off the stage, and communicate with some ladies."

Crume had a brief romance with the teenage Mavis, and Pervis would play pranks on the young couple on the road. One day in the South, Crume awoke to Pops's distinctively loud three-knock rap on his motel room door.

"I open the door getting ready to go into my little act, and it's Pervis standing there grinning," Crume says with a laugh. "'It's okay, Mavis, Blab says you can come out of the closet now.'"

Pervis left the group from 1958 to 1960 to serve in the army at Fort Leonard Wood, Missouri, and then Fort Lee in Virginia. His place in the Staples was taken by Yvonne, who had been working as Pops's business partner, helping book tours and managing the group's finances.

Occasionally Pervis would take leave from his duties to briefly rejoin the group.

"Once, while singing at the Apollo, Pervis came from the army in Virginia to join us onstage," Pops recalled. "Yvonne was the manager and was not too excited about singing, so Pervis replaced her that night. The girls wore pink sheer dresses with long cotton slips. The dresses were straight but flared at the bottom. Instead of sewing a zipper in the slips, the dressmaker made them with hooks and eyes. Cleo would clap, then Mavis and Pervis would do a fancy double clap over their heads."

Mavis clapped and could feel her slip fall. She turned to Pervis and asked him to pick up the slip as he left the stage so as not to attract attention. Mavis stepped out of the slip and exited stage left, Pervis exited to the right.

"He picked up the slip all right," Pops recalled. "Instead of balling it up, he started flagging it full length from the waist. The audience went up for grabs, laughing and hollering. Mavis looked back to see her brother parading her slip."

While performing with the U.S. Army Chorus in Virginia, Pervis met and later married LeNora Anderson. But when Pervis returned from the army to rejoin his family on the road, he and Crume resumed their tag-team tomcat adventures.

"We had this gig in Gary, Indiana, and I drove my personal car from Chicago," Crume says. "We finished the gig up pretty early, around eleven, and we didn't intend to hang out because we were both married, so we went out for coffee. But three or four ladies wanted to hang. We got a hotel room to talk till maybe one, then go home. One thing led to another, then Blab went and got another room. We paired off. The next morning the sun is shining through the window, and I call his room. 'Blab, do you know what time it is?' 'Oh, hell, we in trouble.' His old lady was jealous and mine was, too. We were driving home trying to make up excuses. He was begging me to go in with him, he was so sure

LeNora was gonna go off on him. Instead, everything's cool. I get home, and my wife is smiling, going off to work. Pervis and I never could figure it out. He thought our wives had collaborated. From that day to this day they never said a word about that night. We got away with one—or maybe they did."

11

Modern folksingers

For all the Staple Singers' initial success at Vee-Jay, the group never enjoyed a follow-up hit on the scale of "Uncloudy Day." Pops Staples was a gospel disciple, but he wanted an audience that reached beyond the genre's narrow confines. If he wasn't keen to dive in as deep into the crossover waters as Sam Cooke, Aretha Franklin, and Bobby Womack had, he still wanted to address and win over secular music fans on his terms.

"We started out as a so-called gospel group, but the Staple Singers were not just a straight gospel group in the face of our religion and gospel people," Pops said in a 1973 interview with the *Los Angeles Free Press*. "We've always been a kind of blues-like-sounding group, because I started out playing guitar, playing blues. When we sang gospel, we'd kinda be on that same kick and I'd have the same chords and keys that we played the blues in. The real gospel singers like Mahalia Jackson, Roberta Martin, and Clara Ward, we just wasn't in that category. We more or less was in a kind of modern folksingers bag."

Pops may have been speaking with the benefit of hindsight—it's unclear how aware he actually was of the "modern folksingers bag" at the start of the '60s. By then he was a man in his midforties, immersed in the culture of gospel and the day-to-day responsibilities of being a father, husband, band manager, booking agent, financial planner, song-writer, and tour security guard. But Pops also was a splendid mix of caution and curiosity; he was open to persuasion and logic.

"Pops is someone who could change and adapt, but you had to show him that it made sense," says Bill Carpenter. "It was like law court: You had to present your case, lay out the ramifications, and then he would have to digest whether it was worth those ramifications."

And clearly Pops saw the Staple Singers as not just a musical endeavor, but a business, a livelihood not only for himself but his children that he needed to preserve and nurture above almost anything else.

"[Vee-Jay talent scout] Calvin Carter used to say, 'Pops sure does take care of his kids'—he knew that's what motivated Pops," Jerry Butler recalls. "Whenever there was some negotiating to be done, he was right in the center of it fighting for his kids. It was hard to deal with him on a business level, because his business was his kids. It was always a collective. When you saw one, you always saw the other three. They were gentle, spiritually oriented people, but Pops would circle the wagons if he felt in any way that their livelihood was being threatened or compromised."

In 1961, Pops signed with Gary Kramer, a former Atlantic Records executive, who had opened his own management company, Jubilee Artists Corp. Kramer's clients included gospel singers Marion Williams and Alex Bradford, and actor Billy Dee Williams.

Pops showed up at the Jubilee offices in Manhattan "all by himself, country but super slicked up," recalls Anthony Heilbut, who tipped Kramer to the Staple Singers. Kramer landed them a date at the Evansville Jazz Festival in June 1961, where the Staples performed on a bill with Duke Ellington, Cannonball Adderley, Ira Sullivan, Al Hirt, and Mel Tormé. It was among the first significant dates for the Staples outside the gospel circuit. Though attendance was sparse, the jazz bible *Down Beat* covered the festival, and many of the performers saw the Staples in action for the first time and came away impressed.

"It was a very small audience—Kramer must have lost his shirt—but Cannonball Adderley told me he was big fan of the Staples because they reminded him of down-home singing," Heilbut says. Ellington told Pops he loved what the group was doing; it's where he saw the family play "gospel in a blues key" for the first time.

Kramer urged his friend Orrin Keepnews at Riverside Records to sign the Staples. Keepnews was a jazz aficionado with a nuanced eye and ear for talent; his roster brimmed with heavy hitters such as Adderley, Thelonious Monk, Bill Evans, Charlie Byrd, Johnny Griffin, and Wes Montgomery. He also had an extensive folk catalog, including Bascom Lamar Lunsford, George Pegram, Jean Ritchie, and Bob Gibson. Keepnews was largely unfamiliar with the Staple Singers and gospel music in general when Kramer first mentioned them, but he was sold after he heard some of their Vee-Jay recordings.

"When Kramer got them on Riverside," Heilbut says, "the Staples were very proud—they got something like $24,000 for two years, which at the time was a lot for gospel talent."

On February 18, 1962, the Staples made another appearance designed to stretch their reach. "Gospel: The Soul of Jazz" concert at Carnegie Hall was billed as "a dramatized history of 100 years of Negro Church Music and its influence in the development of Jazz." The other performers included Dizzy Gillespie, the Bobby Timmons Trio, Faye Adams, Alex Bradford, Marion Williams, the Soul Stirrers, the Caravans, and the Choir of the Greater Abyssinian Baptist Church.

The Staple Singers were becoming one of gospel music's most reliable draws. The *Chicago Defender* reported that in 1962 the family took in $60,000; at the time, the average family income in the United States was $6,000.

The group's classy, high-profile appearances started bringing them some serious mainstream media attention. The legendary jazz critic Nat Hentoff praised the group's spooky subtlety: "Rather than exploding in tambourine-whacking euphoria, the Staple Singers are more introspective, so much so that the listener gets the impression he's overhearing a family service. Especially compelling is these vocalists' insinuating beat, which draws the listener into the music as if he were caught in an undertow gathering momentum for more than three centuries." *Time* magazine raved, "Roebuck himself is a first-rate guitarist, but his daughter Mavis is the best vocalist, a contralto whose voice has both a honeyed quality and almost hypnotic intensity." *Down Beat*'s Pete Welding went even further in praising Mavis, describing her as "an extraordinarily gifted singer, with a vibrant, flexible voice with power to spare. Her dramatic sense shapes songs so that their content and meaning leap to the fore. Her performances are less interpretations than they are effusions of her own deep-seated conviction and religiosity." At year's end, *Down Beat* named the Staple Singers its "new star" vocal group.

Two days after the Carnegie Hall concert, the Staples entered New York's Plaza Sound Studios to record their first album for Riverside. Pops didn't stray from the Vee-Jay template. He came armed with traditional gospel tunes and filtered them through the Staples' well-honed sound: his sparse, blues-inflected guitar; Mavis's increasingly nuanced vocals, now brimming with a sophisticated, knowing, profoundly adult melancholy on hymns such as "Hear My Call, Here" and "Nobody Knows the Trouble I've Seen"; and the group's twangy harmonies, with Cleotha in particularly piercing form.

"Pops wanted to be able to broaden the audience without alienating his base," Keepnews told journalist Rob Bowman. "He kept referring to what an important part of their livelihood their regular run of church gigs was. He was nervous about the possibility and didn't want to do anything too extreme with repertoire."

But Keepnews did hire a sharp rhythm section, with Leonard Gaskin on bass and Joe Marshall Jr. and Gus Johnson sharing drums. The session musicians weren't just window dressing as they were on the group's Vee-Jay recordings; Keepnews gave the drums more punch in the mix. Pervis, Cleotha, and Mavis had now developed an intricate array of handclaps, and with the drums they injected up-tempo tracks such as

"Everybody Will Be Happy" and "Great Day" with Holy Roller energy. The polyrhythmic handclapping was commonplace in gospel, but it sent a charge through the gospel novices the Staples began to see in their audiences in the '60s.

"The handclapping started in church. We'd sing something fast and Pervis would do a double-clap, Cleedi would play it straight, and I'd do a syncopated clap," Mavis says. "It's the sound of the sanctified church with the tambourine, but we didn't have that tambourine, so we had to come up with something in its place."

The title track, "Hammer and Nails," was a relatively new gospel tune written by Aaron Schroeder and David Hill. It carried a spiritual message without being overtly religious, propelled by Gus Johnson's drums and the exuberant call-and-response between Mavis and the family.

"I didn't feel like Riverside was trying to change us drastically," Mavis says. "They may have wanted us to sing stuff without using the word 'God' in the song, but something like 'Hammer and Nails'—'It takes more than a hammer and nails to make a house a home'—I could relate to those words. And I think our old audience could, too."

Keepnews brought the family back into the studio in July 1962 to record a Christmas album, this time working out of the Staples' old haunt at Universal Studios on the North Side of Chicago. Cleotha had temporarily left the group, at the request of her husband, Edgar Harris, because she had been away from home so much while touring. Cleotha focused on her sewing skills and started a hat-making business, so Yvonne was pressed into service again as a vocalist for the next two years.

Family friend Jon Shields attended the Christmas album session at Universal. "That was the first recording where Yvonne was taking a prominent role as a background singer on 'There Was a Star,'" Shields says, though Yvonne had also contributed to several tracks at Vee-Jay while Pervis was in the army.

"Pops really rehearsed Yvonne hard on her part; at the end of the tune he was trying to have her hit this high note. Cleo brought that high tenor whine sound for the Staples, and Pops was trying to get Yvonne to play that role."

The homey feel of *The 25th Day of December* album makes it a pleasant, if ultimately marginal addition to the Staples discography. But soon the group would meet the new prince of the emerging folk movement face-to-face, and their music and lives would take a turn.

12

For the love of Bob Dylan

While growing up in Hibbing, Minnesota, during the '50s, Bob Dylan got a late-night crash course in blues, country, folk, R&B, early rock 'n' roll, and gospel by traveling across the AM radio dial. He picked up stations as far away as Little Rock and Shreveport to absorb the mysteries and provocations of everyone from Odetta and Hank Williams to Little Richard and Jimmy Reed.

"We'd listen to the radio, usually late in the evening," Dylan said in a 2002 PBS documentary on the Staples. "*Dragnet* and *FBI in Peace and War, Inner Sanctum* and Jack Benny. And then after the radio shows would come on, we used to pick up the station out of Shreveport and they used to play rhythm and blues, Bobby 'Blue' Bland, Junior Parker, and Muddy [Waters] and [Howlin'] Wolf, and all that. But then at midnight the gospel stuff would start. I got to be acquainted with the Swan Silvertones and the Dixie Hummingbirds, the Highway Q.C.'s and all that. But the Staple Singers came on . . . and they were so different."

He was particularly enchanted by the Staples' stark reading of "Won't You Sit Down (Sit Down Servant)," which they had recorded for both United and Vee-Jay.

"Mavis was singing stuff like, 'Yonder come little David with a rock and a sling, I don't want to meet him, he's a dangerous man,'" Dylan said. "I thought, 'Oh, my goodness!' That made my hair stand up. I thought, 'That's how the world is.'"

The group's sparse but haunting sound also staggered him. Pops's "easy flowing, gentle voice" stood in vivid contrast to Mavis's fierce contralto, and his guitar "tremolo made the listener tremble and shake . . . he made you feel the trembling that was inside yourself," Dylan said.

The singer had arrived in New York in January 1961 and released his debut album a year later; largely made up of cover songs, it sold only a few thousand copies. But in 1962 he began performing the newly written song "Blowin' in the Wind," which soon was adopted as a protest anthem by the emerging folk movement. Dylan acknowledged that "Blowin' in the Wind" was adapted from the old Negro spiritual "No More Auction Block," and his songwriting bore the imprint of gospel in originals such as "Ain't Gonna Grieve" and "Paths of Victory."

His keen interest in the music brought him to the Gospel Music Festival on September 7–9, 1962, at Downing Stadium on Randall's Island in New York. He accompanied Robert Shelton, who was covering the event for the *New York Times* and would become the singer's first biographer. Dylan was taken aback by the ostentatious arrival of Mahalia Jackson in a limousine, her gown lifted by aides. He was drawn to the more unassuming and approachable demeanor of artists like the Staples.

Shelton introduced Dylan to Pops and his children, who were impressed that the young folk prodigy was on such intimate terms with their music. "We were just shocked this little white boy—and he was little—knew our stuff," Mavis recalls. "And then we'd hear him sing and Pops would say, 'Wait a minute, y'all, listen to what this kid is saying.'"

The Staples patriarch was struck that a young white man from the North had so accurately reflected how Pops felt as a Southern black man. The opening lines of "Blowin' in the Wind"—"How many roads must a man walk down / Before you call him a man?"—took him back to his days growing up in Mississippi, when he was sometimes made to feel like something less.

The Staples family and Dylan crossed paths frequently in the next few years. In March 1963, the Staples taped a Westinghouse TV special in New York with Dylan and several other folk acts, including the Brothers Four, Carolyn Hester, and Barbara Dane. At the taping, the Staples performed Dylan's favorite, "Sit Down Servant," and Dylan did "Blowin' in the Wind." All the artists came out for the finale, Woody Guthrie's "This Land Is Your Land."

"Blowin' in the Wind" and "This Land Is Your Land" would be included on the Staple Singers' next album for Riverside, *This Land.* It was recorded in Chicago on June 12–13, 1963, only days after Dylan's second, breakthrough album, *The Freewheelin' Bob Dylan,* was released with his own version of "Blowin' in the Wind" leading off. When the folk-pop trio Peter, Paul and Mary released their quaint cover of "Blowin' in the Wind," it sold more than a million copies in a few weeks, turning folk music—and, by extension, Dylan—into a pop-culture phenomenon. Singers earnestly strumming acoustic guitars and searching for answers in a troubled world became the new language of youth protest.

Folk music meant almost nothing to the African-American inhabitants of the Northern ghettos and Southern farms, but the musical movement did ignite a hunger for "authenticity" and substance among young white listeners, who became increasingly conversant with blues and soul. Over in England, a host of young, white rockers essentially reconfigured American roots music and resold it to the American public. Veteran black artists were pulled out of irrelevance by the surge. Muddy Waters, John Lee Hooker, Son House, and Howlin' Wolf were among the African-American artists who enjoyed second acts in their careers, in large measure due to the exposure their music received on albums by the Rolling Stones, Cream, the Animals, and other U.K. bands. For the first time, the aging blues artists found themselves playing and selling music to a largely white audience.

The folk and civil rights movements symbolically merged on August 28, 1963, when folk artists including Dylan, Joan Baez, Odetta, and Peter, Paul and Mary appeared at Martin Luther King's historic human-rights March on Washington. It was to this audience that the 1963 *This Land* album was clearly directed, a balancing act between the gospel upon which the Staples had built their reputation in the '50s and timely message-oriented songs that spoke to audiences buzzing on the pop currency of Dylan and Baez.

"The Staples themselves have never seen any point in limiting their own musical interests," Orrin Keepnews wrote in the liner notes. "They see nothing surprising in numbers like 'Old Time Religion' or 'Swing Down, Chariot!' being simultaneously considered 'gospel' by some, 'folk' by others, and 'spirituals' by still others. And Roebuck Staples has become increasingly fascinated by the fact that a good deal of music in the folk vein is thoroughly consistent, both in mood and in message, with the kind of thoughts and ideas the group has been expressing in its music for a long time."

Pervis, as usual, put it in more practical terms. He, of all the family members, had been itching to move the group into more secular terrain. "I was always like, 'Hey, the gospel is not selling,'" he says. "Yeah, we could play this on the five-thousand-watt gospel station or we could play this on the fifty-thousand-watt commercial station. I was having beers and stuff with cats who made a step up above where we were. We started singing the folk songs. We ran into Dylan, Baez, and Johnny Cash, people we respected. We saw this was a whole different market we could be a part of."

But the Staples didn't pull off those ambitions right away. Their version of "This Land Is Your Land" opens the album and presents it as a leaden, personality-free sing-along. Its most controversial, confrontational lyrics are chopped off. Almost any group could have recorded the song, so bereft is it of any kind of detail that would have stamped it as a Staples song. An overdubbed piano imposes an incongruous jauntiness and further distances the performance from the Staples' classic sound.

Pops sings "Blowin' in the Wind" with heartfelt melancholy, but the strummed guitar does little to distinguish it from Dylan's version, or anyone else's, for that matter. Even worse is a straight reading of Lead Belly's "Cotton Fields" with more piano sweetening. The song's lighthearted feel imbues sharecropping with a kind of nostalgic glow that should have infuriated the Staple Singers (to their defense, the song had been covered numerous times, part of the repertoire of respected black artists such as Odetta and Harry Belafonte). Even Keepnews's liner notes dismiss "Cotton Fields" as "good-natured folk nonsense."

Years later, when questioned about the song, Mavis laughs. "I remember when they came to us with that song and I thought, 'That sounds like black people watermelon music.' But Pops talked to me about it. He fixed it so I didn't mind singing it. It was one of those moments where I had my doubts, but I trusted my father. We all did."

Pops defended the group's expanding repertoire of folk songs in a 1964 interview with the *American Folk Music Occasional* as "good material" and jumped off into a long, passionate explanation of the meaning behind "This Land Is Your Land."

"I think it's time for the whole nation to start listening to something that means something . . . this is everybody's land, this is not just my land, this is our land. This land belongs to everybody; if they would think like that we'd have a better United States. You know it's really rough what the colored entertainers have to go through sometimes in their travels."

He recounted incidents where he and Reverend C. L. Franklin were insulted by a gas station attendant on a gospel tour in Yazoo City, Mississippi. Stopping at a food counter, the proprietor ordered them to enter through the back entrance. A disgusted Pops said everyone left without eating: "You'd be hungry, too, but you don't feel like eating after they tell you something like that. . . . That's why the colored people sing the blues, that's why they sing with soul."

Blues and soul had little to do with tripe like "Cotton Fields," though. The soul of the *This Land* album was found in its more traditional gospel songs, with Pops at his mesmerizing best in "A Dying Man's Plea" amid washes of ghostly guitar, and "A Better Home," which straddles gospel and country. The music has greater punch than ever, thanks to a rhythm section handpicked and rigorously rehearsed by Pops at his

Chicago home on 89th Street before the sessions: drummer Al Duncan, a holdover from the Vee-Jay days, and bassists Johnny Pate and Phil Upchurch.

Upchurch was only twenty-one at the time and already a rising star on the Chicago scene, working with jazz, doo-wop, and blues artists and scoring a hit with the song "You Can't Sit Down." But he set aside his guitar to play electric bass for the Staple Singers, and would continue to back them on subsequent tours.

Typical of musicians in the Chicago scene, Upchurch was curious about how Pops arrived at his highly individual sound and was eager to work with him. "He played a Fender Stratocaster and a Fender Twin Amp," Upchurch says. "He used the tremolo effect on the amp. It was a rural style used by Delta blues musicians like John Lee Hooker. A great deal of the songs were in the key of E. We rehearsed at Pops's house so that when we arrived at the studio there was no time wasted working on the music."

It was Upchurch's impression that nothing was foisted on the Staples by Keepnews or anybody else. "The Staple Singers songs were not much different than the other material," he says of the decision to mix folk and gospel. "There were never any displays of ego; they rolled as a cohesive, tight-knit family group."

Six weeks after the *This Land* sessions, the Staples appeared at the prestigious Newport Folk Festival in Rhode Island, along with Baez and Dylan, who closed his rapturously received Newport debut with "Blowin' in the Wind."

"It was new territory for us," Mavis recalls. "We had met Dylan, heard folk music on some TV shows, but the music and the audience were different than what we were used to. We realized after listening to some of these singers that their music was close to what we were singing, that in our own way we were folksingers, too."

Judy Collins, another rising folk star, was mesmerized by the Staples' performance. Mavis and Yvonne wore silk tops, "their hair done to a T with sparkle and shine to match their clothes."

"This was deep-dish soul served to the kids who were yearning, I thought, for something to replace the religions most of them had abandoned," she recalled in her autobiography. "The night was full of shouts of 'amen' and 'hallelujah,' rock and soul. Pops and his daughters won an audience new to the beat of the Christian drum."

She painted Newport as an idyllic oasis in the segregation era. At a time when the rights of blacks to vote, register at a hotel, or marry a white person were still severely restricted, "the community of folk music seemed to be one of the only places it was common to be in mixed company."

Newport Folk Festival founder George Wein and his wife, Joyce, became lifelong friends of the Staples family. "A mixed-race couple, back then that blew our minds," Mavis says. "They were music people, and it didn't matter whether you were black or white, folk or gospel, they were welcoming." Dylan's proselytizing on their behalf certainly helped make the Staples feel at home. He lauded them in an essay for the *Hootenanny* folk magazine alongside such revered figures as Miles Davis, Paul Robeson, and the Freedom Singers' Bernice Johnson.

During the festival, Mavis happened to share a car with Dylan and Johnny Cash. "Johnny Cash and Bobby were big fans of each other and that night John gave Bob a guitar," Mavis says. "Johnny would tell these amazing stories about how he was so drunk one night, he got out of the car and starting staring at a cow in a field because he thought it was Hank Williams. We were all laughing. Bob was begging Johnny to stop, he was laughing so hard: 'Okay, John, no more, no more.'"

Dylan also was thoroughly charmed by Mavis, and publicly proposed marriage. Robert Shelton reminisced in the mid-'80s: "Oh, those great old days, when Bob got an instant crush on gospel singer Mavis Staples, and even though Pop Staples chided him, he went after Mavis anyway." The most widely circulated story is that Dylan approached Mavis about marriage at Newport, but Mavis says the proposal came earlier that year, at the Westinghouse TV taping in New York.

"He told Daddy, in front of everybody," she says. "We were waiting to get food at the cafeteria, and we were in the front of the line. Next thing, I hear this voice from the back. 'Pops, I want to marry Mavis.' Out walks Bobby, and everybody's laughing. Pops says loud enough for everyone to hear, 'Don't tell me, tell Mavis.'

"From that day, Bobby and I, we started talking. The Newport Folk Festival was our first kiss, I'll tell you that. I haven't told anybody that. We sat out on the stump outside the hotel room and just talked. Him and Pervis would talk for hours and drink wine at Newport, they were extremely tight. The next day, we're at a pool. Bobby was so happy that he took a running start onto the diving board and jumped. All of a sudden, he was yelling, 'Pervis, Pervis, you got to come in.'"

Pervis was at first reluctant to do his friend's bidding. "I'm looking at him, he dove in there wearing his boots. I said, 'Man, I ain't coming in. You crazy.' But he wouldn't quit yelling, so finally I jumped in, and he tells me, 'Pervis, ya gotta help me. I lost my trunks.' He was so skinny they slipped off when he hit the water."

During the weekend, an exhausted Dylan fell asleep in the room shared by Mavis and Yvonne. "We were friends—I was talkative and Dylan wasn't at all," Yvonne recalls. "I would tell him, 'You're shy, you got to talk and tell Mavis how you feel.' And they got together. The marriage proposal, it was no joke. Later he'd still come through me to get to Mavis when she was married, but I'd tell him, 'Bobby, it's time-out for that now.'"

Mavis says she still has pangs of regret about turning Dylan down. "Six, seven years, we would write each other and call, and see each other occasionally. It got serious. It was boyfriend-girlfriend stuff. We loved each other, and still do. But in 1969, I stopped the relationship."

She was well aware of Dylan's other girlfriends, including Baez. Judy Collins believes that Mavis was skeptical about Dylan's proposal from the start. "Dylan didn't look like the marrying kind to me, and Mavis knew he was having her on," Collins said.

Mavis eventually married a prominent Chicago mortician, Spencer Leak, in 1964. Their marriage lasted eight mostly difficult years.

Dylan remains one of her greatest advocates. "It was always in my mind that I couldn't marry a white guy," Mavis says. "I was so young and stupid. All I had to do is look around. We had plenty of white people marching with us. Dr. King loved that. So why would it be a problem marrying Bob Dylan? To this day, I could kick myself, because we were really in love. It was my first love, and it was the one I lost."

13

"If he can preach it, we can sing it"

Pops Staples had first heard Martin Luther King speak on the radio in the 1950s and was moved by what he heard. A few years later, he would finally meet the man who was leading the march toward racial equality, a concept that once seemed absurdly out of reach when Pops was growing up on Dockery Farms in Mississippi.

Pops called King to arrange a meeting in 1963 and was delighted to receive an invitation from the minister to attend an 11 a.m. Sunday service at the Dexter Avenue Church in Montgomery, where King was pastor. The Staples were in the midst of another tour, scheduled to play a show in Montgomery that same weekend. When they arrived at the church, King's wife, Coretta, was singing in the choir while cradling their newborn, Bernice. During the service, King formally welcomed Pops and his children to his church. Afterward, Pops and the leader of America's civil rights movement clasped hands as parishioners filed past to exit the church. They smiled and exchanged pleasantries, then turned earnest, huddled for several minutes with furrowed brows and conspiratorial voices in the back of the church.

"We began to talk about the condition of the world and our people," Pops said. "I said to him, 'Dr. King, you preach love, peace, and happiness all over the world. I strongly believe in what you are doing and the price you are willing to pay.'"

King was familiar with the Staple Singers, and he saw a reflection of his values not only in the music the Staples performed but in the way Pops in particular spoke and carried himself. King mingled easily with his parishioners and neighbors, yet he radiated a confidence and dignity that made him a natural leader, said Doris Crenshaw, one of King's closest lieutenants and a friend of the Staples family. In the same way, Pops was an "ordinary" man doing extraordinary things. He seemed approachable, humble, matter-of-fact, even though he had performed in front of adoring crowds and become acquainted with presidents and rock stars.

"They became stars, but like low-hanging grapes of the vine, they were stars that we could touch," Jesse Jackson, who would soon become one of King's most ardent allies, said of the Staple Singers. "I mean, they never got disconnected from our stratosphere. The Staples became kind of an everyman's group."

Pops returned from his meeting with King and gathered his family at the hotel. "If he can preach it, we can sing it," he said, essentially setting the group's course for the next ten years.

"By the time we met Dr. King, I had seen how it was in the South," Mavis says. "I had seen how people were treated down there. For someone to be speaking for us, someone of his caliber and character, I was just totally ready to join forces with him. We all were."

It was hardly a stretch for the group to embrace the new possibility for African-American life that King outlined in his words and actions. Their music was being embraced by the emerging folk and folk-rock movements, and they were endorsed by tastemakers such as Dylan, Johnny Cash, Joan Baez, and the founders of the Newport Folk Festival. Pops in turn was open enough to let these new experiences and influences seep into the Staple Singers' music for the Riverside label.

Just as the Staples were starting to find their new audience at River-

side, the label imploded. Cofounder Bill Grauer died in December 1963
and the company would sink into bankruptcy by mid-1964, leaving the
Staples once again briefly adrift. But the Riverside years had hardly been
wasted; the music the Staple Singers recorded there put them in the
middle of the cultural conversation the country was having about civil
rights and the Vietnam War. Only weeks before Grauer's death, President John F. Kennedy was assassinated while the family was on tour,
driving through the South.

The Staples had performed at Kennedy's inauguration in 1961 and
were invited back the next year to a State Department event with Dinah
Washington and Howlin' Wolf. "We loved President Kennedy," Mavis
says. "We sang for him, we shook his hand. Pops would always talk
about his speeches. After he'd get through with one, Pops would say,
'That's my president.'

"When word came down that he'd been killed, we were on our way to
Washington, somewhere in Virginia. We stopped at a service station to
get some gas and that's when we found out. Somebody said, 'They just
assassinated the president.' And this white man pumping our gas said,
'Good!' Pops just lost it. 'Man, get your pump out of my car. Get it out
right now.' Daddy got in the car and drove off, he was mad. He said,
'These people, this world . . .'"

The distraught family checked into a hotel near Washington, D.C.,
then Pops called the promoter to cancel that night's show. "Washington
was in an uproar and nobody was coming to anybody's show anyway,"
Mavis recalls. "Pops said, 'Pack your clothes, we're going home. We can't
sing on a night like this.'"

Against that dispiriting backdrop, the Staple Singers returned to Universal Studios in Chicago in January 1964 to finish work on what would
be their final album for Riverside, *This Little Light*. Their resolve was
palpable, particularly on a scarifying version of the Dylan song "Masters
of War." Whereas their first attempt at interpreting Dylan with "Blowin'
in the Wind" had come off flat, their investment in the folksinger's bitter

takedown of corporate greed and corporate-sponsored war is chilling. Pops's guitar conjures bluesy doom. His quiet, unassuming voice barely contains the rage just beneath the surface. Yvonne, Pervis, and Mavis provide a haunting, wordless backdrop, with Al Duncan's drums rippling like distant cannon fire.

Dylan's song "A Hard Rain's A-Gonna Fall" also made the cut. Dylan and Pervis had become friends, sharing bottles of booze whenever they met while talking long into the night about the music business, women, and songwriting. In September 1962, Pervis recalls entering Dylan's room one afternoon at the President Hotel in New York and seeing a list of song titles scribbled on a shirt cardboard. "A Hard Rain's A-Gonna Fall" jumped out. "Just the way the words were put together caught your eye," Pervis says. Once Dylan showed him the song, Pervis lobbied Pops to have the Staples record it. It's hardly a "typical" Staples song, wordy and nearly eight minutes long, but Pervis, in a rare lead vocal, gives it an effectively understated reading, a touch of vibrato in his voice as the surreal, often horrifying images parade past: the well-hidden executioner's face, the poison pellets flooding the waters, the young child beside a dead pony. Mavis and the others ring out on the yearning chorus: "Oh, where have you been, my wanderin' son? Where have you been, my darling young one?"

The song is both specific and universal, conflating Cold War paranoia with images of biblical Apocalypse. "What I call gospel is truth and nothing else but," Pops said at the time. "Though Bob Dylan is classical 'folk,' to me he's inspirational. His message is truth—he's true gospel as anything you would ever see."

The Staples' increasing comfort with Dylan's songs made them more of a piece with the group's hard-core gospel tunes: the bedrock traditionalism of the stately "Will the Lord Remember Me?," the dexterous swing of "I Can't Help from Cryin' Sometime," the road-to-glory handclapping of "Let Jesus Lead You."

The song "This Little Light of Mine" was particularly significant.

Composed as a children's song during the era when Pops Staples was born, its simplicity and biblical allusions made it an endlessly malleable part of black and folk culture for decades. Sam Cooke covered it, and Ray Charles secularized it (with his '50s composition "This Little Girl of Mine"). In the '60s, it had reemerged as an anthem for the civil rights movement. It was sung at meetings, rallies, and marches, its self-empowering lyrics tweaked and adapted to suit the situation.

"I don't have any sense of the civil rights movement existing without the singing we did in marches, mass meetings, and in jail," Bernice Johnson (later Bernice Johnson Reagon), one of the original Freedom Singers, said decades later in an NPR radio interview. "There is no separation. . . . If we were there, then we sang."

In 1962, the Student Nonviolent Coordinating Committee had set up the Freedom Singers to spread the message of nonviolence nationwide. The group, consisting of Johnson, Rutha Harris, Charles Neblett, and Cordell Hull Reagon, traveled a hundred thousand miles in 1962–63 spreading the gospel of civil rights. They had appeared with Mahalia Jackson and Odetta at King's March on Washington in August 1963, and performed at the Newport Folk Festival. For the finale, they linked arms with Dylan, Joan Baez, Peter, Paul and Mary, and the Staple Singers, among others, to sing the movement's anthem, "We Shall Overcome."

"This Little Light of Mine" was one of the songs that made the movement run: easy to sing, easily adaptable, defiantly optimistic. On the Riverside album, Mavis tears into the song with a don't-back-down fervor. "Everywhere I go," she sings, and Pops, Pervis, and Yvonne answer, "I'm gonna let it shine." She doesn't let up for the song's two-and-a-half-minute duration, flying above the onrushing tide of voices, bass, and drums.

The Staples were living these words as they sang them. The family toured extensively in the South because their records were most popular there, and they could draw substantial audiences in a string of towns and churches throughout the region. But in between those gospel music oases, they were subject to the indignities and insults that were daily routine for African Americans in the Deep South.

The region could be especially perilous for black entertainers, whose livelihood depended on their ability to navigate back roads bristling with guns, racist taunts, and deep-seated resentment while traveling from town to town. The sight of well-dressed blacks driving Cadillacs was a sign to some whites that the world they had known for generations was ending, or at least changing for the worse. Their resentment and fear sometimes bubbled over into verbal abuse or physical violence.

Artists on package tours often traveled in caravans for safety, but that also turned them into more inviting, high-profile targets. "One time they [police in the Deep South] stopped a caravan we were in—a bunch of cars and a bus," Pervis says. "The police were just messing with us. One of the boys in the Sensational Nightingales had a big Adam's apple, so the police would walk up to him and feel it. They would just detain us long enough sometimes to make sure we would be late for the show and miss that night's pay."

"Pops knew what we were in for, because he had been through it growing up, and there were times he looked like he just wasn't going to take it anymore," Mavis says. "White kids would come up on us and look like they were gonna run us right off the road. Pops would run right back into them."

Once, Mavis, Yvonne, and Cleotha left the black boardinghouse where they were staying in Jackson, Mississippi, to shop downtown. "We saw these shoes that we wanted for the stage, and we went in to try them on," Mavis says. "But the lady at the store told us we'd have to go behind some raggedy, dirty curtain. Cleedi just said, 'In that case, we can't take these.' The lady looked at us and said, 'Y'all aren't from here, are you?'"

Even on the rare occasions when the Staples found lodging at an integrated hotel in the South, they weren't always made to feel welcome.

"The first time we were able to stay in white hotels," Mavis recalls, "a white man came up to me and Cleedi and said, 'I need some towels.' And Cleedi said, 'We do, too.'"

Naïveté occasionally insulated the teenage Mavis from the South's segregationist customs. The Staples were driving from Meridian, Mississippi, to Yazoo City to sing, and on the way stopped in Forest to see Grandma Ware's ex-husband, Thornton. While there, Mavis decided to catch up on her laundry and took a sack of clothes to a coin-operated laundry in town. When she found the machines occupied in one room, she went next door and did her wash there. If it struck her as odd that one side of the facility had only black customers and the other only whites, it didn't register right away. Afterward, Grandpa Thornton crowed, "My grandbaby 'Mabel,' she done integrated that washeteria."

The Staple Singers' closest brush with Southern backwoods justice came in November 1964, after a show in Jackson. A cigar box stuffed with $1,200 in concert earnings was in the trunk as they pulled into a service station in Memphis to fuel up for the long night ride back to Chicago. Mavis was behind the wheel of the green Cadillac Fleetwood, with Pops in the passenger seat, and Cleotha in back with Pervis, who was snoozing beneath a pile of coats.

After a fill-up and window wash, Mavis asked the attendant for a receipt. He refused and said she'd have to come to the office if she wanted one. Pops seethed, the barefoot boxer that he was as a teenager rising to the challenge. "Maybe it bothered the white boy to see a young, pretty black woman like Mavis driving a Fleetwood," he mused.

Pops followed the attendant inside to get the receipt. "I told him, 'My daughter would not have been asked to come inside for this receipt if she had been white.' He jumped in my face pointing and shouting, 'Nigger, let me tell you something.' That is as far as he got. . . . I could have been the boy's father. But I was in good condition and had a 'bad' right hand, so I hit him. Cleotha woke up Pervis, and he ran in fighting."

During the tussle, Pops slipped in his slippers on the oily floor and fell. The attendant scrambled into his office. "I thought he was going to get a gun," Pops recalled. "We ran for the car and left in a hurry."

Pops instructed a nerve-racked Mavis to drive out of Memphis and across the Mississippi River to West Memphis, Arkansas. They didn't get far. Upon crossing the cantilevered Memphis-Arkansas Bridge, they were pulled over by three police cars, loaded with armed officers and police dogs, according to a report in the *Chicago Defender*. The police opened the trunk, confiscated Pops's gun and the cash, and handcuffed Pops, Cleotha, Pervis, and Mavis. They were being held on suspicion of robbing and beating the gas-station attendant, who had phoned the police with his version of the incident.

"It was just like the movies, but without actors, and I was scared to death," Cleotha said.

"When they put us in different cars to drive us away, I just knew they were taking us out into the woods to lynch us," Mavis recalls. "I've never been so happy to see a jail."

The family was marched in handcuffs into the two-story brick West Memphis police station, where they were recognized by the police captain, identified by the *Chicago Defender* as Bobby R. Keen, and an African-American custodian.

"The police captain recognized Pops as soon as he walked in and says, 'My wife loves you,'" Pervis said with a rueful laugh. "They knew us from being on TV [by then the group had appeared on such national programs as *Hootenanny, The Tonight Show Starring Johnny Carson,* and *The Steve Allen Show*]. Pretty soon they had us autographing albums we had in the trunk."

The family was cleared after Pops produced the receipt that he had stuffed in his pocket before scuffling with the attendant. Their valuables and cash returned, the Staples drove back to I-55 with a police escort.

Nobody slept for hours as Pervis drove home in the early morning hours. "We had to pull the car over three times for Cleedi to throw up, she was just so scared," Mavis says. "And the next time we go to Memphis, we were at Mason's Temple for a concert, and over to the right are some box seats and there's the [West Memphis] police chief and a whole row of about ten or twelve policemen, dressed all nice in their uniforms. Pops went over there and said, 'Well, Chief, it's mighty nice of y'all to come out and see us. But who's minding the town?' "

On December 12, 1964, the Staples family was in Shreveport preparing for a show when they heard the news that their childhood friend Sam Cooke had been killed the previous night at a Los Angeles hotel. According to conflicting reports, Cooke was searching for a woman who had accompanied him to the hotel, and got into a dispute with the hotel manager, who shot him in the middle of an argument that turned physically violent. Cooke was found wearing only a sports jacket and shoes in the manager's office-home. He was thirty-three years old, at the height of his fame.

Cooke's body was taken to a funeral home run by Mavis's father-in-law, A. R. Leak, at 7838 Cottage Grove on Chicago's South Side. A huge crowd swarmed around the mortuary and was so tightly bunched that it accidentally broke a plate-glass window. For the December 17 funeral at Tabernacle Baptist Church on 41st and Indiana, two thousand people overflowed the service and thousands more milled in freezing temperatures outside, shutting down the streets.

The Staple Singers offered up the hymn "The Old Rugged Cross" for their old friend. Mavis began to cry almost as soon as she opened her mouth to sing. Outside, a devastated Leroy Crume tried to make his way through the crowd into the church to join his group the Soul Stirrers in paying tribute to their former lead vocalist.

"My mind was gone," Crume says. "I had to park a few blocks away from the church, there were so many people in the street. A policeman saw me and said, 'Crume, you're supposed to be inside.' He took my arm and dragged me through the crowd. I was wearing a brand-new, eggshell, full-length leather coat that a girl in Baltimore had just given me, and my button got caught and ripped my coat. But he got me inside. It was time for us to go onstage, and I marched up there, and it was then I realized I didn't have my guitar. Pops bailed me out and let me use his. We sang 'His Precious Love' [a song Crume had written for the Soul Stirrers]. I can't remember if I intended to bring the guitar with me or not. I can only remember standing on the stage and looking down on Sam's casket. The casket was open, and I think I might have been in shock seeing him that way. I couldn't see anything else."

14

"Freedom Highway"

Like Pop Staples, Sam Cooke was stunned upon first hearing Bob Dylan's "Blowin' in the Wind." Though it was not explicitly about civil rights, the song resonated with many African Americans: "How many roads must a man walk down / Before you call him a man?" They were outcasts in their own country, and a white kid from the Midwest sang like he knew exactly what that meant and how it felt. In response, Cooke wrote and recorded "A Change Is Gonna Come." It captured the frustration so many African Americans felt as they struggled to stand as equals among their fellow citizens. The song's narrator pleads with his "brother" for help, "But he winds up knockin' me back down to my knees."

Cooke had never been quite so emotionally transparent in his recordings as a solo pop performer, and he sang like the redemption the Soul Stirrers had so ardently pursued was slipping from his grasp. The singer wrestled with misgivings about what the song could mean for his career, however, potentially costing him the audience he had worked so hard to cultivate. Its outspokenness, a departure from the genial party and love songs that had made him a fixture in the Top 40 since 1957, filled him with pride but also made him uneasy. Nonetheless, he prepared the song for release near the end of 1964.

A few days after Cooke's death, "A Change Is Gonna Come" was finally released as a B-side to his single "Shake." The song became a hit in its own right, ascending into the Top 40 and joining a chorus of topical songs bubbling up from the front lines of the African-American musical community.

For decades, the church was the voice of black protest, both from the preacher's pulpit and the choir box, where the hymns and spirituals said what many African Americans felt and experienced in their everyday lives but could not necessarily express out loud in a world where they were still largely treated as servants and laborers. In Chicago, the music and the message were deeply intertwined; one of the city's most storied ministers, Reverend Clay Evans, would sing his sermons with shattering power. It was a message that did not carry far beyond the South Side and other black ghettos or rural communities, though; whites never ventured there and the mainstream media ignored or dismissed it. But now that voice was filtering into music that had a platform outside the black community; R&B, blues, soul, and jazz artists were articulating what it meant to be oppressed. Social consciousness became part of the vocabulary of popular music.

Curtis Mayfield, who had sought out Pops Staples's advice when his group the Impressions was first signed to Vee-Jay in the late '50s, led the way. The Impressions' "Keep on Pushing" (Top 10 hit in 1964) and "People Get Ready" (Top 20 in 1965) became synonymous with the movement.

"We were young and didn't know these songs would have that effect," says Fred Cash, who joined the Impressions in the '50s and has carried on their legacy ever since. "You realize that songs like 'Keep on Pushing,' 'We're a Winner,' and 'Choice of Colors' inspired people. I was talking to Andy Young [civil rights activist and former congressman] and he told me how they would sing 'Amen' and 'Keep on Pushing' during the freedom marches. It gave them inspiration to keep on doing what they were doing."

Some artists spoke in thinly veiled code: Little Milton's 1965 blues hit, "We're Gonna Make It," can be read as a relationship song, but it also addresses the aspirations of the black community. Some spoke as bluntly as a brick thrown through a window: Charles Mingus's 1960 screed "Fables of Faubus" railed against Arkansas governor Orval Faubus, who had called out the National Guard to prevent black students from integrating a Little Rock Central High School. There was John Coltrane's moving "Alabama," an evocative tone poem about the 1963 bombing of an Alabama church in which four black girls were killed, and "We Insist! Freedom Now Suite," the 1960 jazz masterpiece in which Max Roach, Oscar Brown Jr., and Abbey Lincoln combined activism and musical improvisation.

"History has never known a protest movement so rich in song as the civil rights movement," *Newsweek* declared in 1964. "Nor a movement in which songs are as important. Martin Luther King called them 'vital.'. . . At nightly get-out-the-vote meetings singing always came first, the singers gilded with sweat starting off with 'We've been 'buked and we've been scorned . . . but we'll never turn back.'"

The Staple Singers had recorded their own version of "I've Been Scorned," released as a single by Vee-Jay in 1961. As the violence and angry rhetoric rose around the civil rights struggle, the traditional gospel song and its Apocalyptic imagery sounded chillingly of the moment. "Two white horses running side by side / Me and my Lord / Gonna take that ride," Pops Staples sang with withering certitude.

In 1965, the group brought the song to Carnegie Hall, as part of the first New York Folk Festival. "When the Staple Singers performed, I got to experience the real meaning of a standing ovation," promoter Herb Gart recalled in an interview on the Berkshire Fine Arts website. "They were doing a steamy ballad called 'White Horses' [referring to "I've Been Scorned"]. The Staple Singers were so intense that in the middle of the song the audience stood up and stayed standing the rest of the song. They stood up not to say, 'Bravo!' but because they couldn't stay seated. It was an incredible experience."

After Riverside's demise, Pops moved the Staple Singers to Epic

Records, a subsidiary of CBS, which already had Dylan under contract at Columbia Records. Epic paired the Staples with in-house producer Billy Sherrill, whose lush productions and deft songwriting skills would eventually score huge hits for country artists such as Tammy Wynette ("Stand by Your Man"), George Jones ("The Grand Tour"), and Charlie Rich ("The Most Beautiful Girl").

But Sherrill's background as a Southern blues musician was his primary credential when he began working with the Staple Singers on their Epic debut, *Amen,* released in 1965. It's essentially a continuation of their Riverside albums, with slightly more elaborate production. The set reprises songs from their years at Riverside ("More than a Hammer and Nail") and Vee-Jay ("Nobody's Fault but Mine"). Pops's storytelling skills come to the fore on the biblical tale of lust and vengeance "Samson and Delilah," with its defiant proclamation: "If I had my way, if I had my way, if I had my way, I'd tear this building down." Pervis plunges deep into the melodrama of "Be Careful of Stones That You Throw," a spoken-word morality tale originally sung by Hank Williams. Pervis gives an ultradry reading, impersonating a finger-wagging preacher: "Gossip is cheap, and it's low," he intones, drawing out the silences between words like a thespian. "So unless you've made no mistakes in your life, just be careful of the stones that you throw."

With the next album, the Staples put their first major musical imprint on the civil rights movement. Pops was an avid news watcher and reader. "If you want to write songs for us," he said at one point, "just read the headlines." He and the Staples were on the road as they watched images of Martin Luther King's series of protest marches from Selma to Montgomery, Alabama. The first, on March 7, 1965, arose in response to the slaying of civil rights worker Jimmie Lee Jackson at a protest in Marion, Alabama, a week earlier. As the six hundred marchers crossed the Edmund Pettus Bridge in Selma, they were attacked by police, armed with clubs, dogs, and tear gas. The "Bloody Sunday" carnage stirred nationwide outrage; one of the freedom march leaders, future congressman John Lewis, suffered a fractured skull.

"The things we did were mostly inside with Dr. King," Pervis Staples says. "We didn't do too many marches because we were touring so much. But we were paying attention to the movement, and we all saw what happened on that long walk from Selma. When they got to that bridge, and the white folks had taken some big ol' nuts off the tractors and put them on sticks and they were hitting that bridge. Then the horses came and people were running and screaming. That was something we never forgot. It hit Pops hard."

A five-day march from Selma brought twenty-five thousand protesters to the capitol steps in Montgomery on March 25, where King spoke. "The end we seek is a society at peace with itself, a society that can live with its conscience," he said. "And that will be a day not of the white man, not of the black man. That will be the day of man as man."

That tumultuous month sent Pops Staples to his guitar, crafting the chords, melody, and lyrics for one of the era's most profound songs: "Freedom Highway."

The next month, the group would debut the song at New Nazareth Church on Chicago's South Side, and Sherrill flew in to record the concert. Pops advised the producer to go straight to his hotel from the airport, and then had him picked up and delivered to the church. "Pops Staples was a cool guy," Sherrill told *Mix* magazine. "He said, 'You're not riding around Chicago by yourself.'"

Sherrill may have been out of place, a white man on 79th Street in the heart of Chicago's African-American community as civil rights tensions were escalating, but he did a splendid job of documenting what transpired when the Staples performed at New Nazareth. *Freedom Highway* is not only one of the finest Staple Singers releases, it's one of the best live albums ever made.

It opens with Pops introducing one of the first public performances of the title song: "And from that march, word was revealed, a song was composed." A clarion Pops guitar riff rings out, and the family and the congregation begin to clap the rhythm. From the get-go, it's apparent that the Staples have become a ferocious funk-blues group with drummer Al Duncan and bassist Phil Upchurch pushing the tempo. Then Mavis, singing Pops's words, lays down the law. "Marching on the freedom highway . . . I made up my mind, and I won't turn around," she sings in a tone that declares anyone who tries to stop her had best step out of the way.

Pops packs a handful of lines with philosophy, history, biblical allusions, rage, resentment, and resolve. In one verse, he references the 1955 murder of fourteen-year-old Emmett Till, who was beaten, shot, and thrown in the Tallahatchie River in Mississippi after flirting with a white woman. Till's body was returned to Chicago, and his funeral was held at Roberts Temple Church of God, only a few blocks from the Staples' apartment at the time. Till's casket was left open at the family's request, and photos of his badly disfigured face shocked the nation. "Found dead people in the forest, Tallahatchie River and lakes," Mavis sings. "The whole wide world is wonderin' what's wrong with the United States."

In "What You Gonna Do," with its spooky riff and Judgment Day paranoia, the Staples warn their people's oppressors: In the end, there will be no place for anyone to hide from his misdeeds. It flows into a staggering version of Thomas Dorsey's "Take My Hand, Precious Lord," a gospel landmark that had previously been recorded by Mavis's idol, Mahalia Jackson, and her friend Aretha Franklin. Mavis's wrenching performance is underlined by Duncan's sensitive, almost orchestral drumming. He makes his trap kit rumble, as if the heavens are answering Mavis when she sings, "O Jesus, lead me on."

"Help Me, Jesus" throws Pops into a reverie about growing up in Mississippi and the revival meetings at the ramshackle wooden church near his home. "Some of those sisters began to moan . . . and I saw my soul has got that moan. He keep on praying, and she keep on moaning . . . My soul has got to mooooooan." The performance escalates into a frenzy of double-time clapping, Upchurch's bass rising and then receding in the mix, the music going on and on as the audience audibly comes unhinged.

"We Shall Overcome," by now the theme song of the civil rights movement, doesn't move quite like the songs that came before. It's drained of surprise, but it doesn't matter. Everybody in the church recognizes the song's import, and they're shouting the words. One member of the congregation simply screams "Yeah!" over and over again. The song may be almost a cliché by now, but to the congregation it has become something much bigger than a song. It's a symbol.

Things briefly wind down after an ebullient "When the Saints Go Marching In," with Pervis doing another dramatic reading of yet another Hank Williams country tearjerker, "The Funeral." Then it's back for the one-two-three punch of "Build on That Shore," "Tell Heaven," and "He's All Right," on which Mavis improvises in classic gospel fashion—"worrying" lines and stretching words, breaking into wordless exultations—while Pops, Upchurch, and Duncan fire away like a blues power trio. "Play it, boy!" somebody screams as Upchurch briefly takes the wheel, his bass hammering out a lead like gospel's answer to Motown's James Jamerson.

In the New Nazareth Church concert, Pops connects the themes of gospel music and the civil rights movement more explicitly than ever before. It presents him not just as a musical innovator, but as a philosopher, preacher, and visionary, a melding of black church music and black popular music for a common cause. Church music was no longer just about making it through this world to get to the next one; it was also about living right now in the streets all African Americans shared.

"We got a better home, children," Pops says at one point. "And in that land over there, we have friends and loved ones. . . . I have a mother and father. They're waiting and watching for me. I don't know when the Lord is gonna call . . . I want to make heaven my own, but I want to enjoy myself a little down here, too."

And finally, he makes explicit what his own life might be about: "I just want to leave a record so that someone might follow in my footsteps."

15

"Why Am I Treated So Bad?"

By 1965, the Staple Singers ruled the North American gospel circuit. *Ebony* proclaimed them "The First Family of Gospel," and stated, "With the possible exception of Mahalia Jackson, they are the hottest property in the gospel field today."

The magazine focused on a typical performance, at King Solomon's Baptist Church auditorium in Detroit. The family looked little changed from their Vee-Jay days: Mavis and Cleotha in gospel robes, Pops and Pervis in dark suits and ties. Mom Staples, Oceola, is among those attending, and a photograph shows her "overcome by emotions" and passing out. It's more likely that the heat from all those bodies stuffed in the auditorium got to her; King Solomon's was packed, with more than three thousand in attendance.

Pops's songwriting was pushing the family beyond the gospel circuit, however. After the anthemic resolve of "Freedom Highway," he wrote the plaintive "Why? (Am I Treated So Bad)," his long-simmering ode to the Little Rock Nine, a group of black students who were physically barred from entering the racially segregated Little Rock Central High School in 1957, even though the U.S. Supreme Court had ruled three years earlier that segregated schools were unconstitutional.

"Pops was sitting in his recliner watching the news on TV, and as those kids walked up to enter the school, a [National Guardsman] told them to turn around," Mavis says. "And Pops says, 'Why would he do that? Why are they treated so bad?' And he wrote that song that night."

"Why? (Am I Treated So Bad)" led off the Staples' next album for Epic, *Why?*, released in 1966. The song and the album open with Pops playing a swampy blues riff and gently rapping about his disconsolation: "My friends, you know this ol' world is in a bad condition. Just the other day, I saw a group of little children trying to ride a school bus. By them being of a different nationality, they weren't allowed to ride the bus. I imagine if you would ask them about this matter, they would have words like this to say, [sings] 'Why am I treated so bad?'"

The song insinuates rather than shouts and is all the more powerful because of it. Steady but unobtrusive handclaps and ghostly wordless vocals waft over a breezy bass line perfect for shuffling down a sidewalk on a sultry summer evening. That bass line would be picked up a year later by saxophonist Julian "Cannonball" Adderley, who met the Staples at a 1961 jazz festival, for his own mesmerizing instrumental version of the instant gospel-blues protest classic. It would become the Staple Singers' first hit, albeit a minor one, eventually punching into the upper reaches of the pop Top 100 a year later (Epic had the Staples rerecord the song in 1967 with rock producer Larry Williams, to give it a more emphatic rhythm on the heels of Adderley's successful instrumental version.)

Martin Luther King also was enthralled by "Why? (Am I Treated So Bad)." "Stape," King would say nearly every time he saw Pops, "you gonna play my song tonight?"

Just as they did in the late '50s with Reverend C. L. Franklin, the Staples would perform two or three songs whenever they appeared with King at a rally in a church or auditorium, essentially serving as his opening act. They now had a trove of topical songs that would amplify whatever topic King wanted to address.

As ardent as King was about music, Mavis says she never recalls him singing along. "He was always looking serious or sad, so when I think back on him, I hold on to his laughter, the sound of his laugh." King didn't laugh much, but when he did, he did so robustly, and everyone around him delighted in it. Other groups were more intimately involved with King in his civil rights campaign, in part because the Staples were touring constantly and by now had contractual commitments for concerts around the world, often playing two hundred shows a year.

"There were all these reviews making it seem as if they were working with Dr. King, and it's not fair to the Loving Sisters who did the lifting," says Anthony Heilbut. Gladys McFadden and the Loving Sisters were preachers' daughters from Arkansas who in 1965 toured with King and later recorded a tribute album to him. The folk-gospel group the Freedom Singers played hundreds of shows and participated in countless marches on behalf of King; Charles Neblett, one of the group's founders, was arrested twenty-seven times in civil rights protests.

But the Staples, like Curtis Mayfield's Impressions, played a key role in creating a sound track for King's work. Their concerts were, in effect, extensions of King's rallies. "The Staples were the forerunners of taking the music message to another level," Jesse Jackson, one of King's future lieutenants said. "Most great singers sing love songs or they sing blues songs. But the Staples unabashedly sing songs Dr. King could identify with."

Pops became increasingly determined to spread the minister's message to audiences both in and outside the black church. The notion of a black entertainer speaking his mind about racial equality in the mid-'60s was not necessarily novel, but it certainly wasn't without risk. "Roebuck wrote some marvelous songs, and a song like 'Why? (Am I Treated So Bad)' is quite a progressive lyric for its day," Heilbut says. "It was a very bold move at the time."

Not everyone saw it that way. As the Staples moved into the clubs and coffeehouses of the folk scene, the group was accused of selling out and abandoning gospel much in the way Sam Cooke once was. "When we started singing songs like 'Blowin' in the Wind,' one of the Dixie

Hummingbirds, Mr. Davis [group founder James B. Davis], told Pops, 'Stape, you're straddling the fence, aren't you?'" Mavis recalls. Critic Barney Hoskyns wrote that the group's transition to folk and rock was accomplished by "Uncle Tomming for the flower children."

Even Cleotha, the child most in step with Pops's thinking on almost any subject, had her misgivings. The gospel community "started putting us down," she said in a 1976 interview. "They felt we weren't in the church anymore. And I must have been the biggest holdback when we were making the transition from all-gospel to the nongospel entertainment circuit. I said, 'Daddy, I don't think we should change. I think we should stay in gospel.' But Pops said, 'Boo, I think you should be a little more open-minded about this. It's a tremendous chance for us to give a message. Now, Dr. King is saying it. We can sing it. What's wrong with that?' The music we were then singing had a little too much beat for gospel. And I thought that was wrong. Mavis, Pervis, and Daddy were ready. But somewhere I was lagging behind."

Jerry Butler, who had embraced R&B before he established a career in gospel, says he never thought the Staples turned their back on their principles or beliefs: "Pops Staples was adamant about not doing rhythm-and-blues love songs. Even though some assumed he crossed the line, he never did. He stayed with gospel and inspirational songs."

Butler is perhaps being generous in his assessment of where the Staples were heading, but he represented a younger generation of listeners who were coming to the group without the baggage of old-school gospel diehards. To R&B and soul fans in their teens and twenties, the Staples were gospel singers to whom they could relate on a personal level. To this audience, the Staples transcended the church or the notion that one had to be a "believer" to connect with their music. "There are really only two gospel units who white people know to this day, which are the Staple Singers and the Five Blind Boys of Alabama," Heilbut notes. "To a lot of people without a background listening to gospel, those groups are singing gospel music, even when they're not."

As the Staples began to perform on bills with pop, rock, and R&B performers, they won over audiences relatively unattuned to the emotional power of a gospel performance. "It may have been a star-studded rock and roll show but the sensation was the gospel Staple Singers who won deafening audience applause," the *Chicago Defender* wrote of one appearance in June 1965 with the Temptations, Four Tops, Patti LaBelle and the Bluebelles, and Gladys Knight and the Pips at the Uptown Theatre in Philadelphia. The show sponsor, DJ Georgie Woods, "commented that he had 'doubts' at first about putting the Staple Singers on the bill, but . . . [afterward] realized that he would've made a mistake in not including them."

It was a watershed concert for the Staples for another significant reason. Pops and Yvonne were still scheduling many of the family's concerts, with monthly phone bills of $200 or more. But after the Uptown show, booking agents "besieged" the band, the *Chicago Defender* reported. The New York–based Queen Booking Agency struck a deal with Pops to schedule the group's live appearances and continued to steer the Staples toward the more lucrative secular circuit.

The Staples were already highly regarded by rockers and folkies in the know, a foundation of respect that smoothed their crossover. Pop Staples's way with a riff and his distinctive tone were studied by a new generation of guitarists on both sides of the Atlantic. Bonnie Raitt recalls hearing "Why? (Am I Treated So Bad)" on the radio while growing up in Los Angeles in the late '60s.

"For me, it was one of those records that changes your life, like Joni Mitchell's 'Blue' or [Bob Dylan's] 'The Times They Are A-Changin'," Raitt says. "My decade was defined by the Stones, the Beatles, the British Invasion, Motown, soul—but my first love was folk music. At eight or nine I picked up a guitar, and then you hear the Staple Singers—that vocal harmony blend, the folkie sound with the tremolo guitar. That was exactly what I needed to hear right then. 'Why? (Am I Treated So Bad)' made me a fan of theirs for life."

Keith Richards acknowledges that he was playing along with Pops on a 1961 Vee-Jay recording of the gospel traditional "This May Be the Last Time" when he "borrowed" the guitar riff for the Rolling Stones' "The Last Time," which reached number 9 on the pop charts in 1965.

The Stones were "basically readapting a traditional gospel song that had been sung by the Staple Singers, but luckily the song itself goes back into the mists of time," Richards said.

Pops had indeed adapted the old gospel tune as a commentary on segregation, after his family struggled to find overnight accommodations while traveling in Montgomery. Then Richards and the Stones took his riff and some of the same words and turned them into a pop song about a dying relationship.

"I'm just hurt they didn't give me my credit and they didn't give me my money either," Pops said in an 1992 interview, though he didn't really have legal grounds to go after the Stones. As Mavis says, "They used our arrangement, but the song really was out there [in the public domain] for anybody to use. We did that sort of thing all the time, too."

The Staples' update of gospel traditionals continued to show up on their mid-'60s albums, but Pops was also emerging more forcefully as an original songwriter. Sherrill, who would later be known for gussying up his Nashville-based country productions, beefed up the Staples' arrangements without overwhelming them; the Staples retain their stark, sparse essence on the 1966 *Why?* album. It reprises "If I Could Hear My Mother Pray Again" and "Will the Circle Be Unbroken," among the first songs Pops taught his family. He also brings back "I've Been Scorned," the song that brought the house down at Carnegie Hall the previous year. Pops's high melancholy moan peaks on the line that begins, "Talkin' 'bout trouble," then dramatically plummets as he echoes himself: "so much trouble." "Move Along Train" pivots on the interplay between Cleotha's arching background harmonies and Mavis's hard-hitting lead. The biblical references that Pops so loved now took on a timely, more urgent dimension. "You've got to let my people go," Pops demands in "King of Kings," as his children clap hands and fire back "hallelujahs."

The Staples' righteous music coincided with Martin Luther King's move north. In January 1966, the minister rented a dingy apartment on the city's West Side to more directly oversee a campaign for school desegregation and open housing in Chicago. After his arrival, King set up a meeting with Pops and his family at a restaurant on 87th and Vincennes. He was going to appoint Jesse Jackson, a South Carolina preacher who was attending the Chicago Theological Seminary, to head up Operation Breadbasket. The new economic initiative aimed to persuade and, if necessary, pressure major corporations in Chicago to bring more blacks onto their payrolls.

King wanted the Staple Singers to help draw crowds and publicity to Operation Breadbasket by singing at food drives every Saturday morning. "Dr. King said, 'People in Chicago don't know Jesse Jackson, but if they know you and the family will be there to sing, the people will come out,'" Mavis recalls. "Then he said, 'Pops, if you do this for me, I'll owe you one.' Daddy just said, 'Doctor, you don't ever owe me nothing.'"

King's Chicago campaign struggled. His reception was in many ways more brutal than it was even in the South as working-class whites resisted his call to open up housing opportunities for blacks. Marches turned ugly and race riots marred King's stay in the city; during one demonstration, the minister was struck by a rock and fell to his knees. Mayor Richard Daley paid lip service to many of King's proposals as a way to head off the demonstrations, but nothing much changed after the minister left town proclaiming that progress had been made.

Operation Breadbasket, on the other hand, was a success for King and Jackson. King enlisted the help of radio station WVON and brought program director E. Rodney Jones into the fold. The powerhouse station—Chicago's "Voice of the Negro"—began airing the weekly Operation Breadbasket broadcasts, featuring performances by the Staple Singers, Operation Breadbasket Choir, and Operation Breadbasket Band led by saxophonist Ben Branch.

Within the first fifteen months the campaign helped bring two thousand new jobs into the black community and effectively launched Jackson's career in public life—a mix of ministry, politics, and old-fashioned Chicago wheeling-dealing with a South Carolina accent. It also left him a lifelong admirer of the Staple Singers.

The Staples had a "combination of music and message that I call soul and science," Jackson said. "And they were talking that relevant talk. You could demonstrate to their music. Or you could shout to their music. The Staple Singers were unabashedly freedom fighters."

16

"Mavis, you want a hit?"

T he Staples family home was a bit like church: a place where friends and neighbors could congregate and share their stories. Church offered fiery oratory and gospel choirs. But the Staples home had Oceola Staples's kitchen and dinner table.

After the family's initial success at Vee-Jay, Pops was able to break the cycle of slum apartment living to buy a two-story, brown-brick four-flat on 89th Street and Langley at the outset of the '60s. He, Oceola, and their youngest daughter, Cynthia, lived on the top floor, and Mavis (before she was married) and later Oceola's mother, Grandma Ware, shared the first-floor space with Yvonne, with tenants renting the other two apartments. An L-shaped lawn wrapped around the house to the alley and a two-car garage, where Pops parked his Cadillac. Their home became a year-round sanctuary, rest stop, and diner for artists and entertainers the family had met in their travels.

"When the groups would come to town to sing at DuSable or some place, invariably at that time they really couldn't eat downtown, number one," Jesse Jackson said. "But to have a home-cooked meal, we would always end up at the Staples home. And so they became the table to all these great artists."

Stevie Wonder, Aretha Franklin, and Gladys Knight were among their dinner guests. Nancy Wilson would call ahead before she came to town and order her favorites: creamed corn, greens, and hot-water cornbread. When Redd Foxx couldn't make it over to the house for dinner, he'd called to ask Mom to send a plate to him backstage at the Regal Theater; Oceola sent Pops to personally deliver the meal.

Ray Charles became obsessed with Oceola's sweet potato pie and joked that he and Mom Staples should open a franchise together. She wouldn't let the singer leave the house without supplying him with an extra pie to take back to his hotel.

"Mom didn't use nutmeg or any spices in her pies, it was natural ingredients only: the butter, the sugar, the eggs," Jon Shields rhapsodizes. "The crust was so light and flaky. The ice water was the key." Chicago soul DJ Herb Kent raved on the air about Oceola's culinary skills: "The Staple Singers don't need payola, because they've got 'pie-ola.'"

On July 4th, the Staples' lawn filled with entertainers, sports figures, and neighbors to share in one of Oceola's feasts. She and Yvonne rose at 4 a.m. to begin preparing the food. Pops started fires on two large, round garbage-can grills, where he slow-cooked massive slabs of pork and lamb ribs. A procession of coleslaw, potato salad, hot dogs, chicken, spaghetti, black-eyed peas, corn on the cob, and ham hocks began from the kitchen to the backyard at about 11 a.m. as guests started to arrive. Baseball star Jim "Mudcat" Grant, R&B singer Gene Chandler, doo-wop vocalists the Dells, Olympic sprinter Jesse Owens, gospel great Albertina Walker, and Jesse Jackson all shared in the Stapleses' hospitality.

The regulars included Mahalia Jackson, who lived a few blocks away at 81st and Indiana. She'd call Oceola every July 4th morning: "Sistah, you got them bones on?" Mahalia was a national star, showing up in limousines and dressed like a queen for her public appearances. But for the Stapleses' barbecues, she wore sundresses and sandals. Here she wasn't known as the queen of gospel but as "Halie." After filling up on ribs, Mahalia would summon Mavis for Oceola's hand-churned specialty: banana-custard ice cream, often flavored with fresh peaches and ambrosia.

Roebuck Staples, a sharecropper's son, at Dockery Farms in Mississippi during the 1920s.

The family foundation: Pops and Oceola.

Sisters Cynthia, Yvonne, Cleotha, and Mavis (left to right) on Cleo's wedding day in July 1959.

The Staple Singers delivering "stirring spiritual Americana" on Vee-Jay Records in the '50s.

Pops finger-picking gospel blues in the key of E.

Pops leads Yvonne, Pervis, and Mavis at a recording session in Chicago for Riverside: "They rolled as a cohesive, tight-knit family group."

Backyard 4th of July barbecue at the Staples home with Pops, gospel great Mahalia Jackson (second from left), Mavis (center), Oceola (third from right), and gospel singer Albertina Walker (second from right).

Pervis Staples looking suave after
getting back from the army.

Mavis's wedding to Spencer Leak in 1964.

"Will the Circle Be Unbroken": Listening
session around the family phonograph.

The newest Stax Records signing:
the Staple Singers in May 1968.

Mavis finally goes solo at Stax.

Pops and Oceola get down hosting a basement party.

The gold and platinum decade at Stax.

Outtake from the *Staple Swingers* album
cover shoot in 1971.

A family portrait, Christmas Day 1972.

Homespun, four-part gospel harmonies.

South Africa concert 1975: Freedom songs amid barbed wire and police dogs.

Fellow civil rights advocate Harry Belafonte and the Staples backstage at Caesars Palace in Las Vegas, 1973.

"I Like the Things About Me": Staple Singers at the height of their early '70s fame.

Syncopated handclaps in Black Star Square, Ghana, 1971: A vision of Aquarian hipness in the motherland.

Billy Preston in an era of big hits and even bigger Afros.

Mavis testifies: "Touch a hand, make a friend."

Whatever the stage, Pops, Cleo, Yvonne, and Mavis take it to church.

The Voice, produced by Prince, 1993. Mavis "had more music in her, I could hear that and feel that."

First Lady Hillary Clinton honors Pops with a National Heritage Fellowship from the National Endowment for the Arts at the White House in the '90s.

The Staple Singers and Marty Stuart work out an arrangement for "The Weight" in a Nashville studio on the 1994 *Rhythm Country and Blues* album.

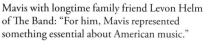

Mavis with longtime family friend Levon Helm of The Band: "For him, Mavis represented something essential about American music."

Pops Staples in the Grammy-winning '90s: "His day had finally come, and he was going to enjoy it."

"You Are Not Alone" at Lollapalooza 2010. Mavis shadowed by Jeff Tweedy. (Photograph by John [Nunu] Zomot)

A Holy Ghost moment, as witnessed by Arcade Fire's Win Butler. (Photograph by John [Nunu] Zomot)

"She'd say to me, 'Baby, could you bring Halie some more ice cream'?" Mavis says. "Then she'd break out a little bottle of vodka or gin and pour some on top."

In 1967, Billy Sherrill produced what would be his last album with the Staple Singers at Epic, *Pray On*. As customary, the family reaffirmed its gospel foundation by rerecording key songs from its Vee-Jay and Riverside years, including "Wish I Had Answered" and the title track. "It's Been a Change" was the latest Pops original, dedicated to the civil rights struggle, an ode to resilience over a chugging John Lee Hooker–style bass line. "One of these days," Pops predicted, "there'll be a man on the moon." And there was "John Brown," another Dylan antiwar song again sung by the group's resident Dylanologist, Pervis.

The album spread the Staples' gospel sound across folk, rock, and another Hank Williams social commentary, "The Tramp on the Street." The split between tradition and topicality, the constant blurring of genre lines, made it difficult for Epic to pin down the band's identity. One of the label's trade-magazine ads for the group declared, "Staple Singers Make You Happy—You may have some trouble deciding which rack to put it in: Pop, Blues, Gospel, Traditional." Epic's wishy-washiness proved contagious; R&B and gospel radio programmers were no longer sure of where to slot the group, either.

Sherrill ended his partnership with the group to focus on the fast-rising singer David Houston and what was rapidly becoming a burgeoning career as a country producer. Epic next turned to Larry Williams, a New Orleans pianist who had written "Bony Moronie," "Dizzy Miss Lizzy," "Slow Down," and other rock 'n' roll rave-ups, to beef up the Staple Singers' sound and take a run at the rock audience. Williams had the group record Buffalo Springfield's antiauthoritarian hit "For What It's Worth." The song passed Pops's test with topical lyrics that could fit the civil rights or antiwar struggles ("You step out of line, the man come and take you away"), even though Stephen Stills has said he wrote the song about youth protests in Los Angeles over restrictive curfews at Sunset Strip rock clubs. Williams gave the Staples a heavier drum sound while preserving some of the group's signifiers—primarily Pops's treble-soaked guitar and the singers' rapid-fire handclaps. Though the performance never quite ignites—Mavis remains restrained throughout—the track reached number 66 on the *Billboard* Top 100, the group's highest-charting hit yet, even as black radio programmers shunned it.

Epic went even further out with the Staples on their sixth album for the label, *What the World Needs Now Is Love.* Ted Cooper, an in-house producer primarily known for working with the garage-rock band the Remains, gave the Staples their most overtly pop-oriented sound yet. Whereas Pops had shared the lead vocals with Mavis on the previous Epic albums, Mavis is pushed to the forefront, a clear attempt to position the singer as the label's answer to Aretha Franklin, riding high with her 1967 breakthrough album for Atlantic, *I Never Loved a Man the Way I Love You.*

At times, the rest of the Staples sound like they're barely involved. The title song, a cover of a 1965 pop hit by Jackie DeShannon, ornaments Mavis's lead vocal with piano, jazzy guitar, and unusually smooth backing vocals. Indeed, one of the tracks from the album was released as a Mavis Staples single, a cover of the '50s gospel-pop ballad "Crying in the Chapel," previously a hit for the doo-wop group the Orioles, country singer Rex Allen, jazz great Ella Fitzgerald and, most recently, Elvis Presley. Cooper erases many of the Staple Singers' trademarks—Pops's guitar and the family's background voices are entirely absent—and replaces them with a bluesy lounge vibe. Mellow jazz licks on guitar and organ temper a typically gutsy Mavis performance.

"They were trying to get me to go solo," Mavis says. "I am the only family member on that song ['Crying in the Chapel']. It was just me. The label went to Pops and told him how much more I could make if I sang by myself. Daddy let me know what they said. 'They want to pay you a lot of money to go solo.' I knew I could sing, but I wasn't ready for that. I'd been singing with Pops's guitar for so long, and my family's voices, I didn't want to sing by myself."

"Crying in the Chapel" didn't chart, in part because there was no context for it. Mavis hadn't really established her name outside the group and had never performed as a solo act. The pop-oriented sound was in many ways a repeat of the way Columbia Records had handled Franklin at the start of her career. As good as Franklin's voice was, the polished, professional, often superbly performed arrangements didn't play to her strengths or the idiosyncrasies that made her distinctive. Similarly, "Crying in the Chapel" sounds workmanlike: a great singer going about her business in a tasteful but dull setting.

The Staples also covered Dino Valenti's "Let's Get Together," which would become a huge hit a year later for the folk-rock group the Youngbloods. With production by veteran soul songwriter Jerry Ragovoy, the Staples turn the future hippie anthem into a tambourine-driven gospel rave-up. The song didn't connect commercially, though white performers like Joe Cocker, Leon Russell, and Delaney & Bonnie would soon score hits with a similar merger of rock, soul, and gospel.

Family friends also get a nod, with a slow, bluesy take on Stevie Wonder's saccharine ode to utopia ("A Place in the Sun"), Curtis Mayfield's timeless gospel-streaked equality anthem "People Get Ready," and yet another Pervis rendition of Bob Dylan's "A Hard Rain's A-Gonna Fall." Amid the onslaught of crossover attempts, Pops contributes another typically thoughtful and troubled mix of philosophy and soul on "I Wonder Why."

It would be the Staples' final album for Epic, an era bereft of major commercial successes. But the group's tenure on the label redirected their career. The mid-'60s gospel programs gave way to shows at coffeehouses and then rock concert halls, venues dismissed by gospel traditionalists as houses of corruption, brimming with booze, drugs, and sin. The Staples had tiptoed into that world and found more common ground than some of their gospel brethren may have anticipated.

"There came a time when gospel shows were being taken off the radio," Mavis said in a 1975 interview. "At that point we realized we weren't going to be heard if we stayed in one bag, one category. We figured our message songs were something that should be heard everywhere. And the big hotel lounges and the streets are the best places for the masses to hear those songs. Let's face it, a lot of people don't go to church. And the young people especially like what we're doing. It's beautiful seeing young people digging what we're into."

It didn't hurt that the Staples weren't exactly hard on the eyes. "They had a unique sound, and the girls were pretty," Leroy Crume says. "Mavis looked like a teenager even when she was in her late twenties, but she had that big voice that was fully grown. I'm not surprised at all that they were able to relate to that younger audience."

The Staple Singers shared bills in the late '60s with such rock hit makers as Jimi Hendrix, Love, Steppenwolf, Traffic, and Janis Joplin. At the time, Bill Graham was among the most innovative concert promoters in the country, booking the Fillmore (later the Fillmore West) and Winterland in San Francisco, and in 1968 opening the Fillmore East in New York. He'd routinely sell out shows with well-regarded rock headliners, which gave him license to open up the undercard to less-mainstream artists he personally valued and championed.

"Mavis Staples for me was in the same class as Aretha," Graham said. "They worked with [jazz artist] Rahsaan Roland Kirk and Love. Rahsaan had finished and I could feel the audience starting to go to the concessions. Back then, I would always do the same thing. Introduce the act and walk to the corner of the stage so I could feel it and check out the first songs. Mavis started snapping her fingers into the microphone as Pops took it all alone on the guitar. She sang, 'You're gonna hear from the Lord . . .' and the entire room turned around and sat back down. No more selling at the concessions. The sign of a great talent to me? No one goes out to buy a thing. They sit and watch or stand and dance or whatever. Watching the room turn around for Mavis and leaving that night knowing the audience had all tasted a fresh new fruit and would want it again, that was the greatest for me."

The experience was equally eye-opening for the Staples, who found themselves immersed in a full-on psychedelic experience when they debuted on April 18–19, 1968, at the Fillmore. The light show alone suggested a church of an entirely different religion, a collage of dancing liquid light and surreal images that mesmerized the audience before and between acts on the triple bill.

The Staple Singers had no trouble communicating, however, their polyrhythmic clapping bringing the fans to their feet. Here was a group of four people essentially electrifying the hall with little more than their hands and voices.

Pops was pleased but hardly surprised by the reaction. He'd been to enough gospel programs that left congregations in a sweat-soaked, sanctified fervor. "Gospel music for the young and old is a music that gets you moving," he said. "People want to move, to rock, so that's what it's become. The old black gospel groups could never read a note of music, but they always had the best beat . . . and still do."

For fans accustomed to rockers pounding drum kits and making electric guitars scream through stacks of amplifiers, the Staples' stark power was revelatory. Instead of stuffing Mavis's pockets with dollar bills as the congregation did back in the gospel days, rock fans enveloped the stage with their own brand of incense.

"A kid who was high came into our dressing room before we went on and he was floating like a butterfly," Mavis recalls. "He offered me and Cleedi a joint. We didn't want to hurt his feelings so we said, 'We can't do that before we go onstage.' But we couldn't avoid it. Once we got onstage, the marijuana smoke was blowing up in our faces and Pops got a contact high. The stage was just a step off the floor and the kids were very close to us. Pops was smiling and shaking his head, and playing this long guitar solo. The rest of us were clapping along, and clapping and clapping some more. I whispered to Pervis, 'Tell him to stop,' he would whisper to Cleedi, and on down the line till we got the message across. He was playing the solo for the wrong song! But Pops was feeling it. 'I'm feeling mighty good up here.'"

Janis Joplin was another ardent Staples fan bearing gifts when she first met the group backstage at the Fillmore in San Francisco. "Which one of you is Mavis?" she demanded in a raspy voice that made Mavis want to curl up in the corner and hide. Eventually the two started talking and Joplin expressed her love of Mavis's voice and the Staples' music. She then pulled a pint of Southern Comfort out of her rabbit-fur shoulder bag.

"Mavis, you want a hit?"

Mavis politely declined, which didn't deter Joplin from taking a long, hard swig of her own on her way out the door.

A few months later, in August 1968, Joplin renewed acquaintances with Mavis at the Fillmore East, this time suggesting an onstage collaboration on a night when her band, Big Brother and the Holding Company, was headlining the first of two concerts. Big Brother's *Cheap Thrills* album was about to be released and soon would become the nation's top seller, confirming Joplin's status as rock royalty. But here she was meeting the Staples on their musical turf, singing a gospel classic suggested by Mavis, "Down by the Riverside." They hardly looked like they belonged together: the miniskirted, cleavage-baring Joplin standing beneath a giant peace sign next to Mavis and Cleedi in stylishly elegant knee-length dresses and Pops and Pervis in tailored mohair suits. But the unlikely combo resonated with the rock audience.

"The Staple Singers had the theater converted into a fundamentalist church with their jubilant, frenetic, poignant religious and topical-protest songs," wrote Robert Shelton, who devoted most of his *New York Times* concert review to the opening act. "The family whipped the crowd into several hand-clapping storms. If one ever needs a quick definition of 'soul,' I submit as an answer: the Staple Singers."

A few weeks later, Pops elaborated to the *New York Times* on his definition of gospel as "truth" and his belief that at their best, rock, folk, and gospel spoke truth to power. "We're not sure what these kids are, but we got a lot of confidence in 'em 'cause they're earnest people," he said. "If the gospel moves them and the black people, and they can get together and smile on their brothers like the song says, we'll be strong enough maybe to go to the power establishment in Washington and get something done."

It would be difficult to imagine any of Pop Staples's gospel contemporaries espousing a similar vision of the hippie dream. But Pops saw an audience ready to accept the Staple Singers on their own genre-blurring terms, and he was glad to meet them halfway. The money wasn't bad on that side of the musical fence, either.

"Gospel goes deeper than entertainment," he said. "It is the word of God. But you can't push that down anybody's throat. All we can do is get as many people to hear us as we can. We've been lucky because doors are opening for us now."

17

The Stax era begins

The Staple Singers were about to leave their hotel in Nashville for a performance the evening of April 4, 1968, when they heard the news. They were still in the parking lot when intercepted by a distressed fan: "Pops, Pops, they just shot Dr. King." The family returned to their room and flipped on the television. Walter Cronkite delivered the sobering message.

"Good evening. Dr. Martin Luther King, the apostle of nonviolence in the civil rights movement, has been shot to death in Memphis, Tennessee. Police have issued an all-points bulletin for a well-dressed young white man seen running from the scene."

And later in the report, Cronkite noted: "There was shock in Harlem tonight when word of Dr. King's murder reached the nation's largest Negro community. Men, women, and children poured into the streets, they appeared dazed, many were crying."

The Lorraine Motel, where King was shot, was well known to the Staples. It was one of the few major motels in the Southeast hospitable to blacks, and the second-floor balcony outside room 306 where King was gunned down was the same one from which the minister had recently called down to Pops in the parking lot with a familiar request: "Stape, you gonna sing my song tonight?"

Pops, Mavis, Cleotha, and Pervis wept as Cronkite's words hit home. "Cleedi, it was the toughest for her," Mavis recalls. "Pops was trying to hold all of us, because we were out of control. We couldn't talk to each other for the longest time about it without crying."

Pops canceled the show that night and the family's plans to travel to Memphis the next day, where they had been scheduled to join King in his battle for the city's striking African-American sanitation workers, who were seeking equal pay and working conditions. Instead they drove the twelve hours to Chicago in a daze.

Memphis was a spiritual and geographic center of Staples family life, as important in many ways as Drew, Mississippi, and Chicago. They would stay at the Lorraine for a week at a time on their frequent road trips to the Deep South, using it as headquarters for nearby shows in Tennessee, Arkansas, and Mississippi. The city was the site of their near-tragic dustup with the cranky gas station attendant on a chilly November evening in 1964. And it was the home of their soon-to-be new label, Stax Records.

Their old DJ friend from Arkansas, Al Bell, had moved to Memphis in the early '60s right around the time Jim Stewart and his sister Estelle Stewart Axton were focusing Stax on the emerging regional R&B scene and striking a partnership with Atlantic Records. Bell was an early King disciple, but he left the fold after he pulled a switchblade in the face of racial taunts during an ostensibly nonviolent march in Savannah. In Memphis, he helped promote Stax's roster on his daily WLOK radio show, where the former Alvertis Isbell of Brinkley, Arkansas, signed on like the larger-than-life character he already was: "This is your 6-feet-4 bundle of joy, 212 pounds of Mrs. Bell's baby boy, soft as medicated cotton, rich as double-X cream, the women's pet, the men's threat, the baby boy Al Bell"—punctuated by the ringing of a bell.

After moving to Washington, D.C., for a couple of years, Bell was summoned back to Memphis in 1965 by Jim Stewart as Stax's first in-house promotion man. By 1968, he had essentially taken over day-to-day operation of the label, and in 1969 was named co-owner, becoming

one of the most powerful African-American executives in the music
industry. After breaking ties with Atlantic, which retained the label's
back catalog, Stax began feverishly rebuilding its musical assets under
Bell's direction. Booker T. Jones, of the label's Booker T. & the M.G.'s
house band, called Bell "our Otis for promotion," after the legendary
Stax singer Otis Redding, who had died in a 1967 plane crash.

One of Bell's priorities was to sign his old friends the Staple Singers
to Stax. On July 25, 1968, he did just that. His newest act, one of his
linchpins for rejuvenating the label, was a veteran vocal group that had
already been performing professionally for two decades. Pop Staples was
then fifty-three years old; Cleotha, thirty-four; Pervis, thirty-three; and
Mavis, twenty-nine.

Yet in many ways, the group's sound couldn't have been more current,
its influence evident in a musical spectrum that stretched from gospel to
soul and into rock. Aretha Franklin's number 2 hit "Chain of Fools"
kicked off with a guitar riff that sounded an awful lot like something
Pops might play. Producer Jerry Wexler later affirmed that he instructed
guitarist Joe South to do just that: "We went for the Pops Staples sound
by tuning the guitar down four or five steps and turning up the vibrato
to the max, creating a deep, mysterious tremolo."

John Fogerty was a Pops fan, too, as evidenced by the slow, steamy,
overdriven guitar riff that cut through Creedence Clearwater Revival's
classic "Born on the Bayou." "I used to listen to the religious hour on
Sunday evenings, they had a gospel show that lasted two or three hours,"
Fogerty said. "I would certainly remember Pops Staples's guitar and the
Staple Singers. That's really why I would tune in, to hear that harmony
sound and his guitar style. I'm just kind of an American sponge of all
things that came before. Pops, and the gospel sound in general, is a big
influence on me. So if you get any of that feel in my records, I am very
proud."

And though the Staple Singers weren't yet a fixture on Top 40 radio
or progressive FM stations, their vocal blend certainly was. The harmonies of Levon Helm, Richard Manuel, and Rick Danko on The Band's

1968 debut, *Music from Big Pink,* were directly inspired by the Staples' mix. Jerry Butler noted the similarities between the Staples harmonies and that of Gladys Knight and the Pips, riding high in '68 with "The End of Our Road."

"Gladys's background singer William [Guest] would tell Cleedi, 'I'm trying to sound like you,'" Mavis says of her sister's distinctive soprano harmonies. "And Aretha wanted to beat up [her sister] Carolyn because she wouldn't sing like Cleotha."

Bell thought the Staples were ideally suited to the rough-edged soul that was Stax's specialty—a rawer, earthier, more down-home sound than the slicker uptown arrangements favored by its Northern counterpart, Detroit-based Motown. As soon as he found that Epic wasn't going to renew the Staple Singers' contract, Bell pounced.

"Another label was bidding for them after their contract expired," Bell recalls. "I was able to convince Jim Stewart that we should sign them. In my conversations with Pops, I think the relationship we had helped—that $1,000 he earned in Arkansas at one of my shows back in the '50s still remained in his mind [laughs]. I never saw them as gospel artists, but as rare, great, and unique singers. The problem I had was since I was making so much noise internally, and so excited in trying to get them, I had to be careful that the other artists didn't think me biased and showing special favor. I really wanted to get into the studio with them from the start [to produce], but I didn't want to show favoritism. So I went to Steve Cropper, who I thought could get them to the next level."

Cropper was only twenty-six when he started working with the Staples, but he already was a veteran of countless sessions and tours. He was not only the guitarist in Booker T. & the M.G.'s, but he had written and produced numerous hits for other artists, including "(Sittin' on) The Dock of the Bay" with Otis Redding, "Knock on Wood" with Eddie Floyd, and "In the Midnight Hour" with Wilson Pickett.

The guitarist was born in Missouri but moved to Memphis with his family when he was nine, and heard the Staples' music for the first time on the local soul-gospel station WDAI. "At Stax, we all knew who they were before they got there, their sound was so identifiable," he says. "The rhythm, the handclaps, I thought we needed some of that on our records. We couldn't get anyone at Stax to clap like that, those sanctified rhythms."

As a guitarist who valued concision, Cropper deeply appreciated Pops's economical attitude toward the instrument and its central role in the Staples' sound. "Pops and I hit it off, in part because we both had a whole different attitude toward guitar. Guitar was meant to be simple, not flashy."

Cropper claims he didn't pay much attention to the Staples' records at Epic, but in many ways he picked up where Epic left off. In the family's first recording sessions in Memphis for the *Soul Folk in Action* album on September 5, 6, 10, and 12, 1968, the producer mixed contemporary material with gospel-flavored, message-oriented protest songs. He placed Pops's guitar and the family's voices at the center of the mix but augmented them with three-quarters of the great Stax house band that had played on so many Southern soul classics—Cropper on guitar, Donald "Duck" Dunn on bass, and Al Jackson Jr. on drums—plus keyboardist Marvell Thomas and the Memphis Horns.

"The whole attitude in the sessions was to move us around Pops, not him around us," Cropper says. "We wanted to keep that sound he had, the arpeggio chords with tremolo. John Fogerty did a lot of records with that Pops sound and was having hits, so there was no reason not to keep that."

The producer also introduced Pops to Homer Banks, a twenty-seven-year-old songwriter who would become one of the group's most valued foils during their Stax tenure.

"Homer was an up-and-coming songwriter who had an open door at Stax," Cropper says. "We were pulling from anywhere and everywhere for quality songs because Al Bell was basically rebuilding the catalog. Homer was a perfect fit for the Staples. He would tell stories for the time, but they would still make sense as pop records."

Banks's "Long Walk to D.C." dovetailed precisely with Pops's vision for the group; the song commemorated King's 1963 March on Washington, sung from the perspective of a poor but determined African American. The "long walk" to the rally turns into an extended metaphor for the black community's struggle to overcome all hardships "no matter what it takes." Pops's guitar ushers in a spirited call-and-response between Mavis and the family, the urgency underlined by bursts of tambourine.

Another Banks tune, "The Ghetto," elicits a heart-rending Mavis vocal over a bed of mournful voices, strings, and organ. Banks's imagery was so vivid that Mavis says she "felt like I was singing a movie," taking her back to her childhood growing up on Chicago's South Side and the Dirty Thirties.

"At night, at night, at night, you are awakened by the sound of a downbound train," she sang, a line that reminded Pops of the elevated train that used to screech past one of his apartments when he first came to Chicago.

Equally timely was "Got to Be Some Changes Made," written by the Staples' old friend Leroy Crume, who was now playing bass with the family on tour. The boisterous demand sounds like a street slogan in the immediate aftermath of King's assassination, with counterpoint horns. The recording sessions were happening so quickly that Crume didn't even get to finish the song. "Al Bell called and said, 'We need this song on the album, but it only has one verse,'" Crume says. "We had just finished a tour in California and I was getting on a plane to come home when he asked me to write another verse on the plane. I did, but by the time I landed, Mavis had already recorded it—she just sang the first verse over."

Cropper also had the band take on Redding's "(Sittin' on) The Dock of the Bay," which only a few months earlier had given the soul legend his biggest hit, rising to number 3 on the pop chart.

"Otis and I both said the song could use some background vocals," Cropper says of the December 8, 1967, recording session with Redding, his final day in the studio with the singer. "The first words out of my mouth were that the Staple Singers were coming in to Memphis and would be perfect for it. Otis just smiled and said, 'Fantastic.' The idea was to get them on there. But Otis's plane went down [on December 10] before they got to town. So having them record it brought the song full circle. So many artists would've been intimidated, thinking they can't sing an Otis Redding song, because at that point he was like God. But it was their way of paying tribute to him. Mavis, when she feels a lyric, can sing anything."

Another relatively new song, "The Weight," was unfamiliar to the group when Cropper brought it to them. It had come out only weeks earlier on The Band's debut album, *Music from Big Pink*. Pervis was game to record it, though he snickered to Mavis, "It's a drug song." Pops related to it as a biblical parable set in Nazareth (which Robbie Robertson of The Band later explained actually referred to the town in Pennsylvania, not the childhood home of Jesus). With Marvell Thomas's rollicking gospel piano, counterpoint strings, and the Staples' harmonies, the song came off as though it were written specifically for them to sing. Indeed, The Band was thrilled to hear the Staples cover it since the roots rockers had borrowed many of their ideas about vocal harmony from the gospel group.

"I thought 'The Weight' seemed like a perfect blend for them, a song that seemed carved out of the earth," Cropper says. "It was very visual, a Pictionary type of song, an old country, backwoods-farmer kind of deal that fit right in with the Staples and how they sing to the common person, whether on a farm or in the ghetto. To me, Pops just laid right on that one. That was his kind of song."

Mavis says that if Pops approved, the songs got recorded. "We didn't start singing songs like 'The Weight' and 'For What It's Worth' because we wanted to. It started with Daddy. If he said it was all right to sing, that's what we did. I wanted to please. But I had to feel it, in order for it to be sung the way it needed to be sung. I had to feel I could say it."

In retrospect, Mavis's relatively tentative performance on "The Weight" sounds like a sketch for the staggering versions that would come later. Over the years, as Mavis absorbed the song, soaked in the lyrics, and began to apply them to her own life, "The Weight" would become integral to her persona as a singer. But for the moment, it represented an adventurous leap for the Staples that they weren't yet ready to make.

Cropper made sure Al Bell heard the in-progress recordings. "I ran everything by Al," the guitarist says. "He didn't hang in the studio. When we got something good, he would tell me, 'This is great, keep going.'" Ultimately, Bell had final say over what songs made the final cut and how the album would be sequenced and packaged. One outtake, dubbed "Pop's Instrumental," is classic old-school Staple Singers: The family patriarch lays down some intricate, blues-based guitar riffs and fingerpicking over the three-part handclapping of Pervis, Cleotha, and Mavis. It's a spectacular example of the family at its intimate, roaring best, a snippet of the exuberant interplay they would pull off in concert.

But the performance was left on the cutting-room floor; perhaps it was deemed too down-home, too old-school to cut it with the rock crowd. Instead, the album leans toward more experimental arrangements that push the Staple Singers' range. Pops's hopeful vision of a world that one day might be, "I See It," swims in a lush sea of strings and horns, resolving in a queasy instrumental coda of "The Star-Spangled Banner." It segues into "This Year," an episodic composition that jumps between cautionary declarations by the group and Pops's brooding, narrative-like orations. Cropper's electric sitar further enhances the track's mystical, dreamlike feel.

"Long Walk to D.C.," "(Sittin' on) The Dock of the Bay," and "The Ghetto"—the three singles released from *Soul Folk in Action*—failed to crack the charts. But Al Bell was undaunted. In February 1969, he not only had the Staple Singers back in the studio again with Cropper, he put Mavis and Cropper to work on the singer's first solo album.

18

"When Will We Be Paid?"

To fans of the Staple Singers in the '60s, the relative anonymity of Mavis Staples was puzzling. With an improbably deep voice bursting out of a diminutive five-foot frame, she projected the deepest commitment to whatever she was singing, losing herself in every word as though reliving a critical moment in her personal story.

And yet she still wasn't a marquee name like Aretha Franklin, Gladys Knight, Diana Ross, and Dusty Springfield. Part of this was by design—Mavis enjoyed singing with her family and preferred to melt into the group. Even when her father brought her out front to sing lead after Pervis's voice changed in the '50s, she did so reluctantly. "I loved singing those baritone harmonies, I always thought that was the best job you could have," Mavis said. She also felt a certain comfort being guided by her father, who had essentially taught her how and what to sing. Little had changed in the decades since, even as it was apparent that Mavis had star power. "Mavis was and is a quartet singer," says Anthony Heilbut. "From a very early age she grew up singing harmony or singing lead in a group with four voices and her father's guitar. She was trained to sing with the guitar, whereas Aretha sang with the piano. It's a very different approach."

Not only that, Pops's idiosyncratic guitar style made it difficult for

Mavis to easily adapt to a different context. So, too, was the unspoken communication between Mavis and her siblings, the way they harmonized with her, even the way they clapped hands together, a high-speed ripple that approximated an entire percussion section by itself. "I've been singing a long time," Mavis says, "and I could never find anyone to clap like Pervis and Cleedi."

But Al Bell never forgot the day in Arkansas when the teenage Mavis's voice bowled him over and left him in tears in what was essentially a solo performance of "On My Way to Heaven" during a Staple Singers show.

"In signing the Staple Singers, I thought of it as signing three acts in one," Bell says. "I wanted to record Pops and Mavis as solo artists. I knew it would add more to them from a personal appearance standpoint, bring them a broader, more diverse audience. I would hear Pops sitting around and just playing his guitar at Stax, and I thought, 'I've got to get this man down on tape.' His singing, I knew there was a lot more songs that could have been done with Pops as a vocalist, because he was so distinctive. With Mavis I saw no boundaries at all—I saw her walking past all of them."

Steve Cropper had already won the Staples family's trust while recording *Soul Folk in Action,* so Bell had him produce what would be Mavis's self-titled debut album.

"The attitude at Stax was that she's a superstar who nobody really knows about, and we have to figure out how to get her out there," Cropper recalls. "But it wasn't easy, because she put limits on herself. There were only certain songs she would try. Her upbringing, her feeling about what songs would or wouldn't go down with Pops, gave me the impression she didn't want to go too far too fast. So I approached the whole thing with kid gloves. I didn't want to lose her trust or do something damaging."

Cropper found Pops a thoughtful and willing collaborator in the studio, but there was no question his word still counted more than anyone else's in the family, even though his children were now well into adulthood. "Every now and then, Mavis would reference Pops in terms of putting his foot down about dating," Cropper says. "He was still on top of her when she got older. There were lines he didn't want to cross when it came to his family's well-being, and that included what kind of songs they would sing, what message they would put out."

The guitarist knew he was running a risk presenting Mavis with a set of secular songs that didn't have any of the gospel or message-oriented underpinnings favored by Pops and the Staple Singers. Whereas her first attempt at cutting a solo single, a cover of "Crying in the Chapel" for Epic, had some tenuous religious imagery, the tracks chosen for the *Mavis Staples* solo album were the sort of pop-oriented love and relationship songs that Pops typically shunned.

But Mavis was hardly insulated from the pop world as a fan and listener. She swooned over Sam Cooke's "You Send Me" the first time she heard it, and her cover of it on her debut album sounds wistful, as if she were singing both to a newfound love and to Cooke's memory. She took on Dusty Springfield's sultry "Son of a Preacher Man" because it struck a personal chord: She had "a little crush" on Reverend C. L. Franklin's son, Cecil.

Cropper coaxed her to try Otis Redding's "Security," which spoke to her self-doubts about going solo and breaking out of her family cocoon. "I don't want no money, I don't want no fame, just security," the song declared. The staccato horns ratcheted up her anxiety in one of the album's most spirited performances.

"I'd gotten to be a young lady and I wanted to sing songs about my life as a young lady," Mavis says. "Pops said it was all right as long as I believed in what I was singing. Reverend Franklin let Aretha sing secular songs, love songs, so that probably made it easier for Pops to accept."

For Mavis, the biggest hurdle was taking on "A House Is Not a Home," the Burt Bacharach–Hal David ballad that had been a minor 1964 hit for her friend Dionne Warwick. Mavis adored the song, and it resonated more deeply with her as her marriage to Spencer Leak was falling apart. Warwick's interpretation suggested grace under pressure, as if she were trying to keep her heart intact in a home suddenly drained of intimacy. Mavis's performance in turn demonstrates just how much she'd grown as a vocalist, her voice projecting a quiet, understated dignity before building to a devastating final plea: "When I climb the stair and turn the key / Oh, please be there still in love with me."

"When they started asking me what I would like to sing, the lyrics of 'A House Is Not a Home' were so beautiful to me," Mavis says. "I make a movie in my head with lyrics I love. 'A chair is still a chair, even when there's no one sitting there. But a chair is not a house, and a house is not a home, when there's no one there to hold you tight.' I could see all of it. When I heard Dionne sing it, I thought, 'Oh, my . . .'"

But when it came time to sing it at the Stax studio in February 1969, Mavis nearly couldn't go through with it.

"Cropper, get out here, I can't do this by myself," she said, sending up a flare from the studio floor to the control room. The producer came out from behind the glass and stood next to Mavis, draped an arm around her shoulder, then grasped her hand as she poured herself into Hal David's lyrics.

"She made me stand there while she overdubbed the vocal, and it was like it made it okay for her to hold nothing back," Cropper says. "I'll always cherish that moment."

"I needed him because I was scared to death" to sing some of the songs Cropper suggested, Mavis says. "He had me singing, 'I don't know what you got, baby, but it sure is good to me.' I liked the song [Otis Redding's 'Good to Me'], but I thought if the gospel people don't like me singing these love songs, I'm done. Steve made me feel safe singing them. I don't know if I would've made it through that session without him."

"A House Is Not a Home" received airplay on stations in several big markets but was never released as a single and didn't crack the pop charts. In retrospect, Al Bell says, he wishes he'd pushed harder for that song. In contrast to Warwick's somewhat fragile, understated version, Mavis's interpretation amps up the air of desperation and the rhythm section puts some muscle into the backbeat.

"It's a masterpiece in my mind," he says. "It hit me later on when Luther Vandross did the same song [in 1981], and it started his career. I didn't think it compared to what Mavis did with it, especially since he modeled his version after Mavis's, not Dionne Warwick's. It hurt me. That should have been a hit on Mavis. She lived it."

Cropper looks back at his solo sessions with Mavis and realizes that the singer was in many ways growing up in front of the microphone. "We always agreed the day before what songs she'd sing, and she was prepared, spot-on, awesome," Cropper says. "But we didn't push her limits, and her confidence was not there yet. I could make the same record today and get twice the performance from her."

Mavis made her live solo debut later that year in the middle of a set by the Staple Singers, who were opening for Isaac Hayes at Detroit's Municipal Auditorium. *Jet* magazine reported two standing ovations from the capacity audience of seven thousand when she performed Cooke's "You Send Me" and "A House Is Not a Home."

"I had a lump in my throat as big as my head and it wouldn't go away," she said afterward. "I was scared I would not be able to sing. My knees were practically knocking together. I had a pretty good case of stage fright for a person who has been in show business as long as I have been."

Decades later, Mavis still remembers how ill prepared she was for the moment when the family left her onstage by herself to sing two solo songs with their backing band. "I was in the dressing room crying beforehand," she says. "My name was on the marquee outside. The response from the audience was amazing, and I was able to get through it, but it wasn't something I was ready for at the time."

As Mavis's solo career got off to shaky start, Stax and Al Bell kept plowing ahead. Every artist, producer, engineer, executive, and songwriter associated with the label was multitasking in an effort to fill retail shelves with new music. Mavis, along with Pervis and Cleotha, was enlisted to sing on tracks for another Bell-inspired idea, the *Boy Meets Girl* album, which paired the label's artists in a series of coed duets. Pops participated in an album, *Jammed Together,* with the label's two other famed guitarists, Cropper and blues legend Albert King. Pops takes the lead on an ominous version of John Lee Hooker's "Tupelo," and then calls out for King and Cropper to take solos. But Cropper says the three guitarists were never in the studio together.

"That was another rush job, an Al Bell project with Al Jackson, and he brought us in separately to overdub our parts because we were all too busy—Pop and Albert were on the road constantly, and I was in the studio all the time," Cropper says. "When Pop sang about that 'flood down in Tupelo,' I about died when I heard that, it was so good. But it got lost in all the music we were putting out at the time."

In late May 1969 alone, Bell saturated the market with twenty-seven albums and thirty singles. During the entire Atlantic partnership from 1961 to '68, Stax had put out a mere forty-three albums. The extra workload pushed the core Stax producers to the brink of burnout, so Bell began farming out work to additional studios, particularly Ardent in Memphis and Muscle Shoals in Alabama. Bell, who was increasingly playing a hands-on role as a producer on top of his executive duties, felt more comfortable working away from home.

"When you have people working for you as producers like the members of Booker T. & the M.G.'s, I was a bit intimidated," Bell acknowledges. "I was really good at hearing things and coming up with ideas, but I couldn't sing, play, or dance, and my sense of timing was bad [laughs]. They'd kid with me about it, and so I'd keep my distance, let them do their thing their way. At Muscle Shoals, they were happy that I was bringing in great artists for them to work with, so I felt more freedom to be myself and do what I thought needed to be done."

Bell liked what Cropper had done with the Staple Singers on *Soul Folk in Action,* however, and he reunited them for the 1969 follow-up, *We'll Get Over.* "We were game for anything at that point," Mavis acknowledges. "Nothing seemed to scare us. The only thing we didn't want was to sing any garbage."

The album opens with the title song, another Staples message-with-a-beat ready-made from the songwriting team of Homer Banks, Bettye Crutcher, and Raymond Jackson, a mix of funky horn-spackled soul and gospel harmonizing, with Mavis preaching to the choir about resilience. Then Cropper tries to shake some Top 40 dust onto the Staples' down-home earthiness: the 5th Dimension–like pop-soul of "Give a Damn," a cover of Joe South's hit "Games People Play," and a bit of payback to Gladys Knight and the Pips in an interpretation of the Motown hit "The End of Our Road," which borrowed heavily from the Staples' sound. The group also enthusiastically channeled Sly and the Family Stone's mix of male and female voices on "Everyday People," over a driving Duck Dunn–Al Jackson rhythm topped off by Cropper's wah-wah-soaked acid-rock guitar solo.

Mavis had been summoned to Los Angeles around that time to meet Sylvester "Sly" Stewart himself; the soul star told her that he'd modeled the Family Stone's harmonies after the Staple Singers. He had promised to get Mavis into the studio for some recording to help launch a new label, but nothing much occurred except an unwanted introduction to Sly's increasingly decadent lifestyle.

"I went all these places with him over a few days in California—he kept on moving, but we never went in the studio," Mavis recalls. "His manager had us over to his house, me and Sly. He was cooking out on the patio, some steaks and potatoes. Sly hung out in this room, and I saw this white stuff everywhere. I didn't know what it was. I was young. But I knew it was time to go home."

Just as he had with *Soul Folk in Action,* Cropper took some chances, using the studio as an instrument while tucking the Staples inside the lushest arrangements of their career. Electric keyboards, strings, and horns cushioned the elliptical fairy-tale-like lyrics of Randy Bachman's chamber-pop "A Wednesday in Your Garden," originally recorded by the Guess Who. A poetic Banks-Crutcher-Jackson message song, "The Gardner," made a fitting bookend.

"I loved those songs so much," Mavis says. "I gave it my own interpretation. I felt like it was about whites not letting blacks into their lives.

[Chicago soul radio DJ] Herb Kent fell in love with 'A Wednesday in Your Garden,' too. Herb used to close his show with that song."

There was also a splash of weirdness, the Japanese folk tune "Solon Bushi," which the family had learned on a tour of Japan in 1968. "It was different enough; the hope was to get people's attention," Cropper says with a laugh. "We were shooting in the dark in how to handle albums. Stax had been a singles-oriented label, and we were good at it. 'Dock of the Bay,' 'Walking the Dog,' 'Green Onions'—we knew these were hits the day they were cut. But when you've got ten, twelve tracks on an album, and you're trying to make them all sound like singles with unique approaches, great intros, top-level arrangements and performances, it was a whole new world for us and I'm not sure we were ready for it. We had to split up the rhythm section, farm out work to New York, Chicago, Los Angeles, and bring in outside producers. We were working on fifteen, sixteen songs to get ten for a record, instead of one hit that you could build from the bottom up until everything was exactly the way we wanted it."

Both Staple Singers albums with Cropper contain plenty of worthwhile moments, as they document the group's transition from gospel to pop. "If there was a downside to working with them, there were restrictions from going all-out at first because Pop wasn't ready to make the leap to what he considered pop music," Cropper says. "I should say lyrically reluctant because they had that dance element creeping in with our rhythm section, you almost couldn't avoid it. But they didn't want the street shit. And I wasn't really sure in talking to Al Bell where he wanted to take them. I tried to maintain the original feel of the Staple Singers as a gospel group and do lyrics that weren't quite gospel but still had the feel. I think we were all learning about each other. It wasn't until later with Al Bell that they got more down-and-dirty sounding, with meaningful lyrics, and the hits started to come."

The Staples era at Stax with Cropper is often ignored, but it contains several crucial songs, none better than "When Will We Be Paid?," the final track on *We'll Get Over*. The song, written by the former doo-wop singer Randy Stewart, framed the civil rights struggle as an unpaid debt by America for three centuries of labor and service: "We have given our sweat and all our tears / We've stumbled through this life for more than 300 years."

Horns answer the family's unison voices as they chant the chorus— "When will we be paid for the work we've done?"—underpinned by Cropper's typically terse, rhythm-lead guitar fills. The Staples turned the song into a piece of theater in concert, with heads bowed and arms raised. Ignored by radio, the song accrued anthemic resonance when performed in front of largely black audiences, who would applaud between verses and sometimes demand that the song be sung twice.

When Pops sang it, he'd think about his grandfather spending most of his young life as a slave in Mississippi, and about his years as a youth spent sharecropping only to see his family fall deeper into debt. The song anchored the Staple Singers' shows for years, and Pops always made sure to give it three centuries of context.

A few years after it was recorded, Pops introduced the song to a capacity audience at the Apollo Theater. "We were in Africa a few months ago and we went to see where the African people were sold and then brought into the States to be working for over three hundred years—for nothing!" His voice rose, the trademark Pops gentility momentarily shoved aside for some Old Testament sternness. "They helped build the U.S. and make it what it is today. And still we're second-class citizens."

The fans who weren't out of their seats already, now stood. Pops was reminding them of their collective past, and it rang true. "Preach!" one cried.

"We've got to fight and get our respected places where we belong— first-class citizens just like anybody else. We want to be respected and get just what the other fellow gets because we've been the horse and worked all those many years for nothing. A young man wrote a song asking the question, 'When are we gonna get paid for all the work we've done?' All of that back time,"

Now Pops, ever the preacher, lowered his voice for dramatic effect. He turned confiding, conspiratorial.

"Well, we won't get paid for that job, but I don't live for that day. What I want y'all to get hip to is try to get paid from now on in. Not only in money but in every respect. Go where you want to go—be recognized—and in every respect we need to get paid in every kind of way."

19

Mahalia passes the torch

Mahalia Jackson was born in New Orleans and grew up in a three-room shack near the Mississippi River. She scrubbed floors as a child, singing the songs of Bessie Smith to take her mind off her aching knees and back. She would bring the emotional transparency of the blues—expressed in slurs, moans, and wordless interjections—into gospel, her most enduring musical love. At sixteen, she moved to Chicago, where she made do as a factory worker, florist, laundress, and beautician. Eventually, her one-of-a-kind voice earned her a recording contract and the guidance of the great gospel songwriter Thomas A. Dorsey.

As a gospel singer, Jackson was a revolutionary who tested Dorsey's patience; rarely did she sing any of his carefully plotted compositions the same way twice. She would draw out and slow down the métier, and stretch or contract words, syllables, lines as the moment dictated. Few singers could rival her combination of range and emotional investment. Little wonder that little eight-year-old Mavis Staples was rocking back and forth with excitement when she first heard Sister Mahalia's voice calling out from her father's phonograph in the family's South Side apartment during the '40s.

Longtime familiarity, with Mahalia assuming the role of neighborly mentor and surrogate mother dispensing health and professional advice to young Mavis ("Now, baby, don't forget to put on a dry shirt after you sing"), did little to diminish Mavis's awe. Even as an adult well into her own career as a singer, Mavis never thought of herself as Mahalia's peer but as her student and disciple fetching her ice cream at backyard barbecues.

Jackson was a dominating figure in gospel, but not because she was above it all, the voice on the mountaintop. She could be as diva-like as any of them, but when she was performing there was little separation between her and the congregation. She walked the aisles, reaching into the pews and clasping hands. The music seemed to be flowing through her, a lightning rod acute to every movement in the room. "I'm used to singing in church until the spirit comes," Jackson said, which meant that as a singer she was willing to take her time, to bend the song, venture off course, until she found what she was looking for. That sense of embodying the song, not just emotionally but also physically, was what made Mahalia Jackson so beloved. She had a way of contorting her body at the waist when a note hit her just so.

Mavis had been studying Mahalia from an early age, and she responded to and then absorbed the singer's most compelling attribute as an artist: a total giving of the self to the song, intimate knowledge not just of the notes but also of the poetry, the ability to will herself inside the narrative. Pops saw it, too: "Sincerity, it's something you can't fake. The people can sense how genuine you are. It's the main thing I taught Mavis from an early age: If you sing it, believe it, and people will believe you."

Great singers all develop their tics and mannerisms for selling a song. By the late '60s, Mavis and Mahalia were both well-established artists who had spent years on stage, learning what to do and what not to do to move an audience. But whatever scripted moments had crept into their routines briefly disappeared when they stood shoulder to shoulder onstage in July 1969, sharing a microphone and a common purpose. The occasion was the second Harlem Cultural Festival in Mount Morris

Park. The performers at what became known as the "Black Woodstock" included a who's who of African-American arts and entertainment: Sly Stone, B. B. King, Nina Simone, Abbey Lincoln and Max Roach, the 5th Dimension, Olatunji, Gladys Knight and the Pips, Stevie Wonder, Moms Mabley, Pigmeat Markham.

Over six weeks, they performed in front of audiences in the tens of thousands that spanned generations and cultural allegiances, from black militants to Holy Rollers. It was a confused and confusing time; the era of nonviolent protest had ended tragically when Martin Luther King was assassinated the year before, followed only months later by the slaying of presidential candidate and racial-equality advocate Robert Kennedy. In the summer and fall of '69, eight bombings rocked New York City. Violent crimes topped a hundred thousand annually for the first time in the city's history; murders and rapes were at an all-time peak and would continue to rise over the next few years. Unemployment nationwide was at its highest point in nearly a decade.

It was not a time of celebration on July 13, when the Staple Singers performed with a full band and horn section. Mavis, Cleo, and Yvonne wore paisley dresses and hoop earrings and neatly trimmed Afros. Pops wore a black suit and tie, looking improbably cool on a humid, overcast afternoon as he hunched over his Les Paul guitar. Pops wasn't much for idle banter. Each moment onstage was precious, whether delivering a melody with a message or a minisermon between songs that amplified their meaning. He was in an especially serious mood this day.

"You'd go for a job and you wouldn't get it," Pops said to the audience. "And you know the reason why. But now you've got an education. We can demand what we want. Isn't that right? So go to school, children, and learn all you can. And who knows? There's been a change and you may be president of the United States one day."

Standing in the wings was a future presidential candidate, Jesse Jackson, who served as master of ceremonies. Jackson looked like a sheriff out of an alternative Western with his scarf, vest, and star. Indeed, Harlem in the summer of 1969 had turned into something of a Wild West town; police refused to provide security at the festival, so the Black Panthers were enlisted. The concerts went off without incident and yet were barely acknowledged in the mainstream media, even though their scale and artistic ambition rivaled that of any of the era's major rock festivals.

The Staples finished their set but lingered to lend support for Mahalia Jackson's headlining appearance. "At the gospel festivals, when the singers get off they stick around onstage and clap for the others to make it sound like church," Mavis says. "So I came back and changed my clothes and sat next to Sister Mahalia."

Jackson, in a salmon-colored gown and white shoes, entered singing "Oh Happy Day," marching up and down a long walkway into the audience. The breaks between songs got longer as the set continued, as if Mahalia were giving herself time to recover. "I'm trying to see what's going on," she said at one point, while leafing through sheet music on a grand piano. She was only fifty-seven years old at that point, but she was suffering from diabetes and her health had deteriorated markedly since her second divorce a year earlier.

After one break, she delivered a magnificent "Let There Be Peace on Earth," her eyes squeezed shut as she sailed atop the piano and organ accompaniment. Mahalia held nothing back, only to drift to the back of the stage, exhausted, and find her seat next to a beaming, applauding Mavis.

"Baby, Halie don't feel too good," she said to Mavis. "I need you to help me sing this song."

"Yes, ma'am, whatever you need me to do," Mavis replied.

"She never told me what the song was, but as soon as the piano and organ started, I recognized it," Mavis recalls. "We were all church people up there."

The song was Thomas Dorsey's "Take My Hand, Precious Lord," which Mahalia had widely popularized in the '50s with her definitive studio recording; she also performed it at Martin Luther King's funeral in 1968. In the wake of the minister's assassination, the hymn "seemed the truest song in America," Anthony Heilbut wrote, "the last poignant cry of nonviolence before a night of storm that shows no sign of ending."

Mahalia knew nothing less than transcendence was expected, but she wasn't physically up to delivering it. So she passed the microphone to her protégé. Mavis had no time to think about anything other than making sure she did right by her friend and mentor. She knew the song in her bones because it had been a part of her since childhood, and she swept in over the stirring Hammond organ chords: "Lead me on . . . take my hand . . . and lead me home," her left arm raised. Jesse Jackson draped an arm around Mahalia and led her to Mavis's side at the bottom of the first verse. Mavis stepped back to let Mahalia belt a few more lines, before passing the microphone back again. Mavis began jumping in place, driving into the last verse; Mahalia, with hands on hips, exhorted her. At the last instant, Mavis slipped the microphone back in front of Mahalia's lips, and the legendary singer got the last word. "Take my hand, precious Lord, lead me home."

Thirty months from that moment, Mahalia Jackson would be dead. More than forty thousand people would show up to honor her at her longtime parish in Chicago, Greater Salem Baptist Church on 71st Street, and then six thousand more would pack the Arie Crown Theater at McCormick Place the next day for her funeral. Aretha Franklin would be called upon to sing "Take My Hand, Precious Lord."

But the torch had already been passed. The teacher had honored the student. Years later, a tape of the "Black Woodstock" performance was hand-delivered to Mavis by an anonymous fan.

"I put it on and I was in shock, and then I was in tears," Mavis recalled. She shared the tape with her family at Thanksgiving, and they were similarly moved upon seeing their old family friend in such a fragile, vulnerable state. "My father, everybody, there wasn't a dry eye in the house. Pops said, 'Mavis, I'm telling you, I didn't hear it like that at that concert. That was really beautiful. You keep that and you'll have her with you all the time.'"

20

"You talk to me like I'm a kid"

When the Staple Singers performed in Harlem in July 1969, Pervis Staples was not in his familiar position onstage between Mavis and Cleotha. His place was taken by Yvonne, the family's most business-minded sibling and reluctant fill-in singer. A few weeks earlier, Pervis had told Pops that he wanted to leave the group to devote his time to the business side of the music industry. He would open Perv's Music at 8125 S. Cottage Grove in Chicago; he'd already lined up his first client, the Emotions, another family vocal group out of Chicago consisting of three teenage sisters.

Steve Cropper, who worked with the Staple Singers on what would be Pervis's final album with them only weeks before, didn't detect any dissatisfaction or restlessness from the singer.

"He was a group player from the word 'go,'" Cropper says. "He loved being in the studio, and he and the family had a lot of respect for each other. Cleedi would keep the energy level up. They were all about the group. The records sound like they were made by a family, not a bunch of call people. Pervis helped me in production, the harmony parts especially. If I had an idea, he would work with the girls and stretch the idea. He would become the band leader, work with them over and over.

Every idea wouldn't work right away, so he'd work on it until they got it right. They were like horn players, each of them knew what part to take. He never threw up any flares, and neither did Pop. Pop would walk away and let us do what we needed."

Pops rarely clashed with Cleotha, his strongest advocate in the band. Mavis and Yvonne used to teasingly call her "Roberta" because she was so closely aligned with Daddy Roebuck on so many issues. Though Mavis could be more stubborn, she depended on Pops for guidance and stability. When recording her solo album, Pops's absence in the studio was as big a factor as any in her anxiety. Pervis respected Pops, too, but the son was nearing forty years of age, and he surmised that his role in the Staple Singers had been defined for perpetuity.

"Pervis left because he didn't want to listen to Pops all the time, he wanted to do his own thing," Yvonne says. "We were all in the car one day driving to a show down south—me, Pervis, Mavis, and Daddy. Pervis was arguing with Daddy about something, and he jumped out of the car and ran down the highway with Daddy following him waving a Coke bottle. Two grown men wearing their suits, running down the highway, yelling at each other. Mavis and I couldn't help but laugh."

Pervis "was up and down on the accelerator," Mavis recalls, "and Pops would say, 'Drive steady, Perv.' Finally, Pops had enough: 'Stop the car!' Pops is swinging this bottle up in the air, chasing Pervis. Pervis said, 'You talk to me like I'm a kid.' He had been in the army, and he was standing up for himself as a man. Pervis just got tired of only being thought of as Daddy's son."

Pops relied on his son the way an army officer might a sergeant; he was assigned to protect his sisters, venture into segregated towns to buy groceries, and help develop the vocal arrangements in the studio. There was immense responsibility, but also accountability to the man in charge. Pervis was mildly frustrated that the group didn't adapt more readily to the pop music of the day, the way his childhood pals Sam Cooke and Lou Rawls had. "We finally got the old man to turn around and do this pop stuff," he confided to a friend, but he felt it might've been too late, that they were already too old to compete with the younger, fresher voices on the soul scene.

He provided plenty of musical input; Pervis often led the way in persuading Pop to nudge the group outside its traditional parameters. He was Bob Dylan's strongest advocate within the group and often sang lead when the group covered one of the folk iconoclast's songs. His dramatic monologues on "Be Careful of the Stones You Throw" and Hank Williams's "The Funeral" provided a change of pace at Staple Singers shows. If an oddball track like "Solon Bushi" made it onto an album, it's a good bet Pervis had something to do with it.

Yet he never felt a part of the decision-making inner circle. Often his father would consult with respected peers outside the immediate family such as Reverend C. L. Franklin and Martin Luther King when mulling his next move in music or business. Whenever hotel rooms were booked for the group's tours, Pops frequently isolated himself at one end of the hotel and put Pervis in the middle in closer proximity to his sisters, who shared a room.

"Reverend King, Reverend Franklin—they were like my daddies, too," Pervis says. "But we knew what was going on with the broads; they'd come around and bring pie. Dr. King and them would be down at one end of the hotel with the sweets, and the kids would wait at the other end. We were obedient but we weren't fools. [C. L. Franklin's son] Cecil Franklin, he wasn't a fool. But the fathers wouldn't share a lot of things with us. Pops wouldn't talk about a lot of things that he would talk about with them, like we were still children, even though we were moving swiftly into adulthood. When I had two children of my own [from his brief marriage to LeNora Anderson in the early '60s] and a wife, I thought Pops was going to 'tat' me up. But there's something sacred about family, and we had a mother that went along with Pops. There was no arguing about what the rules were."

Leroy Crume, who spent many hours with the Staple Singers on the road during the late '50s and '60s, says Pervis had more freedom than his sisters. "Pop let Pervis do his own thing, but he tried to keep his daughters on a string," Crume says. "It wasn't that he was that tough on them, but let's just say he was concerned about who they were seeing. Pops was a grown man, you never forgot that, and his sternness would come out in rehearsal. When I was playing bass with them in the '60s, he would want to rehearse two or three times a week and don't you dare be late. Pop was loosey-goosey otherwise. He never let his kids see him like that, which is why he'd often ask me to drive him somewhere. Me and Blab [Pervis] never disrespected him when the girls would hawk us right off the stage. We'd hide it, but Pops knew what we were up to. Ain't nobody saints on the road. You respect your religion, but none of us were saints."

Pervis was in many ways still the enterprising teenager who concocted his own ice-ball business on the South Side streets. And now he figured he knew enough about how the music business worked after twenty years on the road and in recording studios to strike out on his own as a talent scout, artist manager, and agent. He first got to know Sheila, Wanda, and Jeanette Hutchinson when the three teenage sisters were known as the Hutchinson Sunbeams. "Pops felt they needed to be heard and we took them on the road with us in the '60s," Mavis recalls, just as the Staples had done before with Aretha Franklin and the Womack Brothers. The Hutchinsons' father and guitarist, Joseph, approached Pervis about managing the group after they transitioned into R&B and changed their name to the Emotions. The group won a talent competition at the Regal Theater in Chicago and got a huge break: an opportunity to record a single for Stax, produced by Isaac Hayes and David Porter. Sheila Hutchinson's debut songwriting effort for the label, "So I Can Love You," reached number 39 on the pop charts in 1969, higher than any Staple Singers' song had climbed to that point. Pervis wrapped up his duties on the Staples' *We'll Get Over* album and then told Pops he wanted to devote full-time to managing the Emotions and running Perv's Music.

"There was no argument," Mavis says. "I hated that it had to happen, and Pops hated it, too. But Pervis thought he could make these girls big, and that was it—Pervis was gone. Pops told Yvonne it was time to come home."

Yvonne had done her best to forge a life outside the family since childhood. She stayed with Grandma Ware in Mississippi through high school, she says, mainly to avoid singing with the group. When Pervis was drafted by the army and Cleotha took a hiatus in the mid-'60s, she filled in reluctantly. But mostly she preferred to help Pops run the family's affairs behind the scenes.

"At an early age, Yvonne was taking care of business and subtly running things," Pops said. In the '60s she moved back to the South, this time to Atlanta, where she worked as a secretary and volunteered at a hospital for the mentally disabled. Now she was called upon again to sing with her family, just as the group entered a make-or-break phase in its career.

"Pressure? I didn't feel any pressure," Yvonne says. "When Daddy asked us to do something, we did it. No questions asked."

21

"I Have Learned to Do Without You"

Mavis Staples was not thrilled with the way Al Bell and Stax had promoted her first solo album. In what Bell called the "craziness" of 1969 with its logjammed release schedule, not every record was going to get the attention it deserved. And one of those albums, Isaac Hayes's *Hot Buttered Soul*, demanded the majority of the company's resources as it ascended the charts and spun off two Top 40 singles, edited versions of the shaved-headed singer's radical reinterpretations of Dionne Warwick's "Walk on By" and Glen Campbell's "By the Time I Get to Phoenix." The album ended up selling more than one million copies and turned Hayes from a highly proficient behind-the-scenes songwriter-producer–session musician into "Black Moses," a larger-than-life star unlike Stax had ever seen (save for the great Otis Redding).

"When *Hot Buttered Soul* came out, they promoted that over my record," Mavis says. "It hurt because I took this chance. I was scared, a gospel singer singing these secular songs. But Al told me, 'Isaac has been with us longer than you have. I have to promote his record.'"

Mavis was incredulous: "You can't promote two records at one time?"

She was eager to give solo recording another shot, though. Her first album with Steve Cropper felt like a challenge she wasn't sure she could overcome, but now she was ready to make a statement. She had Pops's approval. She liked stretching her range as a singer. And she had a story to tell.

Her marriage to Spencer Leak began disintegrating when they discovered they could not have children, Mavis says. Hurtful words were exchanged. While on tour in Europe, Mavis poured out her feelings in a letter to Spencer. When she returned, she found the letter torn in pieces and her husband's wedding ring on the bedroom dresser.

Mavis called a locksmith to change the locks to their two-bedroom apartment at 92nd and Cottage, she says. "Spencer had to live out of his car for a good while and take showers at the funeral parlor. I would stay at Cleedi's till two or three in the morning, because I didn't want him coming near me. When I got that divorce paper that made it final, I rejoiced. I just stopped my crying. I wanted to have as many children as my mother, but that was it for me." Mavis never did remarry or have kids.

For years after the divorce, Mavis was reluctant to talk about her marriage, finally making a general comment about male psychology to *Black Stars* magazine in 1975: "I've seen their egos drop if their wives are bringing in more money than they are. But that doesn't necessarily have to happen. Not if the man's head is together. But it seems that many guys define masculinity in terms of the cave man ethic of bringing home the money and being the leader."

Mavis instead funneled the turbulence into her second album, *Only for the Lonely,* an artistic shotgun marriage of sorts between her and Detroit-based producer Don Davis. He had cut the hugely successful 1968 single "Who's Making Love" with Johnnie Taylor for Stax, and his efficient Motown-influenced approach to making records dovetailed with Bell's need for product, and quickly.

Much of *Only for the Lonely* was recorded on September 29, 1969, at United Studios in Detroit with a six-piece band. But Mavis was used to working quickly, and she turned the opening track, "I Have Learned to Do Without You," written by Davis and his team, into a personal manifesto about the state of her marriage. "Yes, I got over you. Yeah, I have

learned to do without you," Mavis sings. And then she walks out over
ascending keyboards—the women scorned gets the last word.

"By this time I'm getting a divorce, and that song was right on time,"
she says. "I was talking to my husband through it. I started ad-libbing,
'Somehow I got over you, I don't need you no more.' Pervis would tell
me, 'Mavis, that song is the flip side of "A House Is Not a Home."' It
was real. It was my life."

The album as a whole is even more introspective than its predecessor,
with Mavis digging into deep, luminous soul ballads. Drummer George
McGregor and bassist Tony Newton create a sensitive foundation for
Ray Monette's terse guitar fills and Rudy Robinson's electric keyboards.
They enfold Mavis in empathy, giving her voice plenty of room to
explore all the emotional avenues in songs tinged with the ambiguities
of adult experience.

"How Many Times" is even more agonized. "How many more times
do you think I'll come crawling back again?" Mavis cries, before a devastating series of chords plays out beneath counterpoint horns. The way
she stretches the word "I" in "Since I Fell for You" is like a song in itself.
"Endlessly" pushes her into jazzier terrain, her voice languid yet lus-
trous. And there's a bit of sweet payback in her stark, smoky reading of
"Since I Fell for You," which Grandma Ware had forbidden her to sing
as a schoolgirl in Mississippi. The performances are among the most personal of Mavis's career and in many ways represent a breakthrough for
her as a woman and a singer; there's not just sheer vocal power on dis-
play but also a knowingness and nuance that would have been beyond
her only a few years before.

If once there was trepidation about singing secular songs dealing with
love and intimacy instead of straight gospel, it had faded into resolve.
For Mavis, her maturation as a singer and woman meant telling the
truth about the full range of her experiences. "I remember teasing Mavis
about one of her boyfriends," Jerry Butler says, "and she said, 'We're
Christian, but we're not dead.'"

"I felt like a young woman instead of a girl," Mavis says. "I'd experienced heartbreak, I'd been hurt. I couldn't even think of singing these songs before, because I realize I was such a kid in so many ways. But if you live and you've been in love and had heartbreak, that is something to sing about. When Al Bell asked me to make these records, the first thing that came to mind is, I can sing this stuff now. I can sing about the pain in my heart. I learned from Aretha; her songs were all about her love life. She didn't have to act. And neither did I."

I Have Learned to Do Without You rose to number 13 on the R&B chart in June 1970, but again the album fell short of commercial expectations. Mavis was miffed that a dispute with Stax over publishing rights kept two songs she had written under wraps: "I'm Tired of You Doing Me Wrong" and "You're All I Need." Rather than fork over 50 percent of her publishing to the label, she pulled the songs from consideration. "I said, 'That's it. I'm not doing any more albums for you.' I had written three songs and I couldn't get them on my own album. That stopped my solo stuff. Al even asked me to do another [solo album], but I said, 'No way, not after you cheated me like that.'"

Bell blames himself for losing Mavis's trust. "That was an era where the business was more singles oriented," he says. "You needed to have one or two singles before getting appreciation for an album. We didn't get or capture in terms of radio airplay that hit single for her. We worked the daylights out of it. I saw us getting closer and closer. The more popular she became with the Staple Singers, I think she would have exploded if she would have made one more solo record. She would have been in the heads of radio programmers. All that political stuff would've been gone. That becomes the real work."

Davis did a tremendous job with little time to massage the tracks, but Bell plays a game of what-if when he wonders how *Only for the Lonely* would've come across had the singer gotten the opportunity to really develop a relationship and a mutual trust with the producer.

"I knew it was going to take some time for Don to get to know her and find the Mavis that the world should hear," Bell says. "I know that wasn't captured. I was reaching for it. I thought we had a shot with [the

Homer Banks song] 'It Makes Me Wanna Cry.' What Don did with her
on that song was okay, but the Mavis we know didn't get a chance to
perform and live the song."

Mavis never developed a relationship with a producer the way her
friend Aretha Franklin finally did at Atlantic Records with Jerry Wexler.
Once Wexler began working with her, Aretha proved unstoppable as an
artistic and commercial force. "I was talking to Wexler about this," Bell
says. "He allowed Aretha to sit and play piano and tell the musicians to
follow. I think if Mavis could play piano she could have gotten there
quicker. The musicians and Don had to learn who she was first, and we
didn't give them enough time."

22

Muscle Shoals soul

Muscle Shoals occupies a sleepy corner of northwest Alabama along the Tennessee River with the cities of Tuscumbia, Florence, and Sheffield. By 1970, it had become an unlikely epicenter of Southern soul, boosting two first-rate recording studios: Fame Studios and Muscle Shoals Sound Studios.

Fame had been rolling since the late '50s under the direction of Rick Hall. Arthur Alexander's 1961 hit "You Better Move On," recorded at Fame's original location above a drugstore in Florence, helped establish the studio's country-soul template: a mix of black singers and white musicians situated at the heart of the "golden triangle" of Southern blues, country, soul, and R&B—Memphis, Nashville, and Macon—and melding influences from all three.

The white studio musicians at Fame lived in the area, augmented by the occasional ringer (future Allman Brothers guitarist Duane Allman once famously pitched a tent in the Fame parking lot in order to play on sessions). They were schooled in the black music coming out of radio stations such as the fifty-thousand-watt WLAC in Nashville. The sound was simple, earthy. Clipped guitars were played through low amplifier settings, bass and drums danced in the three-quarter time of deep soul, and the vocalists let things simmer a bit before bringing a song to a boil.

Session drummer Roger Hawkins described it as "rhythm and blues with a laid-back feeling."

The approach wasn't all that dissimilar to what was happening at Stax in Memphis at the time, and soon Fame was piling up hits by artists such as Wilson Pickett ("Mustang Sally"), Etta James ("Tell Mama"), Percy Sledge ("When a Man Loves a Woman"), Clarence Carter ("Slip Away"), and Aretha Franklin ("I Never Loved a Man [the Way That I Love You]").

In 1969, several key members of the Fame rhythm section left in a contract dispute with Hall and established their own studio in a two-story, gray stone building on Jackson Highway in Muscle Shoals. The musicians were a bunch of friendly, low-key, long-haired guys in their late twenties, all of them with families in town: Hawkins on drums, David Hood on bass, Jimmy Johnson on guitar, Barry Beckett on keyboards.

They exuded laid-back Southern attitude and generosity. They weren't just hired guns punching a clock and playing prescribed parts, but often worked in tandem with the artists to develop arrangements and flesh out songs. In contrast to the work being done in New York and other northern studios with high-paid arrangers, producers, and songwriters dictating performances, the approach at Muscle Shoals favored spontaneity and interaction in a relaxed atmosphere. "Head" arrangements, a let's-see-where-it-goes air of experimentation, prevailed.

Stax also worked that way for most of the '60s, but by the time the Staples started collaborating with Steve Cropper, an assembly-line atmosphere began to take over. When the Staples came in to sing vocals for their first two Stax albums, the rhythm section had already laid down their tracks, so there was no chance for any interplay between the vocalists and musicians.

Bell had started farming out work to Muscle Shoals for the *Boy Meets Girl* compilation, and he booked the Staple Singers for a session there in August 1970. This time, Bell would produce the Staples himself, a decision nudged along by one of the family's influential advocates in Chicago, Jesse Jackson. Bell had been introduced to Jackson by a mutual friend, Chicago disc jockey E. Rodney Jones, and the preacher called for a change.

"Hey, mate, Steve [Cropper] is doing a good job, but he doesn't know the Staple Singers like you," Jackson told Bell during one Chicago visit. "You need to go in the studio yourself because you know Pops and the family, you know Mississippi, you know gospel, you know where they come from. If you give them the kind of attention you pay to that bald-headed rascal [Isaac Hayes], they would be big for you."

"He told me I was doing them a disservice by not recording them myself," Bell recalls. "I knew there was more there that people needed to hear, and I also knew I couldn't get them where I wanted working at the Stax studio in Memphis. Frankly, the guys at Stax didn't want to hear me telling them how to make records. I had already met the guys at Muscle Shoals working on some of our other sessions, and there was a sound there that fit the Staples, somewhere between what was being called R&B and soul music, gospel, country, and pop. With the Muscle Shoals guys, I thought I could talk to these guys—if I can get them to understand and feel the Staple Singers the way I do, we should be able to come up with something different."

The Muscle Shoals musicians—collectively known as "the Swampers"—must have been a sight to the Staple Singers. Mavis remembers the biracial rhythm section at Stax as "something that surprised us," and now the family was in the heart of the Deep South, sharing a dingy studio with a bunch of white guys distinguished by shaggy hair and thick drawls.

"If you can picture a tiny rat-hole studio in Alabama owned by four young white musicians working with almost entirely black groups—that was the business plan we had," David Hood, father of Drive-By Truckers singer-songwriter Patterson Hood, says. "They'd come in and look at us and there'd be a moment's hesitation because all they usually knew about us is how the records sounded. 'Who are these rednecks?' 'There must be some kind of mistake.' But once we started playing, they would realize we knew what we were doing. With the Staple Singers it clicked almost from the start."

The family flew from Memphis to Muscle Shoals on what Bell calls "a little crop-duster" plane and made the short drive from the airport to the studio, a homely brick building across a two-lane highway from a cemetery. "When we got there, we looked at each other," Mavis says with a laugh. "This was a big difference from Memphis. This is country. We looked around and it let us know there was nothing to do in this town except make a record."

On the agenda was a Pops original about African-American identity, "I Like the Things About Me," that played like a bluesy response to James Brown's "Say It Loud—I'm Black and I'm Proud." And there was a track pitched to Bell by a doo-wop singer and aspiring songwriter named Bobby Bloom; he was working with high-powered London-based manager Robert Stigwood, whose clients included Cream and the Bee Gees. Stigwood would soon become the Staple Singers' manager, and Bloom (along with cowriter Jeff Barry, of Brill Building fame) would provide them with their first major hit, "Heavy Makes You Happy (Sha-Na-Boom Boom)."

Bell heard "Heavy" as "the kind of song I could release in the marketplace as a single and have minimal resistance from the religious community that supported the Staple Singers, but then move over to the general-market arena."

David Hood heard it as the start of a beautiful relationship, a steady-burning, shake-a-tail-feather number that couldn't have been more tailor-made for the Swampers' sound. Barry Beckett's electric keyboard sends a glimmering melody floating atop the steady rolling rhythm, and Mavis enters with an ebullient scream. "Good gosh almighty now!" she shouts. The enthusiasm in the room pops out of the speakers, as high energy as anything the Staples had recorded to that point. And really, that's all it aspired to be: a celebration of taking a load off and getting your groove on. No heavy message, just an exuberant rhythm track.

When the Staples returned to Muscle Shoals in the fall to continue working on the album, they cut an even faster track, "Love Is Plentiful." The songwriter, Stax regular Bettye Crutcher, aimed for a more mid-tempo feel in her demo, but Bell, Mavis, and the Muscle Shoals rhythm section rocked it up. With its rampaging drumbeat and roller-coaster bass line, it was earmarked as the session's first single. It did just fine, hitting the R&B charts in November 1970, but it was the "Heavy Makes You Happy" flip side that made the bigger impact, peaking at number 6 R&B and number 27 pop. It reinvented the group's image, recasting the Staples as a hip soul-vocal group.

"That's what the kids are doing today, they're doing the push and pull and the Tom Jones," Mavis said shortly after the song took off. "'Love Is Plentiful' is a little faster than 'Heavy Makes You Happy,' which has that groove where they can do these particular dances to it. I know that in Chicago when they flipped it over, the kids just—I start from Cynthia, our younger sister. Cynthia came home talkin' about it . . . [because] her friends were tellin' her and askin' her about it."

Terry Manning, the engineer and multi-instrumentalist who mixed the album and added overdubs to several tracks at Ardent Studios in Memphis, says he was as sure about the staying power of "Heavy Makes You Happy" as almost any song he had recorded in a career that has spanned five decades.

"Working on sessions as a producer or engineer you always want to feel what you are doing is the best thing you've ever done," he says. "If you don't feel that way, why are you doing it? But you have to be realistic. You know not everything is going to be a hit. But there are a few rare occasions when I just had no doubt at all. When we did the first recording with the Staples at Muscle Shoals, I just knew these were hits. That's only happened five or six times in my career. 'Sharp Dressed Man' by ZZ Top [a 1983 hit that Manning recorded and mixed] was like that. This was certainly one of those times. I felt it, and Al felt it. Everyone was so excited. There had been lots of success around Stax, so it wasn't new to the label, but for them to get that far, it was happiness intensified."

The track would lead off Staple Singers concerts for years thereafter. The 1971 album it anchored, *The Staple Swingers,* turned the group's career around. The album cover depicted the three smiling Staples sisters in Afros and boots sharing a swing, with a leather-jacketed Pops behind them doing the pushing. Even though the album contained its share of message-oriented tracks, including a brisk remake of Smokey Robinson's "You've Got to Earn It," the emphasis was on the bottom end.

"I wanted to present them in the music and the artistic design as fun-loving people," Bell says. "You could be serious and still get people to move. It worked."

It worked not only in Muscle Shoals and the rest of America, the Staples danced in Iran, too. They were selected by the U.S. government to represent the country at the fourth annual Shiraz Festival in August 1970.

"The shah of Iran fell in love with us, he kept us over another week," Mavis recalls. "He had us do a private show and sing to all of his friends and a bunch of ambassadors at the shah's palace. They were sitting in these big, huge, fine chairs, all these big shots."

The shah put the family up at the luxurious Hotel Versailles in Tehran. "Yvonne, Cleedi, and I went window-shopping one day, and all of a sudden we were hemmed in by a store window, surrounded by a mob of men," Mavis says. "They looked a little scary, reaching for us. We took out these little souvenir daggers we bought and made our way out of there back to the hotel. The concierge says, 'They meant no harm, they were fascinated by your hair.' We looked like triplets. All of us had natural do's, a different color for each of us. They had never seen anything like us."

Sharing a bill at the Shiraz Festival with Ravi Shankar, the Juilliard String Quartet, and the Senegalese National Ballet, the Staples left the audience and at least one critic enraptured.

"Their passionate and sensitive harmonies quickly had everyone clapping the beat," the *Tehran Journal* raved. "It was this beat which communicated itself so strongly to the members of the Senegalese National Ballet, who were among the audience, and had them nearly out of their seats as they responded to the syncopation on stage. The crowd loved it and roared its delight. One girl in the audience was completely 'sent' and was on her feet writhing to the music. And the mood of the mainly youthful audience was only heightened by the absurd attempts of a few minor officials to quiet them all down. Having brought such a famous troupe from the United States [it] would have been silly if these officials had spoiled the fun."

A spontaneous chant broke out that carried through the show: *"Viva les Noirs!"* ("Long live the Blacks!") *"Viva les Noirs!"*

23

Back to the motherland

It was a party fifty thousand feet in the sky, a summit of entertainers from the worlds of soul, gospel, and jazz stuffed into a charter jet with musical equipment and luggage. The sweet aroma of marijuana mingled with impromptu jam sessions in the aisles. There were Ike and Tina Turner chatting with Carlos Santana, the Staple Singers laughing with Les McCann, Wilson Pickett strutting like he owned the place. So many stars, so little room in business class: Roberta Flack, the Voices of East Harlem, Willie Bobo, and Pervis Staples's old pool-shooting pal from the South Side, Eddie Harris.

On March 1, 1971, the Staple Singers were among 130 artists, moviemakers, and roadies aboard a DC-8 at John F. Kennedy Airport in New York City bound for the West African nation of Ghana. They were to perform a major concert at historic Black Star Square in the capital city of Accra, next to the Atlantic Ocean. It would be the Staples family's first trip to what they and many of their fellow passengers called the "motherland."

Many aboard the flight were returning to the home of their ancestors, who had come to America against their will, sold as slaves. Now Ghana was in many ways going through the kind of social and political upheaval that accompanied the birth of the United States centuries before.

In 1957 Ghana had declared independence from Great Britain, the first African country to become a self-contained state in modern times. Guiding this transition into a new era was Kwame Nkrumah, who advocated Pan-Africanism as a way to bring the Third World continent closer to economic parity with the West and link it with people of African heritage worldwide. But Nkrumah was deposed in 1966, and the country had been under military rule ever since. Yet the government gave the go-ahead to stage the concert at Black Star Square, an edifice built by Nkrumah in 1957 to commemorate independence. The connections to the American civil rights movement were profound, right down to the way the word "freedom" had been co-opted since the military coup d'état.

At the Kotoka International Airport in Accra, the musicians were greeted by cheering, costumed locals on the tarmac and the terminal rooftop. Several passengers descended the airplane's steps and kissed the ground, out of respect for their hosts. Pickett was greeted by Ghanaians loudly chanting his name, and then was offered a swig of the local corn-made gin. Ever the showman, the "Wicked Pickett" reeled and pretended to collapse after sipping the homemade libation.

The festive atmosphere extended to the hotel, where the musicians dined on pepper soup, palm-nut stew, and jolof rice, and danced with the townspeople, while attentive geckos gawked at them. Most of the visitors tried to adapt to the new diet, participate in the dances, and fit in with the locals as much as possible. But Ike Turner couldn't be bothered, according to Mavis. "He made quite a scene," she recalls. "He would walk around in these gray satin Daisy Duke shorts, with black hands on each side [of the bottom]. And people would point and laugh. You didn't see anybody in Ghana wearing clothes like that. I think Ike liked the attention or he didn't care, I'm not sure which."

Many of the artists were struck by the commonality they felt between their families back home and the Africans they encountered going about their daily lives. "I felt like I was seeing my relatives everywhere," Mavis says. "I used to watch my grandmother take a twig from a tree and bite it up or dip it in her snuff. She called it a 'chew stick.' And I saw this woman on the ferry doing just what Grandma did. It was like flashing back to your own childhood in another country."

Some of the artists, including the Staple Singers, toured one of the slave castles along the coast and saw firsthand the dungeons where Africans were shackled while awaiting transatlantic transport to America and the Caribbean. "These were thick, brick walls . . . these shackles were still in the stone," Mavis recounted in *Soul to Soul,* a 1971 documentary of the Ghana concert. "That was the most sorrowful and heavy-laden [experience] . . . tears would well in your eyes. There was an eerie, eerie feeling. Sometimes late at night you could hear the moans and groans coming through there. Their spirits are still here."

Decades later, Mavis says she still gets a shiver when she thinks about the darkness of that holding cell, with its narrow doorway looking out to the ocean.

"It brought us face-to-face with our homeland," she says. "My father's grandfather was a slave. We don't know who may have come through there, but he may have come over here on one of those ships."

Pops's thoughts also turned to his grandfather William. "Often I think of my grandfather with pride. He was strong and tough. When I went to Ghana, I went down to the ship's hole, the dungeon. I saw where they took slaves like Grandpa, who opposed being enslaved. Those slaves would be tied with a rope on their arms, like handcuffs. There was something like a railroad spike driven in the wall over the door. We were told that they would hang them there until they got weak. Only then, they would cut them down. The hole had the smell of death."

The next night, the Staple Singers were among the performers at an epic concert, which began in the midafternoon March 6 and continued until dawn the next day, with Pickett taking the stage last. The vibe was generally festive, with high-energy performances from Santana and Ike and Tina in particular. The Staples were still shaken by their experience at the slave outpost, and their songs resonated all the more deeply because of it.

Pops looked like a dapper village elder, black horn-rimmed glasses framed by gray hair and sideburns. Mavis, Yvonne, and Cleo were a vision of Aquarian hipness in blue, red, and purple tie-dyed dresses, with aqua eye shadow and glorious Afros.

The Staples rolled into "When Will We Be Paid?" and the accusatory words rained down like stones: "We've been separated from the language we knew / Stripped of our culture, people you know it's true."

When Mavis landed on the phrase "stripped of our culture," she sounded as if she herself had been violated, her delivery stopping just short of an outraged scream. The last verse became a shared commentary on not just the broken promise of her homeland but the precarious fate of their host's country as well:

"Will we ever be proud of 'My country, 'tis of thee'? / Will we ever sing out loud, 'Sweet land of liberty'?"

Mavis raised her left hand as she and the family joined voices for the final chorus. Despite the idyllic starlit setting next to the ocean, the Staples had briefly peeled away the surface goodwill to look at the deeper reality of what it meant to be of African descent in this world. Even in the motherland, freedom was still not a given.

As the family slipped into the sanctified overdrive of "Are You Sure?" Pops tried to momentarily lighten the mood. "Let me hear you clap your hands, now," he said with a smile. "Y'all ain't got no soul!"

The vast Ghanaian audience of a hundred thousand was highly attentive, greeting the performers with enthusiasm and applauding their efforts. Though they weren't as demonstrative as American concertgoers, the music clearly connected. As Mavis began to sing, a boy in front stared at her wide-eyed with a mixture of reverence and wonder.

"Raise your voice high and the Lord will hear you," Mavis said, as if offering hope to those who had asked, "When will we be paid?" only moments earlier. Then the band fell silent, until only Pops's guitar was heard against Mavis's voice. Her eyes glistened as she peered above the crowd, as if focused on something beyond the horizon. She began to speak her heart, Pops's guitar answering each line.

"My Lord, my Lord, my Lord, it may not come just when you want it . . . but I can say He will be right there." A voice in the background responded, "Yeah!" Then Cleo and Yvonne brought the handclap rhythm rolling back, the family restarted the song, and determination gave way to exuberance.

Decades later, Prince would seek out Mavis and begin to work with her because of that moment. He had seen his grandmother moved by the spirit until she began speaking in tongues, and in the film he saw the same otherworldly investment in Mavis's face that night in Black Star Square.

"I know exactly what Prince saw and what he felt, because that's what I was feeling," Mavis says. "I never forgot what Pops told me, to sing from my heart. There's a part in 'Are You Sure?' where I'm just telling the truth about myself. I felt the spirit. I was getting my praise on. We would sing that song every night, and it would be different every time. I got into a little preaching thing, a little sermonette. The background stops and they let me have it for a few minutes. I'm standing up there and I could see these Africans, just as I'm looking out over Lake Michigan right now from my apartment, and they were as far as I could see. And I wanted to reach them, but at that moment, honestly, I was thinking about the song. I wasn't thinking that somebody is going to make this into a movie. I was singing from my heart. That's what Prince got."

24

"Cleo, you like brownies?"

The Staple Singers returned to Muscle Shoals in 1971 with new confidence, now that they had a legitimate hit on the pop charts with "Heavy Makes You Happy (Sha-Na-Boom Boom)." "The first time we met them, there may have been some doubts about how things were going to work," bassist David Hood says. "On *The Staple Swingers* album we had some loose ends, some rough patches. But the next time, there was a definite sense of excitement that we were building on something. We knew we were cutting tracks that were going to be heard and promoted.

"The Staples were doing a new thing. They had the gospel influence, but they were moving in a more secular direction that almost perfectly coincided with what we had going on. We wanted to be like Motown or Stax—a soul rhythm section—but there was a pop and rock thing in there, too. You can't help your roots from showing, no matter how hard you fight it. I don't think that hurt. In fact, I think it helped them reach a wider audience."

Any trepidation the Staples may have had about recording in Alabama was assuaged by the sound they got at Muscle Shoals. "That was a rhythm section to die for," Mavis Staples says of Hood, Barry Beckett,

Roger Hawkins, and Jimmy Johnson, plus lead guitarist Eddie Hinton.
"They were funky, and they helped make us sound funky."

In between sessions with the likes of the Rolling Stones, Lynyrd Sky-
nyrd, Traffic, and Boz Scaggs, the Muscle Shoals Swampers were frequently employed by Al Bell and his team of producers to crank out
rhythm tracks for Stax artists. Their bond with the Staple Singers was
especially tight, due in no small part to the family's easygoing warmth.

"They were huggers," guitarist Jimmy Johnson fondly remembers.
"We'd all get a hug at the start and the end of the week. They all had
pet names for us. Hood was 'Little David,' I was 'Jimmy Mack.' With
them, it became like family pretty quick." Johnson's mom and dad
would host meals at their home nearby to give the Staples a break from
their nightly catfish dinners at the Holiday Inn. Hazel Johnson was
renowned for her country-fried beefsteak, cream potatoes, brown gravy,
black-eyed peas, and corn on the cob. Her homemade pies rivaled those
of Mom Staples.

Integrated restaurants still weren't widely accepted in Muscle Shoals,
but the Swampers and the Staples didn't let that stop them, and they'd
hit the town for a meal and some laughs after a particularly long day.
"There was a time early on, when we were still working at Fame, it was
sometimes a little uncomfortable for Wilson Pickett to eat with us—fly
in the buttermilk, know what I'm saying?" Johnson says. "But even with
all the racial problems back in those days, we had zero problems in the
studio. Sometimes when we'd go eat at places, we'd get looks from the
rednecks. But no one tried to invade [the studio] or send us threaten-
ing letters about the longhairs and the blacks hanging out and making
music together. We were pretty shocked. I knew some people at Voice of
America from Senegal who couldn't understand why the Ku Klux Klan
wasn't after our butts. And shit, you know what I figured out? The KKK
liked the songs, too! They liked 'Mustang Sally' and 'Heavy Makes You
Happy,' and they didn't want it to stop."

Inside the studio, friendly alliances and sparring contests developed.
"Eddie Hinton was a little skinny guy like Dylan, and he could play that

guitar," Mavis says. "Cleedi loved to mess with Eddie, lots of jokes. They liked each other. So one day he says, 'Cleo, you like brownies? I'm gonna make you some tonight.' Cleedi didn't know they were loaded. None of us drank coffee but Cleedi. They'd have coffee made and the next morning, she had her coffee and started eating Eddie's brownies. After a while she got so quiet. She sat on the piano stool next to Barry and was just grooving to everything Barry played. We're trying to record something and finally it got to be where Barry had to say, 'Cleo, I need this space.' And then she knew. 'Eddie, Eddie, why'd you go and do that?' Everybody cracked up."

During the sessions, which typically ran from about 11 a.m. to 8 p.m., the pace was relaxed but efficient—there was not a lot of downtime or fussing. A typical Swampers session started with the band listening to a demo or stripped-down performance of the song by the songwriter on piano or guitar. Barry Beckett would transcribe the chords, using the Nashville number system to assign a digit to each chord. The system gave the musicians and engineers a rough outline, and left plenty of room for interpretation and improvisation, and also made it easy to fix a wayward note or chord afterward with an overdub.

Beckett set up his keyboards directly across from the elevated mixing board in the rectangular room, with the bass, drums, guitar, and vocal booths arrayed on either side of him. An orange vinyl couch sat beneath the control room, where Al Bell often sat so that he could talk to Beckett and roll his broad shoulders when he began to feel a particular rhythm. Mavis would joke with Bell: "Oh, Montana, all I have to know about how you feel about a record is watch your shoulders."

Dirty white acoustic tile in foot squares lined the walls from floor to ceiling, with splotches of red, blue, and green burlap baffling. Incongruously, a closet-size bathroom sat in the middle of the studio, where a musician could continue to participate in the recording if he chose to multitask.

"You'd look in that room with all the horrible color combinations, and you'd think Walt Disney went in there and threw up," Hood says.

"But there were no windows to the outside, so if you turned down the ceiling lights, it would turn into this sleazy club that always felt like it was two in the morning, even though we usually recorded in daylight hours."

Bell found the vibe energizing and a refreshing change from what he perceived as the increasingly hostile atmosphere at Stax in Memphis. "The Muscle Shoals guys took the time to sit with a guy like me and give me enough respect to let be born what happened there," he says. "Some guys would be like, 'This dummy, he can't even play an instrument, can't sing, and he's here trying to tell us what to do. Why should we listen to him?' At Muscle Shoals, there was no ego involved. They wanted to cut a track that everyone in the room felt was great. And if that meant not playing something, or altering what was played, they did. Barry Beckett was a wonderful, agreeable presence. They all were. He was 'my man,' all the time. If I had an idea, he'd figure it out on keyboard, and then show it to one of the other guys: 'Try this.' "

Bell shaped the songs around the vocals, rather than from the bottom up. He wanted the Staple Singers interacting with the musicians so there was a genuine dialogue; the rhythm track would be nailed down in tandem with live vocals, and then the Staples would go to Ardent Studios in Memphis to refine and overdub the finished vocals with Bell and engineer Terry Manning.

The daily curfew sometimes frustrated Mavis, who was used to working late until a track was wrapped up. "These guys were fantastic to work with, but eight o'clock everybody had to get home to see their families and have dinner," she says. "It was different after the late nights at Stax, where if we were on a roll with something, we'd stay till all hours to make sure it got done."

The pace of the sessions prevented Pops Staples from contributing on guitar—a radical and controversial move by Al Bell that still leaves Jimmy Johnson shaking his head decades later. Johnson and Eddie Hinton played the majority of the guitar parts on the Staple Singers rhythm tracks cut at Muscle Shoals, with Terry Manning adding a few guitar overdubs at Ardent afterward.

"I knew a little bit more about Pop Staples than anybody else in the group because I'd been hearing and studying him since they were mainly a gospel group," Johnson says. "Nobody played like him. Do you know of anybody that played like that? It was like his fingerprint. He picked with his fingers and got this amazing tone. We were just honored he was there and we were going to get to know him and work with him. It was highly a downer that he wasn't going to play. We kept pushing him, but he would say, 'Oh, no.' We found out that Al Bell didn't want him to play on the sessions. They had this understanding coming in. Everybody knew, the girls and he knew. They wanted our playing and us to help them get where they wanted to go. They didn't want to go the old route. It was a disappointment for me and Eddie and the rest of us. But I think Stax wanted to take them in more of a pop and R&B direction. Working with Al Bell was quite an experience, because with the Staples we'd do material that would be spread over four albums in about eight days. It was nonstop tracking rhythms. Al Bell was looking for grooves and he wanted them fast."

Because of that pace, Bell says there was no time to figure out how to integrate Pops's idiosyncratic style with the locked-in interplay of the Swampers.

"It wasn't a decision as much as it was creating a problem, but a positive problem," Bell says. "These guys couldn't feel or play around Pops. He and the family's vocals and his guitar, it was a special thing, a special sound. But what Pops does is so unique and different, the Muscle Shoals guys couldn't fall into a groove quickly, having to feel their way around that. I'd have to start with one of the musicians there, rather than Pops, to show them how to play the song. Somewhere along the way I was going to figure it out, how to get Pops in there, overdub him later, but regretfully I didn't get back to that. If you knew Pops before those records and his sound, you would recognize his absence. But if you didn't, you would not miss that much because of the way we integrated the guitars to come up with a reasonable facsimile of Pops. Maybe if I had been a musician myself, I would have known how to figure it out better than I did."

Manning says Bell made the right call given the time constraints. "Pops was the leader of the Staples, and he's from the old school like a lot of blues-based guitar players were, where you might play a song once and it's twelve bars and then fourteen bars the next time. Al thought, and I think rightfully so, when you get into producing radio-ready modern popular music it needs to be structured to a certain degree. The Muscle Shoals guys were seasoned musicians, and they wouldn't improvise unless called upon to do so. They would do the chord charts and they weren't going to vary. Pops might've varied from that, and the timing might've varied. Pops realized he couldn't follow them, but if he led, would it be a structured radio-ready pop song? His style was just different."

In a 1992 interview, Pops acknowledged publicly that he wasn't thrilled about being asked to set aside his guitar during the Muscle Shoals era. "Yes, I did mind, but I didn't play the guitar [style] they were using," he said. "I played the blues guitar. But I was trying hard to please the producer and we were successful."

In the midst of the recording sessions, Pops was too classy to complain openly. In the broader sense, he understood that the Muscle Shoals team was helping his family sell records and widen their audience. He trusted Al Bell, and in the Alabama summer of 1971, that trust paid off.

25

"Respect Yourself"

Roger Hawkins's hi-hat at the outset of "Respect Yourself" sizzles and snaps shut in clipped, syncopated cadences. It dances. It talks. On the Mack Rice–Luther Ingram composition, Hawkins turns cymbals, snares, toms, and a bass drum into an orchestra. The tone shifts from "wet" to "dry" and back again, depending on how Hawkins accents the eighth notes on his hi-hat. He adds syncopated rim shots and rolling tom fills, all the while maintaining a rock-steady, four-on-the-floor kick-drum bottom. As the drummer works the different combinations, the arrangement effortlessly builds excitement without actually speeding up or becoming discernibly louder or more bombastic.

Terry Manning, who engineered and performed on countless Stax sessions, spent a decade listening to and mixing the tracks laid down by two phenomenal rhythm sections: Booker T. & the M.G.'s in Memphis and the Swampers in Muscle Shoals. Both tight-knit ensembles defined a strain of soul music in the '60s and '70s with a distinctly Southern flavor. But to Manning there were crucial differences, particularly in the approach to rhythm that turned the Staple Singers' songs into hits once they came to Muscle Shoals, none more potent than "Respect Yourself."

"Al Jackson was basically a jazz drummer at Stax," Manning says. "He had a jazz-swing feel. He always played the song—on Booker T. & the

M.G.'s 'Time Is Tight,' listen to the drums and how he plays the song, not on top of the beats. At Muscle Shoals, the drums come from more of a country-blues-rock basis. It was a little more beat oriented, a little more syncopated."

"They were making bass records up there," M.G.'s guitarist Steve Cropper says of his Muscle Shoals counterparts. "The bottom end had that more pronounced dance feel."

Al Bell appreciated the coziness of the Muscle Shoals studio and believes the intimacy bled into the recordings. "The approaches at the two places were similar, but there were differences in the studio sound and mixes—how the drums, particularly, were miked," Bell says. "That was a bit of me and the engineer [Jerry Masters or Ralph Rhods] talking back and forth, trying to capture the little nuances on all the instruments. Stax studio recordings had more of an edge on them, it wasn't as warm as the Muscle Shoals sound. The Stax studio had a higher ceiling and a slanted floor because it was in an old theater building. Inside Muscle Shoals, the ceiling was lower, and the musicians and singers were closer together in the room. You can hear that on the records."

Once they were established, the Muscle Shoals rhythm section became so adept at churning out grooves on demand that they sometimes cut tracks that were funky as all get-out for artists they never met; vocals were often overdubbed in another studio, and the Swampers rarely had a sense of what kind of song they were working on until much later. But with the Staple Singers, Bell wanted everything built around the vocals; keys and tempos were set with the rhythm section in the room, interacting in real time with the Staples' vocalists, particularly Mavis. The producer aimed to build not just rhythm tracks but also the architecture of the entire song, from the top down.

"The basic rhythm there was ultimately the group thing, it was so natural," Bell says. "I didn't want to record a rhythm and then do the vocals later, it was about learning the song so they could sing it their way, and then let the Muscle Shoals guys build the rhythm around it. It was always naturally about the Staples. Their vocals dictated the rhythm."

This marked a crucial break with the way the Staples' music was recorded at Stax studio in Memphis, where the tracks were cut ahead of time, and then the family recorded their vocals on top.

In addition, Bell took extra care in harvesting songs in advance that he felt were appropriate for the Staples' voices and lyrical perspective. After "Heavy Makes You Happy" hit the charts, it became easier to solicit songs tailored for the Staples' sensibility and that could pass Pops's sincerity detector.

"There may have been two or three songs I brought them that Pops didn't agree on, but on most there was immediate agreement," Bell says. "I tried to present them with songs that didn't compromise their integrity in any respect. It was a continuation of what they were already doing before they got to Stax: They were singing songs designed to inspire, inform, and motivate people. I looked for these kinds of songs, because I felt like it was their road to travel. I had seen how people reacted to them when they were on that road and singing those types of songs. That was the natural path. It didn't have a color, a genre, it was just a natural path. If you talk to Pops and Mavis, they are regular people, but they see things the right way, how things ought to be. I'm like that. I could really live through them, and I was—I never admitted that before. It wasn't difficult for me to find the songs for them because I was a part of them."

As often as possible, Bell tried to bring the songwriters to the studio or the hotel in Muscle Shoals to play the song for the Swampers and the Staples before the recording session. Pops in particular loved to dig into the philosophy behind the lyrics. Mavis, in turn, had to believe every word before she could invest herself in the song. She and Pops would consult, and if they came to a consensus—with Mavis usually responding to Pops's lead—the tune was a go. Occasionally, a lyric change would be suggested. Even more radical transformations could occur with proposed arrangements. The Muscle Shoals sessions were very much about feel. A song could start with a particular tone and tempo and wind up in a different place; a lot depended on how the vocalists, especially Mavis, responded to the track.

"Respect Yourself" was one of the few songs during the Staples' hit-making run at Stax that were not written specifically for the group. Mack Rice initially wrote a churchy, up-tempo track in response to an off-the-cuff comment by singer Luther Ingram about how "black folk need to respect themselves." After being alerted to the song by Bettye Crutcher, Al Bell zeroed in on the lyrics and melody as a perfect fit for the group, but he thought the tempo wasn't right. Instead he wanted a flavor similar to that of "Express Yourself," a 1970 hit by Charles Wright and the Watts 103rd Street Rhythm Band.

"Mack Rice got angry at me," Bell says. "He called me and said, 'Doc, you destroyed my song.' Mack had a rhythm feel from the sanctified church. I didn't hear it that way, and it threw him off. It was no longer his song, in his mind. I wanted something along the lines of what Charles Wright was doing, because I felt that rhythm was right in line with what radio wanted at that moment. We sat with the Muscle Shoals guys and improved upon what I was talking about—and I didn't know what I was talking about [laughs]. But they got it and took it to another level."

Roger Hawkins's drums and David Hood's bass percolated underneath Barry Beckett's Wurlitzer piano, creating an appropriately moody lead-in for Pops Staples to deliver some deceptively mellow Mississippi-style preaching: "Take the sheet off your face, boy, it's a brand-new day."

The sisters assume the role of a horn section with their unison scat vocals, which pave the transition from Pops's lead vocals to Mavis's. "We were singing that 'dee-dee-dee' part, and Daddy said, 'That don't sound like the Staples,'" Mavis recalls. "But we [Mavis, Cleo, and Yvonne] convinced him otherwise. 'Daddy, we think it's cool.'"

Afterward, the Staples would fine-tune their vocals at Ardent studio in Memphis, which was Terry Manning's domain. "I did go watch a bit of one session at Muscle Shoals, but I purposely stayed out of the way because that wasn't my territory," Manning says. "I didn't want to impose in any way."

The approach enabled Manning to hear the Muscle Shoals tracks with fresh ears, and he would work the fade switches at Ardent to deconstruct the tunes and isolate individual parts before arriving at a final mix. It was at this stage that Roger Hawkins's drums rose to the foreground of the instrumentation. "You would hear brilliance in what Roger played or what Mavis sang, and you wanted to make sure it wasn't buried," Manning says. The engineer was also a gifted multi-instrumentalist, and he embellished the track with less-obvious but nonetheless crucial touches. He not only enlisted a horn section to mirror the lines sung by the vocalists, he also played a fuzz-toned electric guitar and a Moog synthesizer to thicken the bass line and give everything more of a modern rock texture.

"We were trying all sorts of things that may not be immediately noticeable," Manning says. "Al Bell liked high, tinkling sounds, synthesized combinations of tones and instruments; he was trying to appeal on purpose to kids, teenagers, to prick up their ears. We'd implant things in there that wouldn't get away from R&B or the philosophy and seriousness of the group, but would widen their appeal subliminally."

During each step, "Respect Yourself" was lavished with careful attention. An unassailable balance was struck between the raw inspiration of the artists and the refinement of cutting-edge studio-as-instrument technology. Released as a single in September 1971, "Respect Yourself" hit number 2 R&B and number 12 pop. Mack Rice was no longer complaining about what Al Bell did to his song. "He called me a few weeks later and said, 'How did you make the song so great?'" Bell says with a laugh. "After Mack made the adjustment in his mind, he heard how great it really was."

26

"I'll Take You There"

Al Bell remembers writing the song through tears in his parents' backyard in Little Rock. Mavis Staples vividly recalls working out the lyrics with Bell on the living room floor of her condo in Chicago until a neighbor complained they were making too much noise. The Muscle Shoals rhythm section says the arrangement was developed from scratch in the recording studio, with a little help from an obscure Jamaican instrumental recording.

This is how music legend becomes muddled. If a dozen people are in the room when something extraordinary happens, you can bet you'll get at least a dozen different versions of the truth, most of them self-serving. Such is the case with "I'll Take You There," a song that consists of one verse and nearly five minutes of music as brilliant as anything recorded at Muscle Shoals—or anywhere else, for that matter—in 1971.

At the same August recording session that produced "Respect Yourself," the Staple Singers and Al Bell collaborated with the Swampers on a track that was both of its time in the way it addressed contemporary events and ahead of it, with a Caribbean feel that anticipated the rise of reggae on the American pop charts.

In the summer of '71, Al Bell's younger brother Louis Isbell was murdered in North Little Rock. His youngest brother, Darnell Isbell, had been murdered earlier. Bell says he was consumed by dreams of vengeance and for a long time couldn't come to terms with the tragedy. "I actually went looking for the person who murdered Louis but couldn't find him," he says. After Louis's funeral, there was a gathering at his parents' home, but Bell was in no mood to talk with anyone. He instead went out back and sat by himself on the hood of an old yellow school bus that his father once used to haul cotton choppers.

"I was crying, and that bass-line rhythm came through me, then the words," he says. "I started singing—the rest was just emoting. My mind was on death. The song was about transcending. When I went back to Memphis, I was in the office on a weekend, trying to write another verse but couldn't come up with anything that fit. But thinking about that led me to something else. I came across Second Corinthians: 'While we are at home in the body, we are absent in the Lord.' Then I went back to John, where the Creator of the universe created us in His own likeness: 'God is light, and in Him there is no darkness at all.' I started getting a grip on death. I used to hear my great-grandmother say, 'You sorrow in birth, and rejoice in death.' I never understood that at the time, but now I understood. All of that was in me as we went to Muscle Shoals: We have to move above this as a society, as a people."

Bell had his title and concept for the Staple Singers' next album: *Be Altitude: Respect Yourself.* "They had just built the Delta 747, a big new jet plane, and I wanted to put the Staple Singers on the wing of that plane for the cover image," he says. "It was all about the belief that we have to evolve to another level as people. Politically we have to evolve, as a parallel to the Beatitudes in the Bible. I've never been prior or since as emotionally or spiritually focused as I was in putting that album together, from first note to last."

Bell's private pain also comes with the embellishments of the preacher, storyteller, and salesman that he also often is, sometimes all at once. Without those elements, would the Muscle Shoals sessions have been as productive? Terry Manning believes not. "Al was an incredibly intuitive musical person though he was not a musician, and deeply into production values and sound. He orchestrated emotion through color changes in the arrangement, rhythm, and feel of a performance.''

For "I'll Take You There," Bell tapped into rhythms he heard while visiting Jamaica earlier in the year. One record in particular was used as a template: "The Liquidator," a 1969 instrumental credited to the Harry J Allstars, essentially a rhythm track built on the playing of future Jamaican reggae giants Aston Barrett on bass and Carlton Barrett on drums. The track also shared some rhythmic similarities to an earlier Jamaican vocal hit, Alton Ellis's "Girl I've Got a Date."

David Hood and Jimmy Johnson both remember Bell playing an acetate version of "The Liquidator" at Muscle Shoals for the band as a blueprint for the new track. "He brought a 'dub' version that he found while on vacation in Jamaica," the bassist says. "We did our version of this dub—it was an instrumental track we copied that, we found out later, was a hit record in Jamaica. But it wasn't really a song, just a riff that Al Bell liked, and 'I'll Take You There' took off from there."

The Swampers were already familiar with reggae and its offbeat rhythms, in essence a Jamaican interpretation of American R&B. They had worked with rising reggae star Jimmy Cliff on his *Another Cycle* album, and guitarist Jimmy Johnson had vacationed in Jamaica on the dime of Island Records founder Chris Blackwell.

"We had our Americanized version of reggae," Johnson says. "I went to Jamaica about a year before, where Chris Blackwell had a house. I naturally went into Kingston and Montego Bay, and the music there just blew my mind. I bought records by the hundreds and brought them back and passed them out to the other guys in the rhythm section. I picked up those syncopated little rhythm licks, deadening the strings a bit, that you hear on 'I'll Take You There.'"

Hood agrees. "The sound was already in our heads when Al Bell suggested that reggae groove." He insists that other than the intro from "The Liquidator" and a few lines of lyrics, "I'll Take You There" "wasn't much of a song at all when we started playing it.

"The rhythm section would work together with the singers, and we'd take suggestions from around the room," he says. "It was not just me coming up with the bass line—everyone had input. It was a collaboration because none of us wanted a direct cop of 'The Liquidator' track. There was no definite bass line on the original, just chords. I got a bass pattern, and we took solos. We didn't have a lot of lyrics, so it was a case of, 'We need something here.' The bass solo was a very simple thing, the same lick played twice. I screwed up the second time, but you keep things like that if the overall track feels good. You don't mess with minor details. Al claims he wrote it. He may have written a few lyrics. He once said he made up the bass line. He did not. We did. We took 'The Liquidator' and rearranged the pattern a bit."

Mavis Staples glued it all together. She orchestrates as much as she sings, cuing the solos and urging on the musicians. To each solo, first by keyboardist Barry Beckett, then by guitarist Eddie Hinton, and finally by Hood, Mavis responds with her own vocal riffs and phrases. Here was that moment when gospel singers feel "the spirit enter the room," and Mavis anointed everyone in the recording studio with it.

"Play it, Barry," she urges, as Beckett digs into a keyboard solo.

"David, little David, I need you here, help me now, little David, all right," then scats along with the bass solo, "dum-dum-dum," dropping her voice as low as Hood's concluding note.

As Eddie Hinton begins his guitar solo, she calls out, "Daddy, now, Daddy, Daddy," as if it were Pops on guitar. There is some question whether she called Hinton Daddy on the floor of Muscle Shoals, or overdubbed it later at Ardent studio, knowing that it would be her father who would play the part when the family went on tour.

"Eddie worshipped Mavis Staples," Hood says. "And he loved Pops's guitar playing. That solo was him channeling Pops. He could also sing like Mavis, imitate her voice perfectly. So it was Mavis's little wink at him and at Pops."

Johnson remembers Mavis "acting like it was her daddy playing the guitar solo, which I think she meant as a tribute to Pops. And then she mentioned 'Little David' and Barry, which tickled us. It captured the spirit of that day."

It was also Mavis being protective of her father, who wasn't playing guitar on the sessions even though Jimmy Johnson and Eddie Hinton were ardent disciples and urged him to do so. "As time went on, Pops liked what this boy Jimmy was playing, and Eddie, too," Mavis says. "Pops always had his guitar with him, and he learned what the guys were playing, which in a way sounded a little bit like him anyway. On something like 'I'll Take You There,' I could hear places where Pops could play. Everyone thinks that's Pops playing anyway. The liner notes at the time wouldn't spell it out, so sometimes Pops would take credit for it. People would come up to him and compliment his playing on those albums [recorded at Muscle Shoals] and he'd just smile and say, 'Thank you.' That rhythm section was so good, but Al Bell didn't realize how good Pops was."

Mavis and the Swampers got on a roll. One take of "I'll Take You There" stretched to thirty minutes, according to Bell, as everyone realized they were getting absolutely golden interaction between Mavis and the musicians. She kept riffing on the lyrics, dropping in new inflections, interjections, moans, and ad-libs as Hawkins, Hood, Johnson, Beckett, and Hinton responded to each syllable.

"The 'I'll Take You There' session rates as high as any one we ever did," Johnson says, ranking it above the Swampers' collaborations with the Rolling Stones, Aretha Franklin, and Wilson Pickett, among other legends. "And it was because of Mavis's performance. It was a case of a great artist in the moment, and she spurred us on. We'd always have a pilot vocal on the track, and we'd get inspiration from that. The more the vocalist put into that, the more we'd give back. She ended up going for it—always. There was no such thing as a 'scratch' vocal with her. If she sang, she was going for it."

For Mavis, the "I'll Take You There" vocal came as a natural outgrowth of her singing gospel and observing the way Mahalia Jackson and Clara Ward worked a church service. "That music was so good to me, I fell right into it," she recalls. "I flowed with the music. They say I did good stuff at Muscle Shoals. Well, they did good stuff that helped me. When you've got a good band and you're a creative singer, that's the way it's always been to me since the gospel days. Like 'Help Me, Jesus,' certain things will hit you as you feel the words in the song: 'How am I gonna pay my rent? How am I gonna have a meal? Help me, Jesus.' Gospel isn't set, and our home is gospel. That's what has helped me with where I am today. You can ad-lib forever. From the start, Pops would tell the recording engineers, 'Roll the tape, because you never know what's going to come out.' I'd sing a song once and then a different way the next time. I feel so free, and I'm so grateful that the Lord sends me these things. I just let it go. I'm not going to be that hungry or vain to think it has to be a certain way all the time."

Manning, who was tasked with editing the performance to fit on the *Be Altitude* album and also sculpt it into a single, heard it as a departure from the usual Muscle Shoals session tracks he was handed. "That song more than any of their songs is a bit of a controlled jam session type thing," he says. "It's got only two chords, but it doesn't go all over the place, it grooves. They were set free to just feel. We would often overdub the lead vocal later, but we kept some of the original vocal, especially where she starts talking to the musicians. As I recall, the 'Daddy' part was added on, was overdubbed later [at Ardent]. I don't think she said it originally. But it was all her idea, and we all thought it was wonderful of her to bring Pops in that way."

In those improvised moments, Mavis turned a few lines and two chords into an anthem. What better way to underline the message in a song about community and transcendence?

"That song was the way Mavis interacted with people, period," Al Bell says. "I would watch them in the studio when she would do that part with David. I had my eyes closed and my headset on in the control room listening to this performance, and when she did that, my eyes popped open. And I saw that she had her eyes closed as she was listening

to those musicians. She was living that song, every note they were playing, like she was willing it to happen."

Her family's voices also animated and amplified the sense of common
purpose. "Cleotha's twang in particular placed a unique stripe on the
group," Bell says. "That enhanced the uniqueness and the authenticity
of the other voices; I've never heard any harmony singer sound quite like
that. It was the color, the spirit, and the attitude of Cleotha, too. She was
always complimenting, encouraging, and pushing everyone else along.
In 'I'll Take You There,' you'll hear Cleotha shout, 'Sing your song,' to
Mavis. That was Cleotha the person relating to her sister. I would listen to one voice after another a cappella in the mixing sessions—Mavis,
Pops, Cleotha, Yvonne—and realize the world hasn't heard what the
Staples really are. It's like four voices, one spirit. When you hear them
individually, you can only say, 'Oh, my goodness.'"

Yet what should have been a triumphant moment in the Staple Singers' career remains tainted by the bitterness Mavis still feels toward Bell,
who took sole writing credit for the song. In many respects, it was a
tipping point for the family and its relationship with Bell and Stax, one
that would never be the same from that moment.

"Right there on that floor is where Al Bell and I wrote 'I'll Take You
There,'" Mavis says, pointing to the living room in her high-rise condo
overlooking Lake Michigan. "Al was hitting the floor with his hand, and
my neighbor downstairs finally says, 'Miss Staples, I can't sleep, you're
hitting on that floor so hard.' Al was keeping the beat, and I was singing
the words. We weren't taping. When we recorded it at Muscle Shoals,
they were playing and I sang, and I said, 'David, little David, I need you
here, help me out.' These were things I worked out on my own. We were
in the midst of these guys, and we fed off each other. Pops told me I was
ad-libbing lyrics, and that I was helping write the song. The song [writ-
ing credit] was supposed to go fifty–fifty. Al Bell's part of the song was 'I
know a place' through the line 'lying to the races,' and the rest is Mavis.
It hurts to be cut out of that."

Bell also remembers the session in Mavis's living room, but he insists he was teaching her the song, not writing it with her. How to divide songwriting credits has been a slippery concept at least as long as there have been publishing rights. In the case of "I'll Take You There," the publishing royalties would've been considerable given the popularity of a song that has sold millions. But Bell does not need any prompting to praise what he sees as one of the greatest vocal performances he has ever witnessed.

"We had to sit and determine what of Mavis to use on the final recording, because there must be enough emotional utterances from her on different takes of 'I'll Take You There' to go into the studio now and make a completely different version of the song that is as good as the one we eventually released," Bell says. "It was Mavis, Mavis, Mavis—that Mavis I saw in Pine Bluff in the '50s singing 'On My Way to Heaven' with tears streaming down her cheeks. Whatever was in there emotionally and spiritually came out. She has one verse and then it's nothing but emoting and living it."

Besides skillfully editing and mixing the performance to emphasize David Hood's spine-tingling bass line, Terry Manning added blues-soaked harmonica that weaves in and out of the track like one more spirit in the room.

"Several people came into the studio and heard the song while we were mixing," Bell says. "Theresa Davis of the Emotions walked in and said, 'That's a hit.' It's one of the few times I've ever said out loud that we had just made a number 1 record."

27

Wattstax

The back cover image on *Be Altitude: Respect Yourself* shows Pops, Mavis, Cleotha, and Yvonne clasping upraised hands on the wing of a Delta 747, as if to presage the success of "I'll Take You There." It was the album's second single, and on the heels of "Respect Yourself," it turned the Staples into pop stars. "I'll Take You There" rose to number 1 on both the pop and R&B charts in the spring of 1972. Here was tangible evidence that the Staples' music was cutting across lines of genre and race, and achieving the kind of universality that Pops Staples and Al Bell had envisioned for the group.

Stax marketed the Staples' topical, boundary-busting music with ads that declared, "The Message that Rock Music is Still Looking For." In the mid- to late '60s, soul artists including Otis Redding and Sly Stone made major inroads with the rock audience. But in the wake of Martin Luther King's assassination and the rise of the black power movement, walls began to go up between musical genres. A more strident, urban-centric brand of soul arose in the early '70s, with harder funk rhythms and harsher, more realistic lyrics that spoke specifically to the black experience and a black audience.

But the Staples, who had been playing folk and rock clubs since the '60s, were drawing bigger, mixed audiences in theaters and arenas in the wake of *Be Altitude*. The family was used to living out of suitcases since the late '50s, but demand skyrocketed in 1972. A spring tour saw them playing arenas and auditoriums in Philadelphia, Houston, San Antonio, and Dallas, and five-night club residencies in Cleveland and New York. In June and July, they packed an astonishing thirty-seven shows into thirty-one days, with only four days off.

The Rolling Stones tried to line up the Staple Singers as an opening act for a much-anticipated 1972 American tour to promote the U.K. quintet's masterpiece, *Exile on Main St.* The Stones knew the Staples' music well; in '65, Keith Richards acknowledged nicking Pops's guitar riff for a rewrite of "The Last Time," and Mick Jagger touted "I'll Take You There" in interviews. The Stones were the biggest rock band in the world, with a tour that would play arenas and stadiums across North America. An opening slot would've expanded the Staples' reach.

But the numbers didn't add up to Pops. The Stones offered the Staples $500 a night, said the group's manager, Rik Gunnell. The offer "is a total bloody insult," Gunnell told *Variety* magazine. "To be offered $500 for an act that sells a million singles—that's nerve. It's OK for a brand-new group starting off, but for a group that gets $7,000 a night suddenly to work for $500 a night? Pop Staples is 57 years old. He doesn't want to work more than two or three years. He'd like to retire with some security."

Gunnell noted that the Stones tour would likely bring in more than $2 million in gross revenue. The Staples would have to divvy up their $500 fee among eight people: the four family members, three backing musicians, and a roadie, plus take care of their own lodging and expenses.

"We were thrilled to hear the Stones are longtime fans and loved the idea of working with them, even though it meant holding off on a lot of important dates," Pops told *Variety*. "We really felt honored until our management was told that we'd be paid just $500 a night for a tour that will gross millions. Frankly, we felt insulted. I'd like to think Mick Jagger doesn't know about this. I've never spoken to Jagger and I'd like to think there's some sort of mistake, but [Stones manager] Peter Rudge was very definite in his offer and we're very definite in saying, 'No.' We love music and audiences. That's our life, but we don't like being used."

Jagger says his memory of the business machinations behind the '72 tour are vague. "I don't remember the details, but I do remember that long before that we were big fans of the Staple Singers," he says. "I always liked them since I was a kid. They were the first gospel that I listened to, along with Rosetta Tharpe. Both those women singers—Rosetta and Mavis Staples—had quite a big impact on me. We were very influenced by them early on. Pops's tremolo-style guitar playing was unique. They were very influential, not just on us, but on a lot of our contemporaries in England."

The growing attention from the likes of the Stones as well as secular audiences and commercial radio irritated some influential members of the gospel community, including artists the Staples once considered friends, particularly the Reverend James Cleveland and Shirley Caesar.

"The Staple Singers would like to give the impression that they're still gospel singers, but they're not," Cleveland said in the *Journal of Gospel Music*. "They've decided to do message songs and Mavis has even done a pop album which has no religious things on it at all. I've known the Staples all my life. As little kids we grew up in Chicago together when their father was working in the stockyards. . . . There was never anybody else around who sang like the Staple Singers. They had a fresh, Mississippi sound. I don't personally feel that in their case it was necessary to change over from gospel to rhythm and blues, except to make more money, because they had climbed to the very top of the gospel ladder."

Bill Carpenter says the backlash had been brewing for several years. "When Mavis did 'A House Is Not a Home' on her solo record, she was being called a 'backslider' by some people in the gospel world," he says. "That's when the Staples' audience really began to change. People would come to the shows who didn't have an issue with any of that. That was an important lesson for the Staples: They still had an audience even though a lot of people in their own community were complaining. A lot of gospel artists I work with now are very jealous of the Staple Singers' legacy. They feel they don't deserve the recognition and fame they've received as a 'gospel' act. It's sad."

But the Staples had merged their gospel background with a more secular perspective years before, particularly after allying themselves with Martin Luther King. Pops heard the complaints that the Staples were making a "mockery of gospel," but in an interview with *Black Stars* magazine he was resolute about the direction of the family's music: "Our main aim and objective is to bridge the gap between blacks themselves and get them to stick together and stop ripping one another off," he said. "We need a lot of help. We're a downtrodden people still suffering from the horrors of slavery. We need a force that can fix our hearts and regulate our minds and make us respect ourselves. Now, King Jesus can help us. He is the answer. But we got to and we can help ourselves, too. We got to start by loving ourselves and loving one another."

The message was distilled into bumper sticker choruses and sticky pop hooks—"bubblegum," in the opinion of Anthony Heilbut. But it was hardly the "devil's music," as some of the Staples' critics claimed. On *Be Altitude*, Pops praised "Jesus Christ the Superstar," and Mavis proclaimed, "I'm just another soldier of love."

Stax filtered Pops's words into a full-page concert advertisement: "Tonight the Staple Singers. Doing it the way they've always done it. The right way. Call it gospel, rock, rhythm and blues, or just call it what it is. The Truth. Pure and simple."

The Polynesian Palace in Las Vegas took a slightly different twist in advertising a gig by the new chart toppers: "The Staple Singers: Three Groovin' gals plus 'the big man' rock it heavy with acid-action!"

Somewhere between those twin poles of hyperbole, the Staples were becoming one of the biggest acts Stax had ever produced, in the same league as Isaac Hayes, Sam & Dave, and Otis Redding. The Memphis label opened a West Coast promotion office in Los Angeles and in July landed two songs on the U.K. charts simultaneously for the first time: Frederick Knight's "I've Been Lonely for So Long" and the Staples' "I'll Take You There."

As a way of consolidating and celebrating Stax's gains, an empowered Al Bell set his sights on creating a massive festival for the label's acts in Los Angeles that would be turned into a documentary film.

Wattstax was staged on August 20, 1972, the final day of the Watts Summer Festival at Los Angeles Memorial Coliseum in South Central L.A. Bell picked the venue for several reasons, some symbolic, some practical. Watts was the site of a massive race riot in 1965 and had never fully recovered. It left thirty-four dead, most of them blacks, and more than a thousand injured, and led to four thousand arrests. Tens of millions of dollars in damage was reported as fires raged for days. Though the violence was widely condemned as a rebuke of the civil rights movement's largely nonviolent approach, Senator Robert Kennedy saw it as a fed-up community's desperate response to a seemingly intractable problem: "There is no point in telling Negroes to observe the law. It has almost always been used against them."

By 1972, little had changed. The Watts Summer Festival was created to raise money for the destitute community. Bell wanted to help by explicitly tying his label to the cause, and to show the world that something good could emerge from what many saw as a turning point in the civil rights struggle.

Of course, there was more to Bell's agenda than charity. Los Angeles was the heart of the film industry, and he saw the Watts festival as an opportunity to showcase his artists on a massive multimedia platform. He worked out a deal with two Los Angeles radio stations to broadcast the event live, and he hired Mel Stuart to direct the movie. Stuart was an experienced documentarian who had most recently directed *Willy Wonka & the Chocolate Factory.* To give the music texture and context, he suggested tying in the concert performances with voices of ordinary people (and a few actors) from the streets of Los Angeles. An up-and-coming comedian named Richard Pryor was hired to serve as the MC for this Greek chorus of ghetto commentators.

Stuart, who was white, in turn worked at Bell's behest with a crew and staff that was largely black; forty-five of the forty-eight cameras were operated by African Americans. The security staff was entirely black, and unarmed. And the vast majority of the 112,000 people who attended were also African Americans. Claims were made that this would be the largest single gathering of black people since the 1963 March on Washington.

Tickets were $1, but many in the audience were admitted free. The inner-city communities were sinking beneath a mountain of poverty and neglect in the early '70s, and the optimism of the civil rights era had hardened into a more defiant stance. Public Enemy's Chuck D saw 1972 as a crossroads for the black community and the black power movement. "We fought for something . . . now where are we heading to?" he muses in the commentary for the *Wattstax* movie. "I saw a little bit of cracking of the edges around the term [black power]."

When Kim Weston sang "The Star-Spangled Banner" at about 3 p.m. to officially launch the event, the crowd sat and chatted as if it were just background noise. A series of speakers followed, topped by Jesse Jackson, the Staple Singers advocate and now fellow Stax Records recording artist who would serve as one of the festival's MCs. He looked out at the vast crowd and dropped in a series of Jesse-isms that framed the event not just as a concert but as a state of the African-American union.

"Something new has happened in America," he said, his voice rising. "The government has not changed, politics have not changed, but something has happened to the black man in America. Nation time has come. We say that we may be in the slum, but the slum is not in us. We may be in the prison, but the prison is not in us. In Watts we have shifted from 'burn, baby, burn' to 'learn, baby, learn.'"

With Bell standing next to him, the "country preacher" raised a fist and beckoned the audience to do the same. "I may be poor, but I am somebody," Jackson declared. "I may be on welfare, but I am somebody. I may be unskilled, but I am somebody. I am black, beautiful, proud, I must be respected, I must be protected. I am God's child."

Weston then sang "Lift Every Voice and Sing," which Jackson introduced by its unofficial title in the black community, "The Black National

Anthem." The poem had been set to music at the turn of the century, and in this charged time it had usurped the national anthem itself as the song that most accurately reflected Jackson's notion of a black nation within a nation. "Let us march on till victory is won," Weston sang, her voice cracking with emotion as she reached for notes just beyond her range.

It set the tone for the Staple Singers, who took the stage minutes later as a late addition to the bill. The group was in huge demand and had been booked for a run of dates at the Sands Hotel in Las Vegas with Sammy Davis Jr. But Davis canceled the first of his two shows that day to make a campaign appearance for President Richard Nixon; a few days later he wound up in Miami for the Republican National Convention, where he would hug Nixon and stir nationwide controversy. Davis's last-minute change of plans freed the Staples to fly to Los Angeles that morning in time for Wattstax. The group's performance was further complicated by the absence of Yvonne, who was back home in Chicago recovering from appendix surgery. Yet even though they were at less than full strength, the Staple Singers proved to be a potent introduction to the day's six-hour feast of music.

"Heavy Makes You Happy (Sha-Na-Boom Boom)" opened the set and got the crowd moving, a sea of Technicolor bell-bottoms and hot pants, paisley dresses, zebra-striped flop hats, and extravagant Afros. "Are You Sure?" followed, then Pops took over for some front-porch wisdom on "I Like the Things About Me."

"There was a time I wished my hair was fine / And I can remember when I wished my lips were thin," sang Pops, a white safari outfit matching his white muttonchop sideburns, but now "I like the things about me that I once despised."

About two minutes in, he requested a brief interlude to "rap awhile" about black identity, which he turned into a classic Pops mix of seriousness, levity, and empowerment. Despite a huge disparity in schooling and opportunity, he extolled African-American accomplishment in everything from medicine to music. "I want to tell you one thing. No nationality could go through what the black people went through and still survive like we do." He echoed Jackson's exhortation of "I am somebody," quoted James Brown's "Say it loud, I'm black and I'm proud," praised "Black Moses" Isaac Hayes and pioneering black heart surgeon Daniel Hale Williams, and laughed about his fine natural self, right down to his sideburns. "We got our natural things!"

Pops, Mavis, and Cleotha surely recognized what the festival represented not just to them and their label, but to African Americans. "We felt it was a good song to sing at that event," Mavis told the *Guardian* newspaper. "With Pops saying, 'There was a time I wished my hair was fine.' Well, no. Not any more. We want our hair the way we came here with it—nappy. That's what was happening. Black people were showing they were proud to be black. We were singing songs to lift the people."

The Staples rolled into "Respect Yourself" and "I'll Take You There." "Don't you want to go?" Mavis sang and extended her hand as if ready to lead the march to a better place. A bevy of performers would follow— Eddie Floyd, the Bar-Kays, David Porter, Albert King, Carla Thomas, Rufus Thomas—but none would command the stage as long as the Staples, with the exception of headliner Isaac Hayes.

Later, the crowd spilled onto the football field from the stands at the behest of Rufus Thomas, who was doing the Funky Chicken in pink hot pants and white go-go boots. Yet despite a significant gang presence in the crowd, things never got out of hand. Thomas concluded his impromptu *Soul Train* audition by shepherding the dancers back to their seats. Hayes closed the show in full-on Black Moses mode, with gold chains draped across his bare chest. Some of the artists felt shortchanged later on; at one point thirteen of Stax's lesser-known acts performed in the space of ninety minutes, and several scheduled performers couldn't be squeezed in at all. But the day's only other "crisis" turned out to be a temporary shortage of hot dogs.

Short term, Wattstax was a success. It raised more than $70,000 for the Watts community and spun off the documentary film, which pulled a respectable-at-the-time $1 million in revenue, and two sound track albums, the first of which went into the Top 30. Thanks to a little fudging afterward, the movie also gave the Staple Singers another hit, "Oh La De Da," which wasn't performed at the festival but does play under the opening scenes of the documentary. The track had actually been recorded at the Staples' first Muscle Shoals session in 1970, and engineer Terry Manning later tacked on some audience noise and handclapping to suggest it was a live recording. Studio add-ons aside, it's an ebullient gospel-soul performance, with piano and organ riding atop David Hood's buoyant driving bass line. "If you feel like you wanna sing, come on, come on, come on," Mavis exhorts.

Manning says Bell had been sitting on the track for more than two years because "we were saving it for a special place." To create the audience-participation vibe, "I brought two classes of schoolkids into [Ardent studio], which had a huge hallway that goes all the way around in rectangular fashion with an outside garden in the middle. The kids wrapped around the garden, and their voices were blasting through these big PA speakers, so it sounded like ten times as many people were in there." The single continued the Staples' run of commercial successes, hitting number 4 on the R&B charts in early 1973.

But the long-term aftermath of Wattstax is murkier. Al Bell considers it his grandest achievement at Stax. "To be able to stand there and look up in those stands and see that many African Americans in a family spirit and family environment was amazing. We were able to demonstrate something to Americans who thought if two of us got together there would be a problem; yet here we were able to bring 112,000 of us together without any problems. To go through that day without any issues of that sort, that was the moment of my life."

Yet the lack of major media coverage relegated Wattstax to a lesser place in the history of music festivals, despite its massive scale and the appearance of two of soul music's biggest acts in Hayes and the Staple Singers. Bell was never able to get his film division off the ground, and the movie fell out of circulation for a couple of decades, before finally being resurrected on DVD in 2004. The media indifference ensured that troubled inner-city communities like Watts would remain in the shadows until they once again exploded in anger and frustration, as they did in 1992 in the wake of the court decision to exonerate the police officers who assaulted Rodney King. The same streets that hosted Wattstax at the Los Angeles Coliseum were twenty years later soaked in blood and violence. Sadly, the wry remarks of Richard Pryor in the *Wattstax* movie still rang true: "They accidentally shoot more [blacks] out here than anyplace in the world."

28

"They don't know which category to put us in"

Of all the songwriters who fed songs to the Staple Singers during their hit-making reign at Stax Records, Homer Banks forged the tightest bond. Born in 1941—two years after Mavis Staples—Banks was still only a teenager when he began writing songs for and singing in the Memphis gospel group the Consolidators, which toured the same Southern gospel circuit as the Staples.

Banks's best work as a vocalist wasn't documented on the handful of R&B singles he cut in the '60s. "Homer would put the songs he had written for us on a demo," Mavis says. "He had so much soul in his voice, I said, 'Damn, you should be singing these songs.' He said, 'No, Mavis, I wrote them for you.' He could phrase, though, and sometimes I'd try to copy him. We usually put our own thing on a lot of the songs we got, but with Homer it was like he was reading our minds, he knew our voices and what was in our hearts."

After trying to break through as a singer, and apprenticing at the Stax record store in Memphis, Banks formed a songwriting trio, the We Three, with Bettye Crutcher and his old Consolidators bandmate, guitarist Raymond Jackson. They wrote "Who's Making Love," part adulterer's soap opera, part domestic morality lesson, which became a huge hit for the Staples' friend and Stax label mate Johnnie Taylor in 1968. Banks's protest anthem "Long Walk to D.C." that same year became the Staple Singers' debut single for Stax.

Pop Staples's simple instruction—"If you want to write a song for us, just read the headlines"—resonated with Banks and played to his strengths. As a songwriter, he demonstrated a poetic flair for turning the everyday struggles of African Americans into musical drama. His partnership with the Staples grew stronger over the years: Four We Three tracks landed on the first two Stax albums, and three Banks compositions solidified the classic *Be Altitude*.

In October 1972, the Staples returned to Muscle Shoals for eight days of recording, and Banks was part of the entourage, in a new songwriting partnership with Jackson and Carl Hampton.

"Homer Banks was the guy who got it," Al Bell recalls. "He would write things like 'I'm just another soldier in the army of the Lord' for them. He lived Staple Singers. Mavis knew it. She'd ask, 'Where's Homer?' He would be there with me on sessions, even when they were cutting a song he hadn't written—he was into them that much. He would talk with the group during the sessions, there was a lot of dialogue between him and Mavis and Pops. He would tell them what he heard, and they trusted his feedback. He wouldn't dictate, it would just be communication between creative people."

Banks and the family clicked because the songwriter was coming from a similar place, with his background in gospel music and his maturity, undoubtedly amplified by a two-year stint in the army in the early '60s. "Homer was an excellent philosopher and one who studied what was going on in society, socially with people," Bell says. "He studied how the Staple Singers influenced people. It was almost like he was part of the family. He marveled at what Pops could do, but he lived Mavis. He had these inflections in his voice that would mimic her voice, her style."

Hampton imported his piano from Memphis for the 1972 sessions, and his Muscle Shoals hotel room became headquarters for the three

songwriters. Mack Rice and Bettye Crutcher were also in town, working on songs with the Staples in the studio when Banks, Hampton,
and Jackson weren't. "We were looking at it like this is Al Bell's group,"
Hampton told journalist Rob Bowman. "We knew the money gonna be
behind them."

"There wasn't a whole lot to do in Muscle Shoals after we went back
to the hotel, except eat dinner and work on songs for the next day,"
Mavis recalls. "Pops would tell us, 'We don't rehearse in the studio. We're
gonna have our songs ready before we get into the studio.' So we would
sit and rehearse with Daddy's guitar in the hotel room."

The sessions took on the feel of a music factory, with songwriters,
musicians, engineers, and singers working long days and nights under
Bell's direction. Initially, he aimed to record a double album to capitalize
on the Staples' chart hot streak.

Terry Manning confirms that was the initial intent, "but that's a fairly
suicidal thing to do at times. Things financially around Stax weren't
going well. The difficulties in doing something that ambitious were
external because of a new distribution contract with CBS. They put
their thumb down."

Nothing could dampen Bell's determination to expand the Staples
following, however. "Al was armed in advance with songs," Manning
says. "He had a group of songwriters whose philosophies he liked. Al is a
deeply religious, philosophical man, and he wanted things on that level
for the Staple Singers. He would go to Mack Rice and Homer Banks for
songs, and choose the ones that meant something. There was a certain
standard the songwriters had to meet to get on a Staples album."

Bell's drive ratcheted up the pace in the recording studio. The
Swampers were used to laying down tracks quickly, but nothing quite
like this. "Al was pushing," Jimmy Johnson says. "You could tell it was a
big deal because all of them writers were down there all at the same time.
The Staple Singers were all over the radio at the time, and everybody
wanted to write for them. Before it was just us and the group and Al,
and now it was this army [laughs]. That was just overkill, and it wasn't

as enjoyable this time because we were feeling rushed. We didn't get a chance to dig the groove that long. We liked to hear a track a time or two, and do another pass after hearing it to add some cool things. We didn't have that luxury this time, and it cut back on Mavis's creativity a bit, too."

Bell saw things differently. For him, the 1972 Muscle Shoals sessions realized his vision for how the Staple Singers should be recorded and how they should sound. He provided them with substantive songs that spoke to their lives and let the group figure out how best to sing them; Pops and Mavis usually decided between themselves who would take the lead on certain tracks, with Mavis taking the ones that required more "gut" and Pops handling the quieter, more restrained material. Bell would have the singers interact with the Swampers to keep the raw rhythm feel intact, then refine the vocals and add instrumental embellishments later at Ardent with Manning. Finally, producer Don Davis would top things off by arranging strings at his studio in Michigan.

For Bell, "If You're Ready (Come Go with Me)," a track written by Banks, Jackson, and Hampton, represented the pinnacle achievement. The track is actually one of the songwriting team's more perfunctory efforts lyrically. Its arrangement echoes "I'll Take You There," with its reggae feel, the call-and-response vocals between Mavis and the family, even another David Hood bass breakdown. "Love is the only transportation / To where there's total communication," Mavis sings. Whereas "I'll Take You There" felt like a spontaneous creation, "If You're Ready" repackages it as a more structured song. Mavis heard it that way as well when the song was first presented to the group, but she was persuaded to play along by Pops, who saw the similarities as a strength rather than a drawback for the follow-up to a hit. "Pops said they do it all the time at Motown, James Brown does it, Curtis Mayfield does it," Mavis says. "Why mess with success?"

The studio craftsmanship is undeniable, performance and technology in perfect sync. Roger Hawkins's drumming becomes a focal point, thanks to several precisely positioned microphones around his kit. They reveal a symphony of syncopated rim shots counterpointed by the crash cymbal and hi-hat. Hawkins's performance approaches his genius on "Respect Yourself," and Manning and Bell wisely brought it to the forefront of the mix. Another crucial element was Raymond Jackson's clipped yet melodic guitar lick. His playing on the demo was deemed so integral that he was persuaded to play on the track with the Muscle Shoals rhythm section. Mavis scats alongside the guitar during the song's most dynamic moment.

"Homer worked with me side by side and the guitar player to get exactly what I was trying to get," Bell says. "Raymond Jackson's guitar feel reminded me of quartets like the Soul Stirrers, the Dixie Hummingbirds, the Highway Q.C.'s—that gospel sound—with a touch of country, pop, rock. Raymond and I had talked extensively about the Staples ahead of time, and he understood and delivered everything that I was hoping to get to. It brought me to tears that I couldn't go forward with that."

Jackson's nuanced guitar playing was all over the October sessions, but it would prove to be his final collaboration with Al Bell and the Staple Singers. A month later, the thirty-one-year-old songwriter and guitarist tried to exterminate a rodent in his backyard in Memphis by stuffing paper down a hole and lighting it with gasoline. His homemade extermination scheme backfired and killed him.

"When that happened, life went out of me, too," Bell says. "He held inside himself as a musician what I had in my mind as a producer. That's a rare thing to find with someone else. I remember thinking, 'I'm gonna miss you, Raymond.' It had taken so long to get there. You would have heard that sound going forward because Raymond Jackson was in many ways an unsung hero of those sessions."

Jackson's legacy lived on in his playing and songwriting for what would become the final two Staple Singers studio albums for Stax, *Be What You Are* in 1973 and *City in the Sky* in 1974. "If You're Ready" gave the Staples their second Top 10 pop hit in November 1973 and anchored an album brimming with signature songs. "Touch a Hand, Make a

Friend," another Banks-Jackson-Hampton tune built on the bones of an earlier hit, this time Joe South's "Games People Play," cracked the R&B Top 10 a few months later. The uplifting lyrics draw more sunshine from Beckett's calypso-inspired keyboard and Terry Manning's marimba, which at times suggest the tone of Caribbean steel drums.

Bettye Crutcher brought some grit in "Drown Yourself," a bluesy purgatory for a self-absorbed loner, and the moody "Love Comes in All Colors," which digs into the nature of selflessness and how it occurs only when it's convenient. If you found out you had only one more week to live, Mavis and Pops sing, "You'd run over each other trying to help your brother / But today you turn your back on him."

Manning's "Heaven" closed the album triumphantly, in many ways a rock power ballad with lyrics that suggested both gospel ecstasy and secular yearning. It included an uncredited guitar solo by Led Zeppelin's Jimmy Page, Manning says. The young engineer had met Page in the '60s when the guitarist was still in the Yardbirds, and Page enlisted Manning to work on the *Led Zeppelin III* album, released in 1970.

"I had not written the song necessarily for the Staples, but I really liked it and thought it fit with their general philosophy," Manning says. "I did a quick demo for Al, and he loved it. I was not there for the tracking at Muscle Shoals, but we did the orchestrations on the last two albums in Detroit, with many of the same session musicians who played on the Motown stuff. I had arranged parts for them. I took that track to England and had Jimmy Page play acoustic and electric guitar on it. We're good friends, and I'd worked with him quite a bit on the Zeppelin stuff. He was the number one session guitarist in London before Zeppelin came along, so I knew he'd be perfect—he could play anything. I wanted to start quiet, build up to a huge middle, go quiet, and then finish big. It kind of had a Zeppelin feel to it, and it didn't hurt that he was also a Staples fan."

From the rock flourishes of "Heaven" to the island lilt of "Touch a Hand, Make a Friend," the Staples' music mirrored the crazy-quilt patchwork dresses that Mavis, Cleotha, and Yvonne wore at a Los Angeles concert in the early '70s. "They don't know which category to put us in," Pops told the audience at the Bitter End West, "so just enjoy whatever we do."

With the exception of some grumbling from the gospel community, the Staples' evolution was met with acceptance commercially and critically. They had expanded their audience by crossing genre lines while keeping their integrity intact. Richard Cromelin of the *Los Angeles Times* described the group's mix of political commentary, blues, soul, and rock as built on a "solid foundation in the gospel tradition."

Critic Georgia Christgau echoed those comments after a Staple Singers show at the Beacon Theatre in New York: "The religious straightforwardness of their early records has been transformed into a universal world philosophy ["Love Comes in All Colors," "Be What You Are," etc.], but this homogenizing does not betray a loss of faith or authenticity. It only shows the tactfully sensible approach [the Staple Singers have] had to gaining mass acceptance. As Gavin Petrie notes in his book *Black Music,* 'after all, in another culture, Bob Dylan proved that the audience for a nonreligious sermon was a large one.'"

29

A family tragedy

Even as the Staple Singers expanded their scope as artists, they rarely closed doors behind them. They could still hang with the serious gospel, jazz, and roots-music crowd that had nurtured them, and they were now as nationally recognized as many of the top pop and rock stars. In April 1973, they performed at the Jazz & Heritage Festival in New Orleans with Dave Brubeck, Gerry Mulligan, and Joe Newman. In the next two months they would swing from a nationally televised appearance on *The Mike Douglas Show* to a memorial concert for the murdered civil rights activist Medgar Evers in Jackson, Mississippi, with B. B. King and Muddy Waters.

The Staples helped mark a remarkable transformation in Pops's home state. Since Evers was assassinated outside his home in Jackson on June 12, 1963, the number of black registered voters in Mississippi had grown to 250,000 from 10,000. The state ranked third in the number of black elected officials with sixty-three, including Evers's brother, Charles, mayor of Fayette. In 1963 there was none.

Back in Chicago, the Staples were helping their old friend Jesse Jackson by participating in a series of concerts with Marvin Gaye, Isaac Hayes, and other performers during the minister's Operation PUSH Expo, documented in the movie *Save the Children*. Harry Belafonte invited the group to open for him during a string of dates at Caesars Palace in Las Vegas, prompting a congratulatory telefax from Jackson on October 24, 1973: "Pop, we hear that you are breaking it up in Vegas. Right on. You're looking good here in Chicago in 'Save the Children.' Talent is still talent all over the world. Keep on pushing. Yours in peace and freedom. Rev. Jesse L. Jackson."

But at the peak of the Staples' popularity, devastating news arrived on October 29 from home: Twenty-one-year-old Cynthia had shot herself to death.

A single soft-shelled bullet from a .38-caliber Smith & Wesson revolver that Pops kept at home had entered beneath Cynthia's chin and exited her temple. Pops had loaded the gun only weeks before because unidentified intruders had tried to enter their seven-room home on 103rd Street, according to the *Chicago Defender*.

"Pops gathered us in a room at the hotel and told us Cynthia was dead," Mavis recalls. "Mom was home at the time, and it was rough just thinking about what she was going through. We were all in shock." So was Oceola, who was treated at a nearby hospital after her daughter was pronounced dead. Police found no suicide note or any evidence of foul play.

The family scrambled to make arrangements to leave Vegas for O'Hare Airport, where they were greeted by their friend, local disc jockey E. Rodney Jones, who had arranged for a helicopter to fly the family to Midway Airport on the South Side, closer to the family's residence. The heartbroken travelers stepped into their home to find not only Pervis and Oceola but also Jesse Jackson and Stevie Wonder, who had arrived from Detroit.

"Stevie stayed with my mother till we got home the next day," Mavis says. "He was extremely close with my family and my mother; he'd been to the house for dinner many times. That helped her a lot for Stevie to come and hold her hand. It took a long time to get a flight and it was night the next day by the time we got home. It was such a sad, long flight. When we got home, everyone just broke down."

In the hours before the shooting, Oceola had been with her youngest daughter, a slender young woman with a caramel complexion. At five foot nine, she was by far the tallest of her sisters. She and her mom were laughing in the kitchen, talking about a television show and cooking turkey wings and greens. The mail arrived and Oceola said Cynthia was thrilled to receive a card and an $80 check from Pops in Vegas.

Cynthia promised to send a thank-you card and then went to the family's guest room, ostensibly to pack for an upcoming family trip to Trinidad. A few minutes later, Oceola heard a gunshot and rushed to the room, where she saw Cynthia's feet sticking out alongside the bed.

"I was called to the house as soon as this terrible thing occurred and the body was still on the floor as I arrived," Jesse Jackson told *Jet* magazine. "This is a dark, dark hour for the Staples family and the entire black community."

Cynthia had entered a local hospital four months previously for psychiatric treatment but had "recovered," Pops told *Jet*. In his unpublished memoir decades later, Pops wrote that Cynthia was suffering from depression.

The funeral was held October 31 at Fellowship Missionary Baptist Church, where family friend Clay Evans was the pastor. The ninety-minute service was attended by more than a thousand people. C. L. Franklin, Jesse Jackson, and Al Bell were among those who eulogized Cynthia, who lay in state in a white dress, her wounds obscured by a shroud.

In the years since, the family privately tried to cope with Cynthia's death while struggling with questions that never would be completely resolved. Leroy Crume said he'd never heard his good friend Pervis mention a word about the tragedy. "You could count on Blab to talk about anything and everything, but on this—not a word," Crume says.

"Cynthia was getting bullied at school and in the neighborhood," Mavis now says. "Kids can get so cruel. They would stay on her: 'You can't sing.' 'Why can't you sing with your family?' 'Your family is famous, why aren't you?' Cynthia and I were very close. I was basically her babysitter for years while everyone else was at work. Later, after I moved out, she would get depressed and leave home and come to my house.

"I would take her over to the park and play volleyball with her. I would try to keep her lifted. We'd go get some Chinese food together. She'd stay with me for three, four days at a time. She didn't want our parents to see her sad, she didn't want to bring them down, and she knew I could handle it. I'd keep her laughing. I'd be crazy, act stupid, just to take her mind off things."

Cynthia was working as a receptionist after graduating from high school and helping the family with some of its business affairs, Mavis says. "I would tell Pops, we need to put Cynthia in the group after she graduates high school. But Pops felt the group was set. If there wasn't an opening as a singer for her, I thought we should let her play tambourine, be on the road with us. That would've been better than leaving her at home. But we didn't realize how much she was suffering until afterward. At some point, I just don't think she could take it anymore."

30

Stax crumbles

City in the Sky, the second Staple Singers album from the fruitful 1972 Muscle Shoals sessions, finally rolled out in August 1974. It was once again a superior Al Bell production job, a canny merger of North and South: Stax soul nurtured at Muscle Shoals, and Motown-style production sweetness overdubbed in Michigan, with Terry Manning serving as jack-of-all-trades mixologist and multi-instrumentalist.

The album added yet more shades to the Staples' musical vocabulary. The opener, O. B. McClinton's "Back Road into Town," had a pronounced country-soul feel, akin to the plainspoken storytelling of Clarence Carter's "Patches." In this instance, the notion of a struggling father pitted against "the man in the big house" spoke directly to the Staples' own history: Pops's formative years on a sharecroppers' farm and the family's sometimes life-threatening adventures on the Southern gospel circuit. The title song also reached outside the normal Stax songwriting circles. The husband-wife team of Charles Chalmers and Sandra Rhodes, with sister Donna Rhodes, cast urban reform as a matter of social and spiritual urgency. Mavis gives it an introspective reading, before an extended coda fired by keyboards, horns, and handclaps. "Washington We're Watching" returns to the Homer Banks–Raymond

Jackson–Carl Hampton triumvirate for a protest song shot through with funk, via Clayton Ivey's organ fills, and rock guitar.

City in the Sky ranks among the most overtly gospel-oriented releases in the Staples' Stax tenure, with the celebratory "There Is a God" and the lilting island rhythms of "My Main Man." The last word belonged to Pops, who admonishes an upstart with the kind of gentle firmness he exuded in everyday life on Mack Rice's "Getting Too Big for Your Britches," embroidered by Eddie Hinton's guitar leads.

The Staples added to their hit streak at Stax with *City in the Sky* going to number 4 and "My Main Man" peaking at number 18 on the R&B charts. But by the time "Who Made the Man" was released as a third single from the album in November, the Staples were severing their ties with the label.

Al Bell had earlier worked out a distribution deal with CBS, the most powerful record company in the world at the time, to distribute Stax product. But the deal came unraveled in the midst of a payola scandal that ousted CBS executive Clive Davis. Stax product languished in warehouses rather than reaching retail stores, and the label struggled to pay its bills. Checks bounced to Isaac Hayes, Little Milton, and Richard Pryor. Hayes sued and eventually departed the label, depriving Al Bell of his biggest star. The Staples were next, in large measure because Pops had serious doubts that Al Bell could fulfill his financial obligations after executing an option clause to retain the group's services for another year.

On October 25, 1974—less than two weeks after Bell visited Chicago to solidify the deal with the Staples—Stax filed a $67 million antitrust suit against CBS. The same day, Bell received a mailgram from Pops requesting "a cancellation of our agreement." Bell was stunned and made no effort to conceal that he was taking Pops's rejection personally. When questioned about the Staples departure decades later, Bell says his recollections are clouded by the economic chaos that was only just beginning to descend on Stax and his business fortunes.

"I don't remember how I felt," he says after a long pause. "I was going through so much. I could've been a bit hurt. I felt, wow, with the Staples, irrespective of what was happening to me at the time, that I could come through it all. . . . I had a conversation with Pops alone about that. But I was fighting for my life at the time, and in the end Pops had to do what he felt was right for his family."

Bell was accused of embezzling company funds, the federal government scoured the label's books for evidence of payola, and the Internal Revenue Service investigated Stax for back taxes. On January 12, 1976, a U.S. bankruptcy judge would close Stax at the request of the label's chief creditor, Union Planters National Bank. The bank claimed Stax owed it $8.8 million and had debts of more than $30 million. Bell was later cleared of all charges, but the catalog he had so tirelessly built was sold to Fantasy Records to help repay creditors.

Bell returned with his family to Little Rock to live in his father's basement while he rebuilt his life. Eventually, he would return to the record business to work with Prince, run the Memphis Music Foundation, and win a Grammy Award.

Though he calls the final days of Stax "a near-death experience," he justifiably looks back on the label's musical legacy as a profound and lasting one. Despite the acrimonious parting with the Staple Singers, he still is moved to tears when speaking about the family.

"I saw music as it related to people, period," he says. "It was part of the civil rights movement because of the time. That socio-economic group that African Americans were part of at that time, and today—the music was about our lives, our lifestyle, and our living. . . . I don't think Pops planned it that way, but I heard it as far back as 'Uncloudy Day.' We were singing and living each other, the Staples and me. It's the only act that I've ever been involved with that I had that kind of bond."

31

"Let's Do It Again"

As Stax rose, so did the business prospects of Pervis Staples, who had helped bring the Emotions to the label and established Perv's Music as a management and artist development company partially funded by Al Bell. Pervis had left the Staples in 1969 to work with the Chicago-based Emotions but had never reached a formal, legally binding agreement with the group. A few years later, he and the group parted ways, and as Stax sunk, so did Pervis's fledgling career as a music industry talent scout.

But Pervis was impossible to keep down for long. He reset his sights on opening a nightclub and enlisted Pops to help put together and finance the $500,000 property deal with A. R. Leak Enterprises—the same Leak family as Mavis's ex-husband. Perv's Place opened on Halloween night 1974 in a refurbished banquet room at 79th Street near the Chicago lakefront.

With three bars on two levels, the venue suggested an outdoor club with a garden playground, wicker tub chairs, green turf-like carpeting, and an indoor waterfall—it was the '70s, after all. The opening night celebrities included state senator Charles Chew and singer Oscar Brown Jr. Pops couldn't make it because he was attending the funeral of his sixty-four-year-old brother, Reverend Chester A. Staples, whose Holy

Trinity parish had hosted the first public singing performance by the Staples family in the 1940s. Oceola was there, however, to sing her son's praises for the benefit of the Chicago media: "Pervis, oh, he's really something. Why, do you know he's always had a real head for business? We once, Pop and I, bought him a snow-cone machine to play with. Well, he'd take that machine out to a parade that was going on and come back with his pockets full of money, drop it all out on the table, and tell me to go out and get lots of food for everybody to feast on. He's something else."

Pervis, dressed in green leather, addressed the full house and thanked his family "for a whole lot of money that I'm going to pay back." For a few years before disco changed everything, Perv's Place was a late-night South Side magnet for African-American entertainers, ballplayers, politicians, and business executives. Pervis' connections in the music business enabled him to book a string of top-flight R&B acts, including Teddy Pendergrass, Bobby Womack, Gladys Knight and, not least of all, the Staple Singers.

Like Pervis, the group's career was taking a turn. On April 15, 1975, Al Bell formally let the Staple Singers become free agents, and the group signed with Warner Bros. Records after a dinner with Bob Krasnow, the label's vice president of talent acquisition. For Krasnow, the dinner paid an unexpected two-for-one bonus: Pops brought along a friend and admirer, guitarist George Benson, and persuaded the record company executive to sign him as well. Benson went on to become one of Warner's biggest success stories; his 1976 label debut, *Breezin'*, sold more than three million copies.

Krasnow aimed to pair the Staple Singers with their old Chicago crony Curtis Mayfield, who was writing and recording solo albums, overseeing movie sound tracks, and producing other artists on his Curtom label, a Warner subsidiary. Mayfield was one of the pillars of Chicago soul in the '60s, crafting a series of civil rights anthems for his group the Impressions, including "Keep on Pushing," "People Get Ready," and "We're a Winner." In the '70s, Mayfield shifted into a solo career and

began delivering urban operas steeped in funk and gritty realism such
as the sound track for the blaxploitation movie *Super Fly*. He also collaborated with distinctive vocalists including Gladys Knight and Aretha
Franklin on movie sound tracks, and he relished the idea of partner-
ing with Mavis Staples and her family on a 1975 project he had in the
works, the sound track to the Sidney Poitier–Bill Cosby movie *Let's Do
It Again.*

Though the film was a comedy, Mayfield said he was inspired to write
the title song when smitten by the opening scenes featuring actress Jayne
Kennedy. Its lyrics were fairly explicit, especially by the standards of
mid-'70s commercial radio: "I'm not a girl that could linger / But I feel
like a butter finger / Let's do it again."

Only a few years earlier, in defending the Staple Singers' message-
oriented songs against claims of sacrilege and sellout by the gospel police,
Pops protested that all the songs in the group's Stax repertoire wouldn't
sound out of place if performed in church. Not so with "Let's Do It
Again." Dressed up in Mayfield's Curtom recording studio on Chicago's
Northwest Side with sensual strings, purring guitar, and keyboard lines
atop a smoky groove, "Let's Do It Again" sounded like postcoital bliss—
even without the lyrics.

"The only secular song that we have ever sung was 'Let's Do It Again,'
and Pops didn't want to sing that," Mavis recalls. "It took a lot of con-
vincing by Curtis. Curtis wanted Pops to sing those lines, 'I like you
lady, so fine with your pretty hair,' and Pops says, 'I'm a church man, I'm
not singing that!'"

Mayfield just smiled, his voice remaining low-key and calm as he
assured the man he had once looked to for advice in the '50s. "Oh, Pops,
the Lord won't mind. It's just a love song."

Pops knew Mayfield respected the Staple Singers' legacy. "They
started out with the church music, gospel music, and they'd already
built a great following and name for themselves," Mayfield told author
Craig Wenner. "So they of course made their crossover. But they always
wanted their music to be inspirational. So their style didn't really change

too much. They simply found music that spread them out, allowed them to make a better living."

Mavis, Cleotha, and Yvonne were slightly less philosophical about it. They simply loved the idea of their music showing up in a movie starring Cosby and Poitier. Mavis laughs as she recalls the conversation. "My sisters and I were hoping Curtis could convince him. We just wanted to hear our voices on the big screen—we were even begging Pops to sing it. He finally came around. And then, when we'd do the song in concert, when Pops would come in with his part, the ladies would lose their minds. Scared him so bad he forgot the next line. Then he'd start grinning."

The song anchored an otherwise flimsy collection of Mayfield originals, including three instrumentals, and four more Staples vocal performances in a similarly soft-core vein. It didn't matter. "Let's Do It Again" began selling at a pace of forty thousand a day after it was released in October 1975, ended up selling more than two million copies, and became the group's sole number 1 hit. Next to Nancy Sinatra's "These Boots Are Made for Walkin'" and Petula Clark's "Downtown," it ranked with the top-selling hits in the label's history.

"The 'it's just a little love song' argument worked especially when Curtis told Pops how much money he might make if he said, 'Oh, okay,'" says Bill Carpenter. "The money changed it. Pops would perform that song right up till the last time I saw him in the '90s. Here in Washington, D.C., at an outdoor festival, he and Mavis sang that song and the audience went crazy. Pops always struck me as a trailblazer in the sense that he had deep thoughts and developed convictions about certain things, but he wasn't doctrinaire, a blind follower of the church. If he came to a logical conclusion that flew in the face of the church, that didn't bother him, he would do what he was going to do because he had a good reason for doing it. It wasn't that big of an issue. In the case of 'Let's Do it Again,' he wanted to get things off to a strong start with their new record label, and when people he trusted like Curtis and Mavis made him realize it's not that big of a deal, times are changing, people will accept this, he went for it."

The Staple Singers celebrated by headlining four consecutive nights, October 23–26, 1975, at Perv's Place to packed houses. Each night, the group sang "Let's Do It Again." And each night, the women would scream when Pops delivered his mellow mash note, "Now I like you lady, so fine with your pretty hair . . ."

32

"I was never more scared in my life"

At 3:50 a.m. on January 13, 1976, the Staple Singers arrived on a transcontinental flight at Jan Smuts Airport in Johannesburg, South Africa, the seat of apartheid, to play a series of concerts.

Though the family was keenly aware of the South African government's racist policies, the Staple Singers were revered by the country's oppressed black population. In recent years, the Staples had scored a string of hits in South Africa: The *Be Altitude* album and the singles "I'll Take You There," "Respect Yourself," "Touch a Hand, Make a Friend," and "If You're Ready (Come Go with Me)" had all gone gold.

Little wonder that despite the late hour of their arrival, the Staples were mobbed by hundreds of fans at the airport. Many had been waiting since the previous evening, and when the family emerged from Immigration and Customs, the fans broke through police barricades and tried to hug and kiss the bewildered, jet-lagged singers.

"I was never more scared in my life," Pops said. "All the pushing, shoving and hitting was too much for me to handle. That was real scary the way it happened so fast. We had no idea we were that popular in South Africa, especially at three o'clock in the morning." A photographer for the South African paper the *World* tried to climb into the car promoters had provided to transport the Staples from the airport and snap a picture of the family. After pulling the photographer out of the car, a police officer fired his service revolver in the air to disperse the crowd.

Things worsened later when Pops found out the family was expected to perform in front of a strictly segregated, all-black audience at the Eyethu Cinema in Soweto. "I told the agent to send us back home," Pops recalled. The arrangement, he said, was a "disgrace" to black people.

Promoters decided to stage an additional concert at a soccer field that would allow black and whites to attend, if still in separate sections. It's unclear whether the soccer field concert was staged to assuage Pops or to meet demand—local media reported that even as two thousand fans attended the opening concert at the Eyethu Cinema, thousands more milled outside after they were shut out at the box office, and fights erupted. Though claims were later made that the soccer field concert was a first for South African race relations, there had been previous integrated concerts by the Supremes and Edwin Starr.

The concert at Orlando Stadium in Soweto drew forty thousand fans. The Staples presided over a "Woodstock-type fanfair," according to the *World,* but photographs and personal accounts tell a different story. Fans were separated from the performers by a ten-foot barbed-wire fence, and police ringed the stadium, clutching guns and restraining snarling German shepherds.

The *World*'s review ignored the oppressive context and instead rhapsodized about the performance itself: "The Staple Singers sang love, peace, unity, and freedom. They were like monarchs. Their repertoire included their popular tunes 'I'll Take You There,' 'Are You Ready?' and 'Are You Sure?' When the sentimental appeal that followed 'Make a Friend' touched the spell-bound audience, all and sundry clapped hands."

Pops kept the mood upbeat, in contrast to some of the sterner stuff he would deliver at concerts stateside on the subjects of civil rights and integration. "We went over to South Africa to entertain, not to bring about a revolution," he said. "We don't agree with the way things are run there, but there was little we could do, so we stayed neutral." There was nothing neutral about the songs, though. One of the reasons the Staples music was so popular in South Africa is that the messages within the songs spoke loudly to a population starving for affirmation.

Mavis says the family "wanted to see for ourselves what was going on there. Our trip to Ghana [in 1971] opened our eyes about the situation in Africa and what our ancestors went through." But they weren't fully prepared for the levels of segregation encountered in South Africa. "In Soweto, they had three water fountains," she says. "The South only had two. South Africa had an extra one for people with my complexion. They kept asking me if my mother was white. My complexion was 'colored.' Pops's color was 'African.' Black kids wanted to call us at the hotel, but their calls weren't put through. We couldn't go out without a white escort. So we didn't go out."

The images that linger from the soccer field concert still give her a chill. "Those were the biggest German shepherds I'd ever seen. Police everywhere. But at least it was peaceful. We were singing songs like 'Respect Yourself' and 'Are You Sure?' that meant something to them. When we were singing, 'Are you sure there's nothing you can do/to help someone worse off than you / Think before you answer / are you sure,' you could tell they were taking it in."

It may have been a meaningful connection, but it was made through a barbed-wire fence. In too many ways, it felt like the Mississippi of 1964 all over again.

33

"The Last Waltz"

The best musical moment from "The Last Waltz," The Band's historic 1976 farewell concert, didn't actually occur in San Francisco on the night the six-hour performance was filmed for Martin Scorsese's documentary. It came a few weeks afterward, on a soundstage at MGM Studios in Culver City, California, where The Band reconvened to perform with one of their original inspirations, the Staple Singers.

The members of The Band were thrilled when the Staples covered "The Weight" in 1968, only weeks after it debuted on The Band's *Music from Big Pink*. It was the first time one of their songs had been covered by another artist, let alone one they revered as much as the Staples.

"The Staple Singers doing that song sanctified it for my father," says Amy Helm, the daughter of The Band's drummer and co–lead vocalist, Levon Helm.

When putting together "The Last Waltz," The Band's Robbie Robertson aimed to invite artists from a spectrum of genres who inspired or informed their music: "We got Muddy Waters representing the blues, we got Neil Diamond representing Tin Pan Alley, we got Joni Mitchell representing the woman singer-songwriter thing. We've got Bob Dylan, the poet of rock 'n' roll, Van Morrison for the Irish soul, Dr. John from New Orleans, Eric Clapton who brought the blues into British rock.

After everything was done, we got the Staple Singers representing gospel music and Emmylou Harris representing country music. You take all these ingredients and put them all in a big pot and stir it up and that's the gumbo that made rock 'n' roll. It all seeped into your work somewhere, someplace."

Six weeks before the show, Robertson enlisted his friend Scorsese to make a movie of it. The acclaimed director was on a Hollywood roll, with masterpieces including *Mean Streets* and *Taxi Driver*, and he was in the midst of shooting *New York, New York*. But Robertson's offer was too tempting to pass up. Scorsese was a huge rock fan, and the way he blended music into his movies—not just as background, but as a means of driving narrative and character development—reflected that passion. For *The Last Waltz*, he prepared a three-hundred-page shooting script for his crew.

The concert on Thanksgiving Day 1976 at the Winterland Ballroom in San Francisco represented a huge technical challenge, with seven cameras producing 160,000 feet of stock that required two years of editing. Events at Winterland unfolded at a frantic pace, with artists moving on- and offstage in various configurations with The Band. Scorsese and his camera operators endured six hours of nonstop crisis management under less than ideal shooting conditions. But the supplemental performances with the Staples and Harris shot at MGM enabled the director to flex his artistic chops in a more controlled setting.

The add-on performances came at Robertson's behest. The Staples had been unable to join The Band on Thanksgiving because they had an obligation in Europe. So the family's studio performance became something of a beautiful set piece in the middle of a concert movie.

"I remember this little man, Martin, standing on the tallest ladder we had ever seen to adjust the lights—I was scared for him up there," Mavis says of the MGM shoot. The Staples had met the members of The Band on the road over the years, and they were friendly with all of them. Robertson, Helm, Richard Manuel, Rick Danko, and Garth Hudson were in awe of the Staples; they modeled their own multipart singing in part on how Pops orchestrated his family's voices.

"We worshipped the Staple Singers, plain and simple," Levon Helm said. "We tried to sing with the same kind of delivery in our harmonies. They were who we looked to. We felt like if we gave it that full effort like they always did, we'd come close to where we needed to be."

Robertson likened the Staples' vocal blend to "a lonely train in the distance," in a 1998 interview. "The way that their voices would slide up to the note together. And Pop Staples, I just always thought he had the most amazing, soft, cool delivery."

The feeling was mutual, according to Mavis: "We had a sound similar to them. It's like we came from the same church."

The filming flowed like a family picnic, with easy banter and smiles. "I would flirt with Robbie and those big pretty eyes of his. I overheard Martin saying to Liza Minnelli [with whom he was filming *New York, New York* at the time], 'Watch how Mavis looks at Robbie, that's how I want you to look at him [Robert De Niro, her *New York* costar].'"

The guys in The Band respected Pops, but they also felt comfortable enough to joke with him. "Levon and Danko were the talkative guys in the band," Mavis says. "Danko was a comedian, always jiving around, jumping around. Levon and Pops were pals. He's the only one who called Pops 'Roebuck.' We took a break and Daddy walked over to talk to Levon behind the drums. Levon had a cigarette in each hand and Pops asked him why."

"You need to try this one, Roebuck," Levon said with a mischievous smile, handing him a joint.

Pops cracked up. "Levon, I don't need any of that mess," Pops replied as he walked away with a wave.

Mavis laughs at the memory. "Yvonne used to call Pops a 'robot' because he didn't smoke, didn't drink. He knew Levon was just messing with him."

While waiting for lights and cameras to be adjusted, Mavis, Yvonne, and Cleotha would sit in the dressing room with Helm's mother, Nell, a huge gospel fan, who had taken a bus from Arkansas to visit Levon and granddaughter Amy.

"Mavis and her sisters were family to my father, he felt a kinship to them," Amy Helm says. "Mavis moved him the way she moved everybody. He just adored her, worshipped her, as I do. Her whole spirit, vibe, who she is as a person is exactly what you hope it would be. She and her family spent time during *The Last Waltz* with my grandmother, and my dad was just amazed by that, the way they laughed and got along like they had known each other all their lives."

Levon Helm had grown up in Arkansas during the '40s in a family of cotton farmers and music lovers, much like Pop Staples. Though four-fifths of The Band was of Canadian origin, the quintet's music was deeply rooted in the country, blues, and R&B of the American South that defined young Levon's life. The Staples were by now hip, urban hit makers from Chicago, but their sound remained firmly planted in the rich Mississippi Delta soil that Pops Staples had once tilled. Here were Levon Helm's rock 'n' rollers and Pops's vocal group representing two distinct cultures—working-class Southern whites and black Southern sharecroppers—joined by a love of music.

The connection came full circle on "The Weight," among the most mystical and yet darkly humorous of Band songs, a story with a collection of characters and locations that sound like they could have been drawn from the Bible or an old Western movie but were actually from The Band's cross-country travels. It's a song that Pervis Staples once assumed was rife with drug connotations but that its author, Robertson, cryptically asserts is about "the impossibility of sainthood." Scorsese heard it as an "epic saga sung six thousand years ago by people long gone." Steve Cropper said the song felt "carved out of the earth . . . about common people," which made it a perfect fit for the Staples. But the group hadn't quite fully inhabited that vision when they first recorded it, somewhat tentatively, for their 1968 Stax debut album, *Soul Folk in Action*. Now they were ready, and in *The Last Waltz* they would take the song from The Band, who were effectively retiring, and make it their own.

In The Band's superb original version, Helm, Danko, and Manuel swapped verses. At MGM, Levon kicked it off as usual, Scorsese's camera gently circling The Band as they lock into the song's loping country-soul rhythm, then moving behind Mavis as she hits the verse about "Carmen and the devil." Her serenity blends into impishness as she sings, "I gotta go, but my friend can stick around."

Pops slides in for the verse about Moses and Luke, who is "waitin' on the Judgment Day," while Cleotha and Yvonne look on next to him, basking in their father's molasses-smooth delivery. Danko looks as though he's going to jump out of his shirt as he sings the lament of "Crazy Chester," and then the two groups meld for the final verse and chorus—the music of the white and black South speaking to each other. Mavis claps her hands and demands, "Take the load off Fanny / And you can put the load right on me," with a righteous confidence that wasn't evident when the Staples first recorded the song eight years earlier. With a triumphant final unison wail, the Staples bow their heads. Mavis scrunches up her nose and whispers, "Beautiful."

34

Desperate times

The Los Angeles premiere of the Sidney Poitier–Bill Cosby 1975 movie *Let's Do It Again* sprinkled Hollywood glitter atop the Staple Singers' run as hit makers. Pops stepped from a limo with mink-draped Mavis, Cleotha, and Yvonne and fielded questions from *Black Stars* magazine.

"We can never get away from gospel," Pops insisted. "We will never get away from gospel, because that's what we believe in. Sure, 'Let's Do It Again' is not gospel, but the work we do is crossing over into pop anyway. We have to be entertainers, too."

In September 1976 they were back in Los Angeles as headliners at the Troubadour. The trappings of the gospel era—Pops's suit, the sisters' gowns—were long gone, replaced by white sleeveless dresses for Mavis, Cleotha, and Yvonne, and Bermuda shorts with white shoes and kneesocks for Pops. To underline the transition, they now billed themselves as the Staples instead of the Staple Singers. The music and stage show had been transformed too, as Dennis Hunt of the *Los Angeles Times* noted in a scathing review of what he called the Staples' new "middle-of-the-road soul style geared to attracting a larger white audience."

"If Thursday's Troubadour show is any indication," Hunt wrote, the Staples "are not at all close to being a first-rate pop-soul group. A lot of comedy and choreography have been added and the sisters, who used to dress rather demurely, wore flamboyant dresses. None of these elements, however, really enhanced their show. The oldies, as usual, were enjoyable, but the other material—most of it from their new album, *Pass It On*—was barely passable. The exhilarating, churchy feeling that was always rampant in their concerts was missing most of the time. . . . The most unfortunate aspect of the Staples' change is that Mavis, an extraordinary singer, was largely muted."

The disco era proved a difficult, if not insurmountable, hurdle for many soul and R&B acts from the '60s and early '70s, and the Staple Singers were hardly an exception. Curtis Mayfield was also struggling to adapt and had shifted from the socially conscious themes of his earlier work toward expedient pop such as "Let's Do It Again."

In 1976, he wrote and produced the Staple Singers' *Pass It On* album, which included a transparent "Let's Do It Again" rewrite, "Love Me, Love Me, Love Me." Between 1972 and '77, Mayfield also wrote the music for a half dozen sound tracks, each progressively less compelling. He cut *Claudine* and *Pipe Dreams* with Gladys Knight and the Pips, *Sparkle* with Aretha Franklin, *Let's Do It Again* with the Staples, and then, after Roberta Flack dropped out, enlisted Mavis for a rush job on *A Piece of the Action,* to accompany yet another Cosby-Poitier comedy caper.

The hurried two-day recording session in Chicago marked something of an aesthetic nadir for both artists, with Mavis vamping on trite lyrics such as "Let me do it for you," and chanting, "delicious, delicious, delicious" and "koochie, koochie, koochie."

The next year, the Chi-Lites' Eugene Record took over as the Staples' producer, but the recording sessions were equally light on top-notch material for the *Family Tree* album. Pops was no longer contributing as a songwriter, the group's topical material giving way to flimsy trend hoppers such as "Let's Go to the Disco," written by Aretha Franklin's sister, Carolyn. Mavis made the most of Olivia Newton-John's schmaltzy 1974 hit "I Honestly Love You," turning it into a seven-minute gut-wrencher, and for a brief time it was part of the Staple Singers' live repertoire.

Warner Bros. did not have a particularly strong track record with R&B, and by now it was clear they had no idea how to navigate the new commercial terrain of disco. After two decades of innovation, the Staples, along with soul veterans Aretha Franklin, Ray Charles, Wilson Pickett, and Isaac Hayes, were left behind by the disco vanguard of Chic, Donna Summer, and Giorgio Moroder.

In February 1978, the Staples returned to Muscle Shoals studio in Alabama for the first time in five and a half years in an attempt to stir up some of the gold dust of the Stax *Be Altitude* era. Jerry Wexler was brought in to coproduce with Muscle Shoals keyboardist Barry Beckett. In 1975, Wexler had left his longtime home at Atlantic Records—where he had worked closely with Aretha Franklin, Ray Charles, Wilson Pickett, and Dusty Springfield, among others—for Warner, and he was an avowed fan of the Staples' churchy vocals and Pops's guitar playing. But like the Staples, he had fallen out of fashion, and it had been years since he'd been associated with a hit.

The nine-day session for what would become the *Unlock Your Mind* album produced a handful of strong tracks—certainly the Staples' best work of the Warner era. It featured two songs by emerging singer-songwriter Paul Kelly that played to the group's strengths: "Don't Burn Me," with Mavis pleading, "You've got my soul if you want it," and "God Can," the most gospel-oriented track the family cut during this period. The latter provided room for one of Pops's minisermons, with his daughters' wordless vocals providing subtle encouragement.

"This man could walk on the water, take water and make it wine," Pops raps, then breaks into song, punctuated by a ringing vibrato: "Tell the world that I know the man, and he's all right." The words and pacing, the transition from mellow wisdom to bluesy conviction are pure Pops—a rare showcase moment for him during this creative low point for the Staples. But tracks such as "Leave It All Up to Love," "I Want You to Dance," and a cover of the Electric Light Orchestra's "Showdown" merely reheat disco formula. There's also an absurd banjo-driven, hillbilly-flavored cover of the gospel song "Handwriting on the Wall."

"I remember those as desperate times," says Muscle Shoals bassist David Hood. "Music was changing—everything was disco or country, and I didn't like either one. You do this for a while, you start burning out. We would toss off ideas in the early 1970s, but you start running out of things to toss off and it gets to be harder. That was the end of our golden years. But Wexler had such a good reputation for picking songs, we thought maybe we could hit on something."

Unlock Your Mind produced a minor R&B hit—the ambling title track went to number 16—then sank off the charts. Later that year, Mavis cut a solo record with Wexler at Muscle Shoals, "Oh What a Feeling," that suffered a similar fate.

"That was awful," Mavis recalls of an album loaded with tepid dance tracks and innocuous adult-oriented pop songs. "I made a mistake with that. Warner Brothers had given me a contract, and they wanted me to do a record with Joe Sample and some jazz guys. But I asked Wexler to produce me down in Muscle Shoals instead. Jerry picked the songs, the Muscle Shoals boys played, but it was never a groove like we had. It seemed Wexler was in a hurry—he wasn't all there." In his memoirs, Wexler concurred with Mavis's sentiments of the sessions, calling them "subpar efforts on my part."

The family tried to put a positive spin on the Muscle Shoals sessions in a 1979 interview with *Blues & Soul* magazine, even while acknowledging that the challenges of the disco era and a new label's expectations had thrown them off course.

"It's like going back to where we belong," Pops said of recording *Unlock Your Mind* at Muscle Shoals. "We feel we had become a little too slick for our own good." Yvonne was more forthright: "We had gotten into a rut and we were willing to try anything just to get back out there. And being with Warners was a new experience for us—after the family type atmosphere of Stax, especially. We found we couldn't get as close to them because they are so much bigger and they have acts that sell millions of records. At Stax, we were one of the really top acts."

But no longer. The sound of *Saturday Night Fever,* the sound track to *Urban Cowboy,* and Michael Jackson's solo debut album, *Off the Wall,* were defining the sound of pop music. After "Oh What a Feeling" went nowhere, Warner Bros. and the group parted ways, and the Staple Singers were again looking for a home.

35

"Slippery People"

O ddly enough, the most resonant track associated with the Staple Singers in the early '80s was a leftover from their past. After Stax's catalog was sold in the wake of its mid-'70s bankruptcy, California-based Fantasy Records began combing the vaults for reissues and archival releases.

Among the releases was *This Time Around,* an album collecting Al Bell–produced outtakes by the Staple Singers. One of the songs— "Trippin' on Your Love"—became a deep-soul favorite for discerning DJs in the emerging house music scene. House was a Chicago-nurtured offshoot of disco, and "Trippin' on Your Love" kept the dance floor filled, with Mavis sailing over a clipped guitar, a bumping bass line, and whooshing synthesizers. The backing track sounds like it was tailored for the clubs; Fantasy staff producer-engineers Herb Jimmerson and Richard Corsello are credited with additional producing and remixing. The song would enjoy a second, even bigger revival in 1993, when U.K. singer Kenny Thomas covered it and rode it to number 17 on the singles chart.

The Staple Singers aimed to recharge by signing with 20th Century Fox Records. They booked a spring 1981 recording session in Allen Toussaint's New Orleans studio with longtime U.K. admirer John

Abbey as producer and a local rhythm section anchored by the Meters' George Porter Jr. on bass. Wardell Quezergue, who worked on Jean Knight's "Mr. Big Stuff," among other hits, oversaw the arrangements and orchestrations. Despite this A-list of collaborators, "Hold on to Your Dream" continued the Staples' string of mediocre releases, finding a placid middle ground between the "quiet storm" ballads of adult-oriented R&B and light dance pop. Mavis rarely cuts loose and Pops is reduced to little more than a backing vocalist on his own record, once again contributing no songs and not playing any guitar.

Mavis's sisters began working side jobs, with Cleotha beginning a long and productive stint in insurance sales. Mavis started collaborating with her old friend Carolyn Franklin on a solo album; Brian and Eddie Holland, two of the key songwriters in Motown's hit-making reign of the '60s and '70s, came on board to produce. But the 1983–84 recording wouldn't be released on album till a decade later. Pops also began putting together a solo gospel album.

Amid all this clutching at straws, twenty-three seconds of music surfaced that suggested what was missing: Mavis vamping on Al Green's "Take Me to the River" in a brief "Interlude" on her Holland-produced solo album. Mavis riffs, fingers snap, laughter is heard. "I feel good!" Mavis declares, and then it's over.

In 1984, the Staple Singers returned to the charts with a feisty cover of the Talking Heads' "Slippery People," a song at least partially inspired by sanctified church music. The Heads were coming off the acclaimed concert film *Stop Making Sense,* which helped turn the edgy New York City punk band into rock stars. David Byrne, the band's singer-guitarist-songwriter, was steeped in '70s funk and soul, and brought a danceable feel into even the band's earliest singles. The quartet's excellent agile rhythm section would later be abetted by the funk luminary Bernie Worrell of Parliament-Funkadelic.

Byrne heard the Staple Singers while growing up in Maryland. "I remember thinking the songs fit into what was then the 'conscious R&B' movement—songs that dealt with racism, poverty, drugs, and lots

of other issues, and yet were not hectoring and were always danceable,"
he says. "Pops's guitar playing wasn't as radical and reductionist funky as
what the guitar players in James Brown's bands were doing, but it was
more fluid and flowing. His playing gave the sense of a less aggressive
funk—a laid-back groove that was sensuous and inviting."

When the songwriting-production team of Gary Goetzman and
Mike Piccirillo persuaded the Staples to record "Slippery People," they
enlisted Byrne to play guitar. "Gary was a producer on *Stop Making Sense*
and he was instrumental in helping me get [the 1986 Byrne-directed
movie] *True Stories* off the ground," Byrne says. "He produced records
as well as movies, and he and his production partner had the idea to
find contemporary material that the Staples could cover that would also
sound like something they might have written. 'Slippery People'—just
the title alone sounds like a song they could have written. Musically, it
was definitely influenced by gospel—its very gospel call-and-response
chorus made it a natural fit for them."

Byrne's Gumby-like dance moves for *Stop Making Sense* had been in
part inspired by the way worshippers in Southern sanctified churches
responded when filled with the Holy Spirit, their bodies writhing and
undulating while speaking in tongues. "David's inspiration was seeing
people in church, and that's what I connected with," Mavis Staples says.
"My head went off into the Bible."

With Byrne's chattering guitar skipping atop a grid of percolating
percussion, the Staples' version of "Slippery People" cast Pops in the role
of the preacher and Mavis as the congregation responding to his sermon. She sounds like she's scatting in tongues, a brilliant jazzy take on
Deep South church tradition.

The single rose to number 22 on the R&B chart and anchored the
group's 1984 *Turning Point* album as part of a two-album deal with
Private I Records, a subsidiary of CBS Inc. Pervis Staples was brought
out of retirement from the music business to coproduce the rest of the
album with former Stax engineer Henry Bush, but plodding keyboards
and stiff drum-machine rhythms undercut the vocals on most of it.

"That was terrible—they were using that little drum machine and it was a total flop," Mavis says. "Pervis was trying to get something going, making a lot of noise, giving orders. I was trying to help him, but I could tell midway through the record that this was a waste of time."

The 1985 follow-up, a self-titled album coproduced by Goetzman and Piccirillo, pushed the Staples toward electrocoated rock by covering yet another Talking Heads tune, "Life During Wartime," and the Pacific Gas & Electric's 1970 hit, "Are You Ready?," but sank without charting.

Pops, though, made an impression on David Byrne, who cast him for his 1986 movie *True Stories,* a quirky, surreal examination of small-town Texas life. In a character-stretching role, Pops was enlisted to play a voo-doo priest, Papa Legba, who ministers to the lovelorn.

"During the auditions, Pops wanted to be sure that the song he would sing ['Papa Legba'] and his character—a curandero [shaman]—weren't anti-Christian," Byrne says. "I assured him that though this character may not be strictly Christian, he wasn't casting evil spells on people or evoking the devil. He was a benign healer whose mission was to help people along their path. Pops was ready to refuse the offer if he thought the material was iffy. He was very picky and didn't want to do material that was just a pop song or that might have what he saw as a negative influence on people."

Pops brings a relaxed, bluesy swing to the "Papa Legba" track over an industrial-sounding Latin groove, striking a note of genial weirdness that suits the tone of Byrne's movie. When Pops jumps into falsetto to sing the line, "In the night, come and ride your horse," he gives the song an eerie twist. It's a virtuoso turn, though the Staples patriarch would later express misgivings about the role: "That wasn't sincere. That was just playing. That was acting. I don't think a child of God should really do that. If I had to play a part again, I'd have to be sincere in what I was doing."

Pops wasn't the only one in his family feeling out of place. "Nothing came of those albums we did for Private I—all of us were sitting down for a while after that," Mavis says. "I needed to work, so I tried to get on radio as a gospel DJ. I called Pervis Spann at WGCI [a leading R&B sta-tion in Chicago], but they couldn't find room for me. I called for work singing commercial jingles. I called the Jheri curl company. They said you need to have a Jheri curl if you want to sing for us. I said, 'I can get a Jheri curl wig.' They weren't interested. Nobody was."

36

Prince and the Holy Ghost moment

I n July 1987, Mavis and Yvonne made the familiar journey to Aretha Franklin's home in Detroit from Chicago. They hadn't seen Aretha in years, though they remained close to Aretha's sisters Carolyn and Erma. But when Franklin decided to record a live gospel album as a sequel to her 1972 classic, *Amazing Grace,* she invited Mavis to sing with her.

The performance was scheduled at New Bethel Baptist Church, which had been founded by Aretha's father, C. L. Franklin, in the 1940s. It opened in candlelight, on a stifling August night in the unair-conditioned church. Carolyn, Erma, and their cousin Brenda Corbett provided backing vocals, and a hundred-member choir brought even more firepower.

Jesse Jackson introduced Aretha as "Sister Beloved, the one who wears the coat of many colors." Later in the performance, Aretha took to the pulpit to introduce her old friends from Chicago, recalling the night decades earlier on "a dark Mississippi road" when the Franklins ran into the Staples family on the gospel circuit.

Together, Aretha and Mavis rang out the hosannas on Edwin Hawkins's "Oh Happy Day," followed by the exuberant hand-waving gospel stomp "We Need Power." The two singers worked the aisles together, the fans on their feet. Pianist Nick Johnson danced madly when he wasn't pounding the keys. Nurses attended to worshippers overcome by the heat, the singing, or both.

When the live recording, "One Lord, One Faith, One Baptism," was released in December, the tensions that had always hung over the relationship between the two singers resurfaced. Mavis groused that her voice had been mixed below Aretha's, and Aretha acknowledged as much in her subsequent autobiography: "Well, I didn't play her down, but I sure didn't feel like she should be louder than I was on my own album. Mavis has a very heavy voice and for us to sound equal, I had to put her just below me in the mix."

The three-day gospel fest at New Bethel also proved to be one of Carolyn Franklin's last major public performances. She would die of cancer the following April in Aretha's home, at age forty-three.

"I would call her and we'd talk all night," Mavis recalls. "She'd tell me how she felt, what she was dreaming. I told my sisters we needed to go to Detroit to see Carolyn. Aretha had her fixed up in the basement with a hospital bed and round-the-clock nurses. I took a [stuffed] yellow Big Bird from *Sesame Street* with us, and when I got there, I started acting crazy to entertain Carolyn, saying funny things, getting on the floor and trying to turn a somersault. The nurse said, 'I've never seen her laugh like this. I'm so glad you came.' I could see Aretha peeping down in the basement, but she never came down while we were there."

A little over a month after Mavis sang with Aretha in Detroit, Oceola Staples died at sixty-nine in the south suburban Chicago home she shared with Pops. The couple had celebrated their fiftieth anniversary only three years earlier at Trinity United Church of Christ on the South Side, and now the couple's friends and relatives would gather again at the church to honor the Staples' matriarch one final time.

Amid the sadness, Mavis found herself in demand again: Prince was trying to track her down. In the spring of 1987, Prince had just released the double album *Sign o' the Times,* a masterpiece affirming his status as the pop world's most formidable quintuple threat: singer, multi-instrumentalist, songwriter, producer, and performer. He was selling millions of albums even as he was blending and blurring lines between genres, genders, and generations like few artists ever had. Though Michael Jackson may have been the self-proclaimed "King of Pop," and Bruce Springsteen was the new fist-pumping populist in blue jeans at the top of the arena-rock circuit, Prince was in many ways the decade's most diverse, difficult-to-pigeonhole megastar. He was omnivorous in his cultural appetites, his ongoing obsession with music, new and old, informing a deep respect for his artistic predecessors.

In 1987, Prince fell hard for the artistry of Mavis Staples. When LaBelle singer Nona Hendryx recorded his song "Baby Go-Go," Mavis's fierce backing vocals evoked a "Who's that?" from Prince. He dug back and started listening to and watching everything he could find on her career. The lightbulb moment arrived when he came across the Staple Singers' performance in the *Soul to Soul* movie, documenting their 1971 concert in Ghana. Mavis sings until she is so inside the moment her eyes well and her voice trembles: "My Lord, my Lord, my Lord, it may not come just when you want it . . . but I can say He will be right there."

Prince's eyes glisten, too, when he re-creates the moment: "I've been in love with Mavis since I saw that movie. I would watch her, and the part where they sing a cappella, it's like when you see someone possessed. They get the Holy Ghost in them and they're overtaken by something. My grandmother would pass out because she'd be overwhelmed by that Holy Ghost feeling. It's like you can call something into existence, and Mavis can call that up just like that [snaps fingers]. Just like that. I look at her and I wonder if . . . she goes somewhere else, becomes of what she sings about. When I saw that moment in *Soul to Soul,* I thought, 'This is my mother.' When I met her, we recognized each other. After all these years I'd finally met this person, and it's like I'd known her all my life. That's how deeply that music, her voice, her presence affected me."

In 1987, Mavis turned forty-eight years old. By MTV-era standards, she was already a has-been, and some days she felt like one. She couldn't even land a weekend job deejaying gospel records or shilling for hair products. But her magnificence was undiminished when put in the proper context, and Prince knew he was in a position to provide that.

"Fame is . . . something that comes from outside," he says. "With someone like Mavis, there's another level of consciousness. People can be famous for only a short while, it comes and goes based on the way people on the outside project what they want in celebrity. But it's about music for me. And she had more music in her, I could hear that and feel that."

Mystery that he is, Prince was not much for talk of any kind in 1987, which baffled the garrulous Mavis. His manager, Rob Cavallo, called Pops that spring looking for Mavis. "I said, 'What's Prince gonna write for me?'" Mavis says. "I'd heard the songs he's written for Apollonia and Vanity, and I wouldn't sing that stuff. That's teenybopper stuff. But he [Cavallo] said, 'Prince is very much aware of the nature of your talent, and he will be writing adult contemporary songs for you.' If I could have done a cartwheel right there, I would have."

A few months later, in August, Cavallo called again to say Prince wanted to meet Mavis backstage at a Staple Singers concert at the Los Angeles Forum. "I thought I was gonna be cool when I met him," Mavis says. "But when I met him backstage—with his white suit, Lucite cane, his white pumps—cool went out the window. I just screamed. He was so cute. I said, 'Prince, let me kiss you for my mother.' And he said, 'Kiss me on this side for your mother, too.' He was bashful—rolling them eyes."

The two chatted for forty-five minutes in the dressing room, with Mavis dominating the conversation, in part to avoid the awkward silences that were Prince's specialty at the time. "I was shy and I was in awe," Prince says now. "I was just taken with everything about her."

Pops was more than an interested bystander. "My father came into the dressing room, and he said, 'Young man, it was mighty nice of you to come out here and meet Mavis.' And all he said to my father was, 'You can play.'"

Mavis was thrilled about the opportunity but concerned whether she and Prince would ever break the ice and be able to talk like true collaborators. The next year, Prince asked Mavis to join him on the "Lovesexy" tour in Paris, and she dueted with him on the Staple Singers' "I'll Take You There."

"By the time we got to London, he opened up totally, telling me all kinds of things about himself and what he was trying to do with his music," she says. Mavis began writing eleven- to fifteen-page letters on yellow legal paper to Prince that were ostensibly about her life but that helped Prince just as much in living his.

"When we started working together, she'd write me letters, and she'd want to make sure I was eating properly, taking care of myself," Prince says. "When I got the first one, I thought it was so sweet. Then she wrote another, and another. They were all so encouraging. She was telling me about herself so I could write songs for her, but she was helping me. When you get so much discouragement from the world, to read her words was so valuable to me. She sustained me."

The first Mavis album on the singer's Paisley Park label, *Time Waits for No One,* was written and produced by Prince, with two songwriting contributions from her old Stax compatriot Homer Banks. The album was on point sonically, a sharp-edged slice of Minneapolis funk in the mold of Prince-style hits from the Time, Sheila E., and P-Funk leader George Clinton: whip-crack snare drums, jabbing keyboards, terse guitar incisions, vocals marinated in sass. Banks's Caribbean-flavored "20th Century Express" returned Mavis to the type of topical songs that made the Staple Singers run, and his warmly nostalgic ballad "The Old Songs" evoked a bygone era they both shared. Prince's contributions range from the slamming, witty "Interesting" to the cheesy "Jaguar," which has Mavis growling like a big cat on the hunt. The title track is where it all comes together, a slow-build, bell-ringing anthem about a woman running out of patience.

"I can't just sit around watching my life pass me by," Mavis sings.

Prince began to sync more deeply with Mavis on "Melody Cool," a song for his 1990 movie, *Graffiti Bridge.* Mavis would also play a character named Melody Cool in the movie, in which Prince's alter ego, "The

Kid," and the Time's Morris Day joust for ownership of the Glam Slam nightclub. The hokey plot was salvaged by the music, with Mavis as a voice of plainspoken wisdom. The track turns on a phrase often repeated by her father—"There are no big 'I's' and little 'yous'"—that Prince found irresistible.

"You're just as good as anyone else, Pops would say," Mavis explains. "Don't ever think you're any better than anyone else, but don't ever think anyone is better than you."

The movie was a commercial and critical flop, but Mavis came out of it with her profile raised and her reputation enhanced. Her letters helped Prince build a strong backlog of songs for her next studio album, *The Voice,* in 1993, easily her strongest work since the '70s. "After the first album, the disc jockeys were saying that Prince is trying to make a female Prince out of Mavis, and they didn't like it," she says. "So the second one, he took my letters, and he wrote my life. Every song I'd hear something that was in my letters."

"The Undertaker" strolled through drug-infested streets, with Mavis as an impassioned tour guide. "I told him I married an undertaker, he wrote me a song called 'The Undertaker,' an antidrug song: 'Don't go with the crack, you might never come back.' It was a message song, tied in with this little extra twist to my personal life."

Biblical references peppered "Blood Is Thicker than Time," an ode to family and memory. "He told me he wrote that for my family. I had to stop about three times singing that song, I couldn't get through it. My mother had passed, and that's what had gotten the whole thing started." Like "Melody Cool," "House in Order" came out of an impromptu remark Mavis made, this time advising a couple of female singers she overheard smack-talking about men. The album was a superb melding of Mavis's life, personality, and voice with Prince's craftsmanship and vision, but it got buried as Prince was in the final stages of his long, painful divorce from Warner Bros. It was in 1993 that Prince changed his name to a symbol as if trying to erase his past, and three years later he severed his ties with the label.

Despite the drama, the Prince association restored Mavis's stature as an artist, and by extension the relevance of the Staple Singers. A series of box sets began chronicling the history of Stax Records in the early '90s, prominently featuring the Staples' work, and BeBe and CeCe Winans scored a number 1 R&B hit in 1991 with a remake of "I'll Take You There," with a Mavis cameo. The Winans were a top gospel group at the time, building on the Staples' tradition of tying in religious themes with secular lyrics and contemporary music.

"I think they opened up some doors for everybody," CeCe Winans said of the Staples in a 1992 interview. "You have those who feel that gospel music is only to be done one way," but the genre's broader range is "accepted now because the Staples went before."

For Mavis, the respect from a younger generation of artists such as Prince and the Winans coincided with a renewed appreciation for her family's music. A few years earlier, she felt adrift. Now she felt vindicated—and grateful for a new start.

"We got a lot of flak from the church when [we began singing contemporary gospel], because they felt we had abandoned the principles," she said in a 1992 interview. "It was very flattering that BeBe and CeCe wanted to sing a song that we recorded 20 years ago, when they were 6 and 8 years old. Now, you know that made me feel real good that this generation wants to hear that—you feel that you served a purpose. It's kind of like an artist giving you your flowers while you can still smell them."

37

Pops, the second act

For Pops Staples, the winter of 1990 in Chicago wasn't a heck of a lot different from the Depression-era ones he encountered when he first arrived in the city. Now he had nicer clothes, a solid brick home, and money in the bank. But he needed a job just the same, and his reputation took him only so far.

With a few dozen other gospel singers, Pops waited patiently for a shot at his first acting role with the most prestigious stage company in Chicago, the Goodman Theatre. The audition room felt like anything but a church, with a beat-up piano under fluorescent lights and a handful of talent judges instead of a congregation. But Pops was instructed to make it feel like one: the Goodman was preparing to stage the off-Broadway musical *The Gospel at Colonus.*

Pops was seventy-five years old, but he was as anxious as a novice musician facing his first audience. "If I get this job, I'll be the happiest man in the world," he said. When his moment arrived, he plugged in his red guitar and sang a few bars of pleading gospel. After about ninety seconds, a voice interrupted him.

"Cut! That's fine, Pops," yelled Goodman casting director Tara Lonzo. "Terrific, thanks for coming in! Wonderful! Great!"

Pops headed for the door before the last exclamation point could swat him across the behind. His parting words to a *Chicago Tribune* reporter: "I've performed for 6,000 people without even being nervous. But this thing was really rough. It takes awhile to get the spirit going, you know."

Lonzo spent the day listening to some of the finest gospel singers in Chicago, a city with a still-thriving network of choirs and soloists across its South Side churches. All told, more than two hundred gospel singers would try out. "We're only casting for ten roles here, so most of the people just aren't going to make it in this show," Lonzo said. "So when we finally break the news to these people, we try to do it gently. These auditions, you know, are the things that dreams are made of."

Pops finally heard from Lonzo in May, and the news was good: He'd landed the role of King Creon, Oedipus's nemesis, which provided three months of steady work in Chicago and two more months in San Francisco. Pops's song "Come Home" was included in the production and earned applause from the *Chicago Tribune*'s veteran critic, Richard Christiansen, who called Pops "superbly sly."

Michelle Shocked, a singer who had enjoyed late '80s success exploring various folk idioms, enlisted a variety of veteran artists to join her in recording the 1992 *Arkansas Traveler* album. The lead track, "33 RPM Soul," was recorded in Chicago with Pops; his trebly guitar is the first sound heard on the record.

In a 1992 interview she extolled Pops as "the heart and soul of what our contemporary music is really about. . . . Gospel has been pretty much written out of the history of our contemporary culture and it feels like a very fragile thread, as fragile a thread as Pops' guitar playing. But there's something strong in that fragility. Something that will stay alive until someone comes along and picks it up and carries it to its rightful place at the front of our understanding of our culture. I really feel like the Staple Singers stand alone. I feel like they are the beating heart, the center of our culture."

Yet after those first few quivering notes on "33 RPM Soul," Pops is all but erased from the song, his contributions buried beneath a slick country-pop arrangement, the antithesis of the musical qualities Shocked was trying to underline. In much the same way, Pops's two solo records in the '90s can be seen as uneasy compromises between the rough-hewn sound that made him a national treasure and the requirements of a marketplace unaccustomed to something that earthy.

His 1992 *Peace to the Neighborhood* album was a well-intentioned mix of songs from contemporary and traditional sources. It likely owes its existence to John Lee Hooker's 1989 comeback album, *The Healer,* which paired the blues singer with admirers Carlos Santana, Robert Cray, and Bonnie Raitt. It gave the blues legend his first charting album in decades and earned a Grammy Award nomination.

Hooker's agent, Mike Kappus of the Rosebud Agency, helped connect Pops with the Point Blank label, a subsidiary of Virgin Records that began signing a series of blues acts in the late '80s, including Albert Collins, John Hammond, Johnny Winter, and Hooker. The initial idea was for Pops to preside over a students-meet-teacher blues summit similar to what Hooker had done. But Pops insisted he wasn't a blues singer (though he often played and sang like one) and pushed for a stronger gospel feel and message tracks in the tradition of what the Staple Singers sang in the '60s and '70s.

Jackson Browne's "World in Motion" passed muster, with Browne and Raitt joining Pops to create a latticework of rustic guitar lines. The song "was inspired by the Staples—the fingerpicking style," Raitt says. "He put some Mississippi accents on Jackson's song, and we followed his lead. Pops is a hugely underrated major influence on a lot of guitar players. It's folk fingerpicking, but there's a feeling he brings to the tremolo guitar that he owns. His tone is instantly recognizable. It's not folk, not gospel, not R&B, it's just Pops. You can't divorce the sound of his guitar from the Staple Singers."

That sound is amplified on the album's finest performance, "Down in Mississippi," a traditional folk-gospel song with Pops sinking into the Delta mud with one of his most ardent disciples, guitarist-producer Ry

Cooder. With a trio of backing singers including longtime Cooder associates Terry Evans and Willie Greene, delivering the chain-gang blues behind him, Pops drifts back to the early twentieth century, when the sweat steamed off him as he worked the Dockery Plantation behind a plow horse.

"Hunting . . . season was always open on me / Nobody needed no bail," Pops snapped. Pops also reclaimed "This May Be the Last Time" from the Rolling Stones, with Mavis, Yvonne, and Cleotha on backing vocals, and funky organ fills from Lester Snell. The old Staples song "Pray on My Child" (also known as "Pray On") provided another family reunion, with Mavis on lead vocals.

Though family always came first with Pops, he delighted in the renewed attention on his life and career. He was a postmodern roots patriarch, a master of the gospel-blues-soul-folk vernacular that encompassed everyone from Johnny Cash and Bob Dylan to the hip-hop and R&B artists who were now tapping into his family's songs. Wreckx-N-Effect, Xscape, and Ice Cube repurposed "Let's Do It Again," Salt-N-Pepa sampled "I'll Take You There," and Big Daddy Kane remade it.

When two of the leading producers in the music industry—Don Was and Tony Brown—conceived an ambitious merger of country and soul artists, *Rhythm Country and Blues,* little wonder that Pops and his family got a call. The Staple Singers had been injecting urban gospel with a rural vibe since the 1940s. Was had recently produced albums for mainstream stars including Raitt, Bob Seger, and B-52s. Brown was regarded as a Nashville visionary who had nurtured the careers of artists such as Steve Earle, George Strait, and Rodney Crowell. Together, they used their clout for a high-profile vanity project that would highlight some of their personal musical heroes: Al Green and Lyle Lovett dueting on Willie Nelson's "Time Slips Away," George Jones and B. B. King collaborating on "Patches," Patti LaBelle and Travis Tritt taking on "When Something Is Wrong with My Baby."

Marty Stuart, a bluegrass ace who had played with Lester Flatt and Johnny Cash, and gone on to solo fame, was enlisted by Was to work with the Staples on a track. It was an astute choice. Stuart had grown up in Philadelphia, Mississippi, two generations later and about 135 miles from Dockery Farms.

"The first time I remember seeing the Staple Singers, I was visiting a friend in Indianapolis and *The Last Waltz* was on TV," says Stuart, who was born in 1958, about the same time as the Staples were first riding high after the success of "Uncloudy Day." "The camera panned to Pops, and I said, 'Who is that man?' I didn't know anything about him, where they came from, but I thought I was looking at the Old Testament. There was something cool, profound, old world, and divinely ordered about him."

Stuart became a fan. Besides being an accomplished musician, singer, and songwriter, Stuart is something of a music scholar. His knowledge of American roots music runs deep; he's written appreciations of his musical heroes, and his music openly pays homage to the artists who inspired it. When he fell for the Staple Singers, he fell hard.

"I was maybe twenty, twenty-one when I saw *The Last Waltz,* and that led me down to the empowering force, which is the original family structure," he says. "Their position in American music history is really unique, and they were without question among the most powerful gospel singers, but also cultural icons and rock stars. They got into some trouble with the church people because they moved away from gospel, but everyone knows the greatest rock 'n' roll in the world is in the church, especially if you're from Mississippi. Before the world found them, they were at their zenith, working out their harmonies in the car on the way to those church gigs in the South, and they found something."

Like many from later generations who came to revere the Staples' music, Stuart worked backward from the more obvious reference points—*The Last Waltz,* the hits for Stax in the '70s—to the deep gospel of the Vee-Jay years.

"I found 'Uncloudy Day' and the early version of 'Will the Circle Be Unbroken,' a song that gets crushed beneath the wheels of its own fame," Stuart says. "But outside of the Carter Family and Staple Singers versions, everyone can keep theirs because they did it, they owned it. On a trip back home to Philadelphia, Mississippi, I was driving through a Delta cotton field one night and I was playing their record. And I pulled over in the middle of this cotton field—it was pitch-black in the Delta—and I turned the car lights off, until all you heard was 'Will the Circle Be Unbroken' and 'Uncloudy Day.' It was so spooky. It was almost too much for the heart to take, and beautiful. It was like the ghosts coming down from heaven. It scared me, and it moved me."

Stuart called Pops in Chicago to join the *Rhythm Country and Blues* sessions in Nashville in late 1993. They agreed to collaborate on yet another version of "The Weight," a suicide mission in a way because it likely could never live up to the standard set by the Staples and The Band in *The Last Waltz*. Stuart laughs now at the folly of it all: "Yeah, it was like trying to repaint the *Mona Lisa,* right? There wasn't anything more we could do because it had already been cut exactly right. But it was a piece of common ground and easy for all concerned."

After the initial deal had been verbally sealed, Pops called Stuart a few days later.

"I don't think we can come down and do it for the money we talked about," Pops said.

"Everyone is doing this for favored-nation status," Stuart pleaded. "You get $10,000 for the session to cut the track and split among yourselves any way you want."

"Are we getting what B.B. [King] is getting?" Pops asked.

Stuart couldn't help but laugh. "You are, and tell you what, I'll give you $1,000 extra off my side of the table."

Pops, a man who once negotiated with unscrupulous promoters with a gun in his trousers, had one more request: "I need two other things. A Fender '65 with some shake on it, and a stretch-out car."

Stuart agreed, hung up, and immediately called Mavis. "I said, what is a 'Fender with some shake on it' and a 'stretch-out car'? She just laughed and said, 'He needs a guitar with some tremolo on it and a limousine.'"

38

"Whatever you do, don't give up"

Though the rerecording of "The Weight" proved no threat to the original, let alone the definitive *Last Waltz* version, it began what would become a lasting friendship between Marty Stuart and the Staples. His decades-long respect for Pops, planted by an image on a TV screen in the '70s, deepened when he finally met the soft-spoken family patriarch and they began exchanging anecdotes and memories about life in the South. Stuart also got to observe the family interact, holding tenaciously to a pecking order carried down through the decades.

"When we did 'The Weight,' all his daughters were totally grown women, but Pops still handled them like they were his little girls," Stuart says. "He was the boss. That's the way it was set up. He handled them in a beautiful way, but there was no doubt who the chief was in that tribe."

Pops's second solo album for Point Blank, *Father Father*, was starker than the first. The lone guest stars were his family members, with Mavis coproducing a couple of tracks under her family nickname "Bubbles" (each of the girls had a pet name bestowed upon her during childhood by their mother: Cleo was "Boo" and Yvonne was "Bunny"). The album was stacked with Pops originals, including a funky, slow-burn version of "Why (Am I Treated So Bad)." He covered Curtis Mayfield's Impressions classic "People Get Ready," which underscored how his gentle, conversational delivery had influenced Mayfield's vocal style. Once again, Ry Cooder evidenced the deepest understanding of and empathy for what Pops does best on a pair of tracks; his stark production zeroes in on Pops's forlorn vocals and haunted guitar tone on "Jesus Is Going to Make Up (My Dying Bed)" and "The Downward Road."

In 1995, the album won Pops his first Grammy Award, for best contemporary blues recording. The honor came only a few days after B. B. King hosted a belated eightieth birthday party in Los Angeles for his old friend with Bonnie Raitt, Isaac Hayes, and Sam Moore among those paying tribute. The Grammy was an honor Pops would not dare wish for publicly, but one he had coveted since the Staple Singers' "I'll Take You There" lost in 1973 to the Temptations' "Papa Was a Rolling Stone" for best R&B vocal performance by a duo or group.

"When Smokey Robinson read the winner's name, me, Yvonne, and Cleedi were so sad," Mavis recalls. "Pops said, 'I don't want y'all letting the Grammy get you down. Y'all are not singing for an award, you're singing for your just reward. When it's over, you will get your just reward.' But we were pitiful, our heads were down, we wanted to win. My father always conditioned us to not count on awards."

Occasionally, Pops would let his guard down, and deeper-seated emotions would emerge. He could be a brilliant off-the-cuff speaker, given his deep knowledge of the Bible, the blues, and the gospel of Martin Luther King. At the Rhythm & Blues Foundation's third annual Pioneer Awards in New York in the early '90s, Pops was among peers, survivors of the same chitlin circuit he had traveled in the '40s and '50s. Hometown friends the Dells were there, as was Hank Ballard, Bobby "Blue" Bland, Chuck Jackson, Ella Johnson, and Rufus Thomas.

"I'm so glad to be an African American," Staples declared when he took the podium to receive his family's award. His comments built from there, the cadences and timing pitch-perfect, until finally this: "We've done the impossible for the ungrateful," to which a voice in the audience shouted in agreement. "Enough!"

"Pop was on a mission that night," recalls Bonnie Raitt, who was master of ceremonies. "The speech was like a performance. He's such a gentle guy normally, but after that speech it was like we all got run over."

Bill Carpenter said it would be a mistake to underestimate Pops's outspokenness or his need for attention. "Humble, but never satisfied," Carpenter says. "And," he adds with a laugh, "a man of God who enjoyed the ladies."

"I was working with National Parents' Day in Washington, D.C., and people like Florence Henderson, Barbara Billingsley, and different congressmen gave awards to parental role models, including Pops," Carpenter says. "What fascinated me is that Pops was in his early eighties, and he was still hitting on women. They loved him, too. He would be getting dressed, and this whole process would take place. He was late for a radio interview, and so I went to get him in his hotel room. He's up there looking for an iron so he could iron his clothes—for a radio interview! He had on a pin-striped suit, a crisp white shirt, the cuff links, the tie, and enough cologne to suffocate anyone. We'd go down to the lobby, and he's flirting with the lady at the front desk. We were late, but not so late that he couldn't make time with the ladies in the lobby."

The clothes, the cologne, the charm were signs of vindication, Carpenter concludes. "When a person grows up on a plantation, so much is denied to you from an early age that when you're able, you flaunt it a bit. 'I used to pick cotton, but look at me now.' There's a little bit of that. It's not something he ever verbalized, but it came through watching him work in the '90s. It was like his day had finally come, and he was going to enjoy it."

After recording with him on the *Peace to the Neighborhood* album, Bonnie Raitt developed a friendship with Pops built on their mutual respect for each other's guitar-playing abilities. But there was a personal chemistry, as well.

"He used to call me 'Bunnie,'" Raitt says. "He was delighted that a young woman could play guitar like that. He was such a Southern gentleman. He liked the ladies and he flirted—a lot [laughs]. I think Mavis thought he was flirting with me. That happens when there is mutual admiration. It got heated up when I was singing with John Lee [Hooker] on 'I'm in the Mood.' That happens when I'm playing with someone like Marc Cohn, or Pops. I wouldn't call it lust. It's a more sustainable heat that is a lot more long-lasting."

After things fell apart with Prince's record label, Mavis focused on helping her father: She sang on both of his solo records and produced several tracks. The family continued to tour, but their profile had diminished considerably. They were effectively an oldies act, the fate of countless soul groups from the '60s and '70s. If critics bothered to review the Staples' shows at all, they were mostly respectful, but a younger generation of writers cast them as out-of-step with a musical era heavy on dark humor and irony.

In the *New York Times,* Neil Strauss reviewed a Mavis solo concert in November 1994: "When she hit her stride on Wednesday, Ms. Staples's voice smoldered with a righteous passion, but when her instrument began to wane near the end of the set, she tried to compensate with tears and emotional histrionics as canned as her horn section."

Gospel's emotional transparency didn't resonate with a younger generation enamored with indie rock's disaffected coolness and gangsta rap's studied hardness. Mavis was undaunted. In 1996, she paid tribute to her late mentor Mahalia Jackson on the album *Spirituals & Gospel,* accompanied by keyboardist Lucky Peterson. This is the music she had heard since birth; "If I Could Hear My Mother Pray Again" was among the first songs Pops taught her and her siblings, and "Take My Hand, Precious Lord" was the Thomas Dorsey hymn she had performed with Mahalia at the famed 1969 summer concert in Harlem. The performances are heartfelt, emotionally transparent, and loose—sometimes to the point of nearly falling apart. On "Precious Lord," the fissures in Mavis's tone widen as she cuts loose over Peterson's Hammond B-3 organ. But an a cappella version of "Stand by Me" redeems the album, Mavis's voice double-tracked to create the illusion that she's dueting with herself. The call-and-response patterns occasionally resolve in chilling, wordless unison moans, with the double-tracked Mavis in the upper and lower octaves of her range simultaneously. "I'm growing, growing old and feeble," Mavis sings, but clearly she is anything but in this performance, one of the greatest of her career.

Mavis loved and owned the project like few others in her career. She toured the album for years, her solo sets bursting with gospel songs that were the foundation of her relationship with Mahalia. In 1997, she inducted Jackson into the Rock and Roll Hall of Fame, and roared through the gospel standard "Didn't It Rain" with ferocity in honor of "my mentor, my teacher, and my friend." Later that year, she debuted the album live at the Montreal Jazz Festival, and performed the material in Chicago on Martin Luther King Day at Symphony Hall in 1998. In February 1999, she brought the show to Washington University in St. Louis with pianist Tony Dorsey. There she reminisced about her 1969 performance with Mahalia: "She told me to start it off. By the time I got to the second verse, somebody had brought her up to the microphone. It seemed like there was fire all over. Everything got brighter. I had a time. I was in my world."

At the end, the capacity audience—standing and clapping through much of the concert as if they were at a gospel revival in a South Side church—called for "I'll Take You There."

"You know that's not one of Mahalia's songs," she said. "I can't sing that song without Pops and his guitar."

By that point, Mavis knew that the days of her performing alongside Pops and his guitar were winding down.

"Pops could just smell it. 'I gotta get one more record out,' he'd say," Mavis recalls. "And we thought the same thing. In the spring of '97 we started with another Staple Singers record. We knew we had to do it ourselves. You have to prove yourself nowadays, no matter how long you've been around. We went to Memphis, got with Homer Banks and Lester Snell, all the old people who knew us. We came back with three songs, and then Yvonne, Cleedi, and I put the background vocals on.

"At the time, we didn't know that this was gonna be the last Staple Singers project. But then Pops got sick in the fall of '97, and when he got out of the hospital, he really wanted to record some more. I told Cleedi and Yvonne, 'Let's let Daddy put down his stuff, then we'll put our backgrounds down later.' Pops was putting it down, some old traditional gospel songs. One was his favorite, called 'A Better Home': 'I've started out to find a better home.'"

Pops would fade in and out, motivated to record even as he felt his body denying him. "We drove out to a studio in [the northern Chicago suburb of Waukegan], all four of us, and we let Daddy sing," Mavis says. "Sometimes the mikes would be set up and they'd be ready to go, and Pops would say, 'Mavis, you have to take me back, I can't make it today.' Then he'd call me two, three days later, saying he was feeling better. 'Mavis, get that studio.' He was determined to make another record."

In 1999, the Staple Singers were inducted into the Rock and Roll Hall of Fame. With Bruce Springsteen, Paul McCartney, Billy Joel, Neil Young, Eric Clapton, Robbie Robertson, Bono, D'Angelo, Wilson Pickett, and Curtis Mayfield's widow, Altheida, looking on, Lauryn Hill praised the group as "postwar gospel warriors" who had "single-handedly invented a genre called folk-soul." The Staples, she said, had "unmistakably proven that speaking of faith and spirituality and God is in accordance with being 'fly' and commercially acceptable."

Though he walked unsteadily, Pops played the role of elder statesman with regal panache, his white mustache wrapped to his muttonchop sideburns. All the family members were in attendance, including Pervis, but there was no question who would accept the honor.

"I've been blessed," Pops said. "For forty-four years I've been singing with my family. We drove all over the United States in an automobile for fifteen years before we began to fly . . ." Pops spoke off-the-cuff, as was his habit, and detoured to his childhood. "When I was a boy I loved to hear them blues. In those days that was the devil's music. . . . I said to myself when I was about twelve years old, I'm gonna play guitar. . . . I'm gonna play that guitar and I'm gonna be famous. I went from twelve to seventy-two before I got to make a [solo] record. I went to seventy-two

to eighty-four before I made that hit record and got a Grammy. Whatever you do, don't give up."

The family rolled into "Respect Yourself" and "I'll Take You There,"
Pops and Pervis in tuxes, Yvonne, Cleedi, and Mavis in gowns—the last
time all five of them would be on stage together. The music industry
executives in the audience roused themselves from their white-cloth dinner tables to stand and applaud. Pervis threw his left arm around Pops's
shoulders, and they exited together.

In November 2000, Pops suffered a concussion in a fall outside his
home in Dolton, Illinois. On the morning of December 19, just a few
days short of what would have been his eighty-sixth birthday, the Staples patriarch died. Trinity United Church of Christ on 95th Street was
packed for his funeral a few days later. Gladys Knight sang, and Jesse
Jackson spoke, then Marty Stuart.

"Gladys Knight took the top off the church—she showed up with
everything she had," Stuart says. "I had to follow Jesse Jackson—that's
when I discovered I was a white boy when it comes to talking. But when
I remember that day, I think of being out at the cemetery and it's a text-
book Chicago winter day—sun going down, really cold, gray, icy. As
they lowered Pops into the ground, I started singing the first verse of
'Will the Circle Be Unbroken' to myself. That song yet again came alive,
and it got me through. I saw Pops and Pervis and those babies traveling
the back roads of America, working out their harmony parts, going from
situation to situation, figuring it out, this little family from Chicago in
a car going across the land the same way the Israelites did, across the
wilderness, hacking it out as they went. They'd been through everything
together. If someone from that group, that family, leaves you, you don't
recover from that easily."

39

"My skin started moving on my bones"

Cleotha might have taken Pops's death the hardest of anyone in the family. "Even though she was only a few years older than Mavis, Yvonne, and Pervis, they saw Cleo as the old granny sister," Jon Shields says. "Cleo was always in agreement with whatever Pops's position was. Sometimes her sisters and brother would look at her and think, 'Why does she always take Daddy's side on everything?' She always related to her father, regardless of her sisters' and brother's positions.

"I was in their home one day, and Mom found an eyebrow pencil in Pops's attaché case, and she wanted to know who that eyebrow pencil belonged to. She and Pops were going back and forth, kind of serious, kind of in fun. She was stroking his ego a little. Pops couldn't figure out where it was from and he walked out of the room. Cleo says to Mavis, 'Why don't you tell Mama that's your pencil?' Mavis was giggling and grinning, enjoying all the arguing, but Cleo was very serious, upset that her father's integrity was being attacked, even in a kind of humorous way."

Cleotha had been diagnosed in the early stages of Alzheimer's disease around the time of Pops's death, and afterward she "just couldn't hold it together anymore," Mavis recalls. Cleedi lived in the same condominium complex as Mavis, and Mavis arranged for her sister to receive twenty-four-hour care at home so she would be disrupted as little possible. But Cleedi would never sing again. With her illness and Pops's death, the Staple Singers were done. Without Pops's signature guitar sound and Cleedi's high harmonies, Mavis felt lost—not just personally but also musically.

"I was a pitiful child," she says. "I think I was going a little crazy. I'd go over to my father's house and I think I'd see him sitting there with his guitar. I started talking to him: 'You left me here. I don't know what key I sing in. I don't know music.' People always want me to sing with these house bands, and I tell my manager, 'You know, I don't know how to tell these guys certain stuff. I don't know the lingo these others do. It would be better if you just let them hear my record and let them hear what key I'm in and let them write it out. I don't do good with house bands.' I didn't have the confidence to do it on my own. I still loved to sing, but what could I sing without Daddy? You've been singing with your father for over fifty years, and now he's gone. And I'm a big baby anyway, you know. I felt like it was over for me."

Two people brought her out of her funk, in good-cop, bad-cop fashion. Her pastor at Holy Trinity, Jeremiah Wright, paid a visit and reminded her how she used to make Pops laugh. And get-to-the-point Yvonne basically told her younger sister to "snap out of it."

In February 2002, Mavis made one of her first public appearances since Pops's death in a tribute concert to her father at FitzGerald's, a roadhouse-style club in Berwyn, Illinois, on the western outskirts of Chicago. Otis Clay, the Chicago soul singer who had his greatest success cutting tracks in Memphis with Willie Mitchell in the '70s, was on stage summoning the down-home spirit on "Will the Circle Be Unbroken."

"I couldn't really see the audience, because it was dark in there," says Leroy Crume, who was singing backing vocals with Clay. "I hear this voice, 'Hey, Blab!' It's Mavis. I said, 'Maves, c'mon up here.' She came onstage—the place was jammed and people went bananas. I went down into the audience and escorted her up. Otis was singing Pops's part in 'Respect Yourself,' and then came Mavis's part, and I shoved the mike in her face. She started singing and the place went up for grabs again. I hadn't seen her since moving to Florida about ten years earlier, but that voice still had the power to get people."

Mavis had a ball onstage. It felt good to be in a club packed shoulder to shoulder with her family's fans. She burst into a whimsical, scat vocal tribute to the club's avuncular owner, the gray-bearded Bill FitzGerald.

What motivated her to get back onstage? "Yvonne got me," Mavis says. "Yvonne said, 'Mavis, your daddy would want you to keep singing. You've got to get up. You're Daddy's legacy. Daddy started this, and you can't just stop it.' And that's when she started with the other words: 'Damn it, Mavis,' and worse. It woke me up."

Yvonne just laughs. "It's nothing she didn't already know. I just needed to remind her about a few things. I don't know if she liked hearing it at first, but she stopped moping around the house, I'll tell you that."

Mavis started picking up the phone, accepting singing gigs wherever they came: albums by Los Lobos and Dr. John, tribute compilations to Johnny Paycheck, Johnny Cash, and Stephen Foster, and a galvanizing appearance at the 2003 "Soul Comes Home" concert with Isaac Hayes, Anne Peebles, and Carla Thomas at the Orpheum Theatre in Memphis. One of the calls came from her old sweetheart, Bob Dylan, who invited her and Yvonne to Los Angeles to record a new version of his track "Gonna Change My Way of Thinking" for a 2003 tribute album, *Gotta Serve Somebody.* Dylan had rarely sounded this relaxed or flat-out whimsical on record. He breaks off the music after about thirty seconds to answer a knock on the door and engage in a little bit of off-the-cuff theater with two old friends.

He shouts out to Yvonne about rustling up some chickens in the backyard for dinner. "We gonna go knock a few of 'em off and fry 'em up," he says. Then he confesses, "Mavis, I've had the blues."

Mavis: "Oh, Bobby, don't tell me you got the blues."

Dylan: "Yeah, I've been up all night, laying in bed, having insomnia, reading *Snooze-week.*"

Mavis: "*Snooze-week?* That ain't gonna get rid of no blues. Let's do some singing. Sing about it."

It's hard to imagine anyone other than Mavis making Dylan feel comfortable enough to banter that way in the middle of a song. They come out of the interlude to team up for one of Dylan's fiercest latter-day performances, a seething reinvention of the thinly veiled protest song. Staples shades Dylan's growl with shouts, interjections, harmonies. The band—one of Dylan's best since the '60s with Charlie Sexton and Larry Campbell on guitars—rumbles and rolls through the changes, playing with a savagery that demands Dylan and Mavis respond in kind. And they do.

"Well, we live by the Golden Rule / Whoever got the gold, rules," the two growl.

Just as her father had in the 1950s, before fully committing his family to the music business, Mavis took her time before making her next move. She had been burned by the Prince experience because of what she saw as record company neglect: good work, honestly done, left to wither by indifferent corporate politics. Her distrust of record labels was a carryover from her days with Stax and Al Bell, and she was not eager to deal with that world again. But the words of her father commanded her to push forward.

"Just before he died, he called me to his bedroom talking really soft, 'Mavis, don't lose this stuff,'" she says. "He was talking about the songs we cut just before he got sick. He was listening to them real quietly at his bedside and he knew that he had done something worthwhile. We spent our money making that record, but we never got a chance to shop it."

Yvonne suggested that the best way to bring notice to the Pops recordings was for Mavis to cut a solo album first. But she had no idea where to turn: Curtis Mayfield had died about a year before Pops, and many of the old Chicago studios that she knew were gone. Then a door opened. Songwriter-producer Jim Tullio, who had worked with The Band in the '80s and was operating a studio out of his home in the northern Chicago suburb of Winnetka, had written a tribute song to friends he had lost in the September 11, 2001, terrorist strike on New York City and Washington, D.C. He was looking for a singer, and Levon Helm recommended Mavis. Tullio called Yvonne and faxed over the lyrics to "In Times Like These." That's all it took. "This is me," Mavis thought.

The song is an anthem in the "We Are the World" mold, gussied up with a gospel choir that makes it a distant cousin to some of the Staple Singers' message tracks from the '70s. The session with Tullio was pleasant enough and the producer offered to help Mavis take the next step in the music business, whatever she wanted it to be. Mavis, as always, looked to what Pops had done. The Staple Singers had launched their recording career in 1953 by cutting a homemade single and pressing five hundred copies. If no record company wanted to help her, she would do it herself.

Mavis ended up putting about $40,000 on her credit card to finance the sessions for what would become the *Have a Little Faith* album. She started by revisiting what she knew: a reworked version of "Will the Circle Be Unbroken," among the first songs Pops had taught the family, and then "A Dying Man's Plea," the song that Pops had sung with such chilling conviction on one of the Staples' early '60s albums for Riverside.

"I always loved that song," Mavis says. "I loved to hear Daddy sing it. And when I first heard it when I was a kid, it mystified me. The images of a silver spade, the golden chain, the two white horses. The way Pops sang that song, it was so cool—he knew how to sing. I saw some kids in New York when I was about thirteen and they were singing at the top of their voice. So I started singing like that, and Pops snatched me off and said, 'Mavis, what is wrong with you? What you doing? You don't need no gimmicks. You're singing God's music. You don't need to sing at the top of your voice. You be sincere, and sing from your heart. What comes from the heart reaches the heart. You'll reach the people if you sing from the heart.' And I never forgot that."

Little wonder her performance of "A Dying Man's Plea" is positively Pops-like in its eerie understatement.

Mavis cut much of the album live with Tullio accompanying her on guitar, adding instruments later. Many of the songs revolve around themes of perseverance, an echo of Pops's words at the family's Hall of Fame induction ("Whatever you do, don't give up") and Yvonne's salty pep talk to a downcast Mavis in the months after Pops's death. "God Is Not Sleeping" in particular conflates Mavis's personal struggles with her enduring faith. An old friend, Phil Roy, presented the song to her after a concert in Philadelphia.

"I put on that song, and I'm tellin' you my skin started moving on my bones," she says. "I said, 'Whoa, we got one.' I called up Toos, and I said, 'Montana, I got a song here. We got to put this down tomorrow.' He said, 'Play me the song now.' I said, 'No, I want to see your expression when you hear it.'"

"She called from her dressing room, she was so excited about it," Tullio recalls. "When Mavis believes in a song, to hear her sing it—there's nothing like it. And she believed in that one."

Tullio was impressed with Mavis's preparedness, how she approached each vocal with care and resourcefulness. "With most singers, there are usually a number of flubbed notes in every performance, and you have to patch things together," he said. "But with Mavis it was great, greater, and greatest. She says she doesn't 'know' music, but knowing music has nothing to do with it. She knows as much about music as Beethoven did, in her heart."

Mavis also knew she was singing for her musical life. She had already been cast aside a couple of times by a music industry in constant search of the next new voice. She was now in her sixties, and few artists—let alone female artists—had managed to maintain their relevance at that stage in their careers.

"It's a shame, us at this point, we still have to prove ourselves all over again to the music business," she said at the time. "You feel like you're being put out to pasture. But I still got a voice, and I've got more inside me now than I did when we had hits. Look at what I've been through, and what I've overcome, and what I have to offer to you now. What makes [the music business] think that it's over?"

But after she put together *Have a Little Faith* with Tullio's help, she again found herself met with indifference. She didn't have the resources or the know-how to self-release the music through the Internet. She was looking for a little infrastructure to help push her music. Labels listened and passed, others put her off. Anti- Records was interested but dragged its heels. Only Bruce Iglauer, the founder of Chicago blues label Alligator Records, expressed any immediate enthusiasm for the record.

"I was knocked on my butt—maybe that's not the right thing to say about an inspirational record," Iglauer says with a laugh. "At the end of the '70s, I was able to sign Albert Collins. I never dreamed of having an artist of that stature on Alligator. And the same is true of Mavis. I never thought this company would be good enough, big enough, powerful enough, or establish that level of reputation to have an artist like that on its roster."

Iglauer had specialized in blues artists at Alligator, but he also had ventured into reggae, Louisiana R&B, and zydeco in the '80s, issuing important albums by Jamaican artists such as Augustus Pablo and Pablo Moses and Louisiana greats Professor Longhair, Clifton Chenier, and Dr. John. He heard what Mavis was doing not as pure gospel but as a hybrid that would appeal to fans of the type of roots music that he valued. "The term we use for the music she's doing is 'inspirational,'" he said. "By the definition of gospel music on gospel radio—somebody like Kirk Franklin—this isn't it. Mavis talks about blues and gospel being first cousins. She's very comfortable with the blues because it's also soul-healing music."

In that sense, Mavis was making the kind of music that Pops had always envisioned for the Staple Singers—a style based in gospel tradition but flexible enough to inhabit different genres and attract an audience that had never been inside a church. The blues, folk, and soul voicings that naturally found their way into Pops's music were also embedded in Mavis's sound.

Mavis took the album on the road in 2004 and 2005 and wrung the songs dry. "God Is Not Sleeping" was a centerpiece of most performances, and with good reason.

"Since Pops's death, she's performed regularly, but not a great deal," Iglauer said in July 2004. "I think she may have felt after Pops's death, their mission was done. It was also a measure of her finding confidence as a solo artist. But I would see her in front of blues audiences, and she would get caught up in the performances. After 'God Is Not Sleeping,' people in the audience were crying. To call it artistry doesn't cover it. She swept us up."

For Mavis, those moments where the "Holy Ghost walks in the room" had been arriving since she was a teenager. "God Is Not Sleeping" awakened something in her that she hadn't felt since before Pops died.

"His death took something out of me," she said after one performance in 2004. "I think I was worried that I could never get past that. But that song, when we sing it at our concerts, I remember doing it at Telluride, looking out at the mountains, the trees, all the beauty, God's beauty. And I think, 'This is truly God's work.' He is still working. He is alive. I got caught up in that song. I lost it. I had to apologize to the audience, but when the spirit hits you, you got to let it go, you can't hold it in."

Mavis's little shot in the dark with Alligator Records did its job. *Have a Little Faith* enabled her to start touring regularly again, and in 2005, she appeared on the nationally televised Grammy Awards with a young star who grew up not far from where she still lives on Chicago's South Side, Kanye West.

"People had forgotten about her, but she invested in herself when there was no record deal," Bill Carpenter says. "The Alligator record was a good, decent record. It got reviewed well, and it put her name out there again. If you don't have a machine behind you—and the Staples never really had one—you do things to create buzz for yourself. She did. That CD was the basis of everything that came after."

40

"I'll be the history"

R y Cooder walked into Mavis Staples's high-rise condo like a star-struck kid entering a shrine. Mavis had picked him up at a downtown hotel after he flew in from Los Angeles, ushered him into the living room, and there it was—Pop Staples's amplifier. Cooder barely noticed the view outside—a vision of blue-gray Lake Michigan loveliness stretched out before the thirty-ninth-floor window. He reached down and touched the amp like a sacred object, then he plugged in the guitar he had brought along for the occasion. Out came a spooky, skeletal sound that sent a little shiver up Mavis's neck.

"He started strumming like Pops would do," she recalls. "The same chords, the tone. The sound, it was like, 'Pops, are you here?'"

Ry Cooder had worked with everyone from the Cuban musicians in the *Buena Vista Social Club* to the Rolling Stones in a career that stretched back to the '60s. He was particular about with whom he recorded, and he was particular about the way records should sound. He had a sound in his head, shaped when he was a boy growing up in Santa Monica, California, in the '50s and '60s, a sound articulated by Southern blacks on old gospel and R&B records. When Andy Kaulkin, the president of Anti-, invited him to produce the new Mavis Staples album, he embraced the idea immediately.

"The first gospel music I ever heard was in high school," Cooder says. "It was the Staple Singers. They had their albums on Vee-Jay, and 'Uncloudy Day' had a big impact on me. The sound and the harmony and the atmosphere and the mood, the guitar sound—a big impact. I always refer to that in my mind when I make records or play the guitar."

Mavis and her management, Dave Bartlett and Matt Cornell, were impressed with the way Fat Possum and Anti- Records had handled a 2002 album by soul great Solomon Burke, *Don't Give Up on Me*. Produced by Joe Henry, the album refreshed Burke's career by putting his deep-soul vocals in a contemporary setting, and brought him his first Grammy Award. Kaulkin thought Mavis was overdue for similar recognition. He had just finished reading *Walking with the Wind: A Memoir of the Movement*, by John Lewis, who had been at Martin Luther King's side during some of the civil rights era's most harrowing marches and rallies. The Staple Singers had been elemental in shaping the sound track for that era. What about going back to the source and recording some of the freedom songs that she and her family had performed countless times in the '60s?

The notion resonated with Mavis. She'd been horrified by the images from New Orleans in the wake of Hurricane Katrina in 2005, which left more than eighteen hundred dead and hundreds of thousands homeless.

"That hurt," she says. "When I saw Katrina, I started praying. People floating in that black water, people on the rooftops, and nobody going to help them. Man, tears were streaming down my face. Where is the help? Where is the government? You put thousands of people in a stadium [the makeshift New Orleans refugee camp in the Houston Astrodome] with no water, no food, and it's hot. Babies are up there. An old lady in a wheelchair, and they just covered her up. That hurts to see your race being mistreated and abused."

Her mind flipped through snippets of news footage in recent years, from the racist tirade by comedian Michael Richards to the forty-one shots fired by New York police at West African immigrant Amadou Diallo in 1999.

"It made me think of my father's song, 'Why Am I Treated So Bad?'" she said at the time. "I feel the Lord has kept me around for this reason. I'm sixty-seven years old and I was here the first time around and now I'm still here, and it's still not fixed. I'm here to let you all know that I'm still not pleased. We can't let Dr. King have shed his blood and died for us trying to get us our justice. We can't allow that. It's the twenty-first century. We should be ashamed of ourselves still allowing this to happen in America. We don't teach enough black history in the schools. But I'm the history. I'll be the history. The kids need to know. They need to know what we've been through. They need to know where we've come from."

Cooder understood the context and the singer. What he heard was an artist who was interested not in re-creating an era but bringing it forward. The guitarist is in many ways a musical scholar, and he approached what would become the *We'll Never Turn Back* album as if he were preparing to film a documentary.

"The first question I had was when you deal with these songs from the civil rights era, it's like military music, it's the music of soldiers, they need to be empowered quickly, they need to strengthen very quickly and go out and lay it all on the line," he says. "It's a catharsis that they go through. I was listening to Smithsonian recordings from the era, stuff recorded in little storefronts and meeting halls, prior to these marches and rallies, and it was very daunting. How do we do that? How do we jump-start that impulse forty years later in a recording studio? That's what I couldn't figure out."

The guitarist visited old country churches in Alabama to hear how the congregations sang. "It was very nice, and I could see an abiding faith, an abiding musical culture, but it was no longer about soldiering. We aren't soldiering anymore. People spend most of their time in shopping malls or working now, whereas this music was made for getting ready to do battle with cops and dogs and water cannon."

Mavis and Cooder had several conversations in Chicago about how to proceed before the recording sessions began in Van Nuys, California. "We decided to start with a list of songs and see where they led," Cooder says. "They break into two groups: the old songs, utilized by the move-ment, and the ones originated by the movement. Some we could carry forward."

Backing vocalists were important, as a way of evoking the sound of a community speaking its mind. Cooder heard a connection between the South African vocal group Ladysmith Black Mambazo and "what black community or church singing would've sounded like in the 1880s and 1890s—really old-time. You can't get that here now. Everything here has been changed and imprinted by modern tendencies, but not those guys. They still sound like people used to sound in their energy."

Kaulkin suggested assembling the Freedom Singers, who were part of the formidable Newport Folk Festival lineup in 1963 with the Staple Singers and Bob Dylan. Two of the original members—Charles Neblett and Rutha Harris—were still active, along with Bettie Mae Fikes, who joined the group later in the '60s.

"Those people, the three we had, they are soldiers, and still are sol-diers," Cooder says. "They walk in as soldiers, not as entertainers. They stand there the same way. The world has not changed that much for them. They still see that era vividly. I know Charles Neblett does, because I've seen the look in his face. He starts telling stories in the stu-dio and you look in his eyes and he's still seeing it. I guess you would if you saw the bodies dragged out of the river, all wired up, and heads cut off, and you'd been chained up in prison and a dog set on you, you'd still see this. They can deliver. It was motivational."

The air-conditioned Sound City Studio in Van Nuys where *We'll Never Turn Back* was recorded couldn't have been more removed from the dusty back roads of Mississippi that the Staple Singers and Freedom Singers once traveled. Some of the personalities involved hadn't seen one another in decades—Mavis thinks the last time she crossed paths with the Freedom Singers was at Newport. But one afternoon, she heard Neblett start to sing an old melody, and he was quickly joined by Harris and Fikes: "In the Mississippi River / Well you can count them one by one . . ."

The voices and words raised goose bumps on her arms. She had a vague memory of the song—the mournful, forbidding sound of it awoke memories—but she couldn't place it.

"What are you singing about?" she asked Neblett. "Who's being counted one by one and two by two?"

The song was written by one of Neblett's fellow Freedom Singers, Marshall Jones, after the 1964 slayings of three civil rights activists in Mississippi. During the forty-four-day search for James Earl Chaney, Andrew Goodman, and Michael Schwerner, dozens more bodies were pulled from the Mississippi River, many of them African Americans who had been bound, mutilated, and lynched.

Neblett's litany of "you can count them two by two" and "three by three" and "six by six" and so on becomes a bed of slow-burn outrage. Mavis solemnly narrates the drama as much as singing it. A back-porch trio of Cooder on guitar, Mike Elizondo on bass, and Jim Keltner on drums plays it equally stark and ominous. The small combo approach evoked the Muscle Shoals rhythm section on the Staple Singers' great Stax recordings, and some of the stripped-down sessions at Vee-Jay in the '50s and Riverside in the early '60s.

"In this music, if you play too much, if you start moving around and asserting yourself," Cooder says, "you get past the primal, that primal simplicity that Pops put before us."

Cooder's guitar playing is steeped in Pops's vocabulary of reverb and sparseness, with a shot of rock 'n' roll corrosiveness and urgency. On the traditional song "99 and $^{1}/_{2}$," Cooder and the band push the groove into a double-time march, and Mavis begins to improvise, urged on by Neblett, Harris, and Fikes. This is familiar ground, and she cuts loose: "Broken levees, lyin' politicians, runnin' through hatred, homeless babies . . . Freedom now! Freedom now! Freedom!"

She's spitting out the words, free-associating images. On "My Own Eyes," she and Cooder settle into a gentler, more contemplative framework at first. It begins with Mavis rolling back to the 1964 night when she and her family were handcuffed and marched into an Arkansas police jail, wrongly accused of robbing a service station.

"All right, Pops, it's been almost fifty years though, how much longer must it last? . . . Somebody please tell me, why, why are we treated so bad?" The song builds from its modest beginnings into a series of images that merge her country's history with her own—much in the way Pops once did during and between songs at Staple Singers concerts. "I wouldn't tell ya no lie," Mavis concludes with a wink. "I'll leave that to the politicians."

Spontaneity was built into the performances. Stories exchanged in the downtime between recordings became part of the songs, long-ago images hung in the air like ghosts. The freedom songs had been adapted and reinterpreted many times, much like blues songs, designed to shift with the times. "I'd take an old idea, do some rewriting, and give her a few more lyrics to chew on, a few more concepts to flesh it out, to give it more structure, more content for her to sing," Cooder says. "The soldiers in the day didn't need to say too much. 'We shall overcome' was enough. But we do. We need to embellish it a bit, make it more interesting. We moved ahead, brought it forward. She's certainly mindful of the Katrina topic and had a lot of feeling going for it. She had this one lyric based on her appraisal of that whole thing, and that brought it forward. We didn't want it to seem antique or to be a history lesson. We wanted to make it personal. And once she started testifying and giving this poetic recounting of her own experiences, we had that gas in the tank."

Mavis had been singing like that all her life onstage; the genius of "We'll Never Turn Back" is that it is the first Mavis solo album to fully embrace that improvisatory spirit.

"I've been in rehearsal halls with her where she does these twisty turns with her voice, holds a high note, and it makes your jaw drop," Bill Carpenter says. "And that's at sound check. So I'll ask her, 'Are you going to do that tonight?' And she says, 'I don't remember what I just did.' She was just making sure the band knew their parts. She was just playing around. She sings what she feels, and then it's gone."

Cooder was equally at home in a more spontaneous setting. "It's part of her expression and training, growing up in churches. It seemed to come naturally. Once she did it in 'Down in Mississippi,' I thought that's cool. Some of these takes are not even takes, they're run-throughs, practices, and she worked it out in the moment. It was always sort of telegraphed somehow. So you don't have to spell it out—verse, chorus, then you stop, and play. And if you did that every time, it would all start to sound the same. I didn't want that. I didn't want anybody to be too careful. I wanted her and the people in the room to be reacting and responding."

"I'll Be Rested," on which Mavis and Cooder share the writing credit, is essentially a eulogy, a list of difference makers in Mavis's life. She moves from civil rights activists, victims of racial violence, and spiritual leaders to the gospel singers who influenced her. Finally, she conjures "Papa Staples—and you got your guitar."

"She's always channeling Pops," Cooder says. "You begin to realize that Pops is close at hand for her, always. And it's very good, because his presence is something she can always depend on. On 'I'll Be Rested,' where she goes to heaven and sings with the departed sisters and brothers of gospel music, and all of sudden here comes Pops with his guitar, and the music stops—it's just great. It's a very real thing. In her life, it's a true fact that Pops is right there. He's gone, but not far."

41

Hope at the Hideout

While recording *We'll Never Turn Back* with Ry Cooder in Southern California, Mavis was scheduled to play a concert on July 20, 2006, at the Santa Monica Pier. The opening act was a blues trio led by guitarist Rick Holmstrom, who had previously accompanied Mavis at a quickie duo gig set up by her manager, Dave Bartlett.

"I look to stage right, and the promoter was making a sign for me to stretch: 'Fifteen more minutes,' and we do four, five extra songs before we finally get off," Holmstrom says. "While I'm playing, I notice a guy with big glasses at the side of the stage looking at me and giving me the thumbs-up."

After the extended set, Holmstrom walked off with his bandmates—bassist Jeff Turmes and drummer Stephen Hodges—and found himself in a backstage huddle with the promoter. Mavis's touring band was late arriving, delayed by poor weather back in Chicago. "We've got to do something," Bartlett pleaded with Mavis in her dressing room. What about having Holmstrom's trio play a few songs with Mavis until her band arrived?

"Do you sing any blues?" Holmstrom asked.

"No, I do gospel and soul," Mavis replied.

But they quickly found some common ground. Holmstrom knew

the chord changes for a few songs in Mavis's set, including "The Weight," "Freedom Highway," and "Will the Circle Be Unbroken." He, Turmes, and Hodges turned what could've been a train wreck into something credible until her band arrived to finish out the gig.

"It had me scared—it wasn't what I normally heard onstage," Mavis recalls. "But those guys were good, they could jam."

"We stumbled through some of the changes, but we got through it," Holmstrom says. "The guy standing off to the side with the glasses turned out to be Ry Cooder. When I got done, he tapped me on the shoulder and said how much he liked us. We're used to backing up blues singers: You follow the singer, fill in the holes, build up a song from scratch sometimes. They'll say, 'Do it in G' or stomp their foot, and you have to turn it into something right on the sound stage."

That brief encounter was the beginning of a longer-lasting relationship. Holmstrom's approach lined up perfectly with the type of record Mavis was making with Cooder, and it linked back to the Staple Singers' sound in their pre-Stax era—a sound defined as much by Pops's guitar as Mavis's voice. Holmstrom wasn't intimately familiar with Mavis's repertoire, but he was a big fan of Pops' guitar playing. "I was at a blues festival in the mid-'90s when this friend of mine told me that my playing reminded him of Pops Staples," Holmstrom says. "I didn't think of Pops so much as a guitar player but as a singer. But my friend turned me on to the Staple Singers' Vee-Jay stuff—he put all the 45s on a tape for me. And I would drive back from gigs playing them. It was great music for coming down after a gig: quiet, airy, not jarring. I became a Pops fan, and his sound started seeping into my own songs. That sparse tremolo sound was very appealing to me, and when I got the call from Mavis's manager, I broke out those tapes again."

With the release of *We'll Never Turn Back* in April 2007, and its raw, unfussy presentation, Mavis received more attention from critics and concert promoters than she had in more than a decade. She was being offered tour dates to showcase not just her classics but also the new material—the album would eventually sell fifty-nine thousand copies—

and she needed a band that could play in that style. Cooder didn't like to tour, so Bartlett invited Holmstrom to join Mavis on the road with his band and serve as her musical director. It was an overdue change in many ways. Since the late '70s, Mavis and the Staple Singers hadn't updated their sound as a touring act; their backing bands were suited for the supper club circuit, but to a younger audience they contributed to a feeling that the Staples were essentially an oldies act. Holmstrom, Turmes, and Hodges were a veteran trio—the guitarist had been playing in blues bands since the late '80s—but their approach had a lean, contemporary edge and toughness.

"Ry was playing some dangerous guitar on the album," Mavis says. "The band I'd had for twenty years couldn't play that way. I finally had to tell them good-bye. I told Ry, 'You made me change bands.' He'd been studying Pops for years, and I needed a band that could play in that style. Now I tell Rick, 'Pops is in your fingers.'"

By the spring of 2008, Mavis and the band had turned into a formidable live act. Her sister Yvonne went everywhere with Mavis, including the stage—she was one of three backing vocalists, and she served as a buffer against any hint of anxiety or discouragement.

"When Mavis started to perform again after Pops died, Yvonne was a big part of it," says Marty Stuart. "She needed to have a member of her family up there on the stage with her, because of the loss of Pops and the absence of Cleedi. Yvonne was always the quietest one. But she was the eagle eye that saw every move somebody would make before they made it. She could sum up somebody two seconds after they walked in the room. One time in Austin, we were rehearsing and I said, 'Yvonne, tell me about that drummer in your band.' And she'd say, 'He's new to us. Our old drummer called and wanted to be excused to work with someone else. When he came back, I said, "Oh, no, you're still excused."'"

Yvonne protected her family like a lioness, and with Pops gone she stepped up as Mavis's manager, adviser, and tripe buster. "She's a business gal, but she's also Mavis's closest friend," Stuart says. "She was a reluctant singer, but she knew Mavis needed her, so she sang with her every night onstage. When Mavis and Dylan did that old Jimmie Rodgers routine on that gospel record they did together, Yvonne's credit was 'encouragement.' I don't think it could've been said any better."

A new alchemy was happening in Mavis's stage presentation. Her family relationships had resettled and solidified in a way that made her feel at home again. Her reconfigured band held a sound that echoed what she knew and held dear, and yet pushed it forward. Her old friends saw the transformation.

"When I felt her rumbling that she was getting her mind right after Pops's death and getting steady enough to sing, I called her, I felt her coming back," Stuart says. "I look back to that scene that day that Mahalia passed the torch to her [in 1969]. I felt there was enough time passed, she had been through enough, and she was ready to take on her role. She was suiting up for her destiny, for the queenship of her destiny. A lot of people had come and gone, and it was Mavis's time."

Steve Cropper, who had produced Mavis's first stab at a solo album in the late '60s at Stax, saw a more assured and versatile artist than the one he had met four decades earlier. "We did a show in Los Angeles and I got to play behind her, and it was all there: the attitude, the confidence, the ability to entertain," he says. "She's found her niche. She wasn't scared anymore to be on her own. She always had the tools, and now she's doing it with an ease that was just brilliant."

Anti-'s Kaulkin wanted to capture that new dynamic in a live recording. They tried first at a concert in Denmark, but Mavis's voice was hampered by a cold. The next week, on June 23, 2008, they tried again, this time on the singer's home turf—at an unassuming but beloved blue-collar bar called the Hideout, inconspicuously tucked in a warehouse district off Interstate 94 on Chicago's West Side. The room held a little more than a hundred people, and the stage was only inches above the floor, barely big enough to hold Mavis and her half dozen musical accomplices. But the nearly claustrophobic conditions led to an intimacy and immediacy that made the performance and live recording one of the pinnacle musical moments in Staples history.

Live: Hope at the Hideout was recorded during the summer Barack Obama was running to become the first African-American president of the United States. The freedom songs on *We'll Never Turn Back* sounded more relevant than ever, and the band and Mavis had begun to reshape and expand them live.

The set served as something of a career overview, a mix of homespun tales, righteous anthems, and mournful hymns delivered without fuss or polish. "The stage was so small, we were really cramped, and we were playing really quietly. Oddly enough, it was more powerful because of that," Holmstrom recalls.

A terse treatment of Buffalo Springfield's "For What It's Worth" took Mavis back to the Staple Singers' pre-Stax era. Holmstrom's shivering "paranoia-strikes-deep" guitar spikes the tune with the appropriate tone of foreboding. The guitarist plays with a rhythmic drive that balances restraint and propulsion. Hodges and Turmes lag just a shade behind the beat, leaving plenty of space for Mavis and the backing singers to maneuver. There's a rumble in "Eyes on the Prize," "Down in Mississippi," and "Wade in the Water," and barbed-wire toughness in "This Little Light" that matches the call-to-march urgency in Mavis's voice.

"On My Way to Heaven" is performed at a near whisper, with Mavis and the backing vocalists modulating their voices brilliantly as the song winds down. Mavis even channels Muddy Waters's "how-how-how" at one moment, as if to wink at the godfather of Chicago blues in the afterlife that the song envisions.

Her rasp turns bereft on the gospel lament "Waiting for My Child." Accompanied only by Holmstrom's skeletal guitar, Mavis sings of a mother's heartbreak, at one point drifting off the microphone and singing to the room unamplified. On "Why Am I Treated So Bad," her father's civil rights anthem, the backing vocalists glide over the guitar as Mavis slips into a reverie about how Grandma Ware's moan kept the devil at bay. "Freedom Highway" rises to life over a snaking guitar riff and Hodges's hi-hat flurry, and segues into "We Shall Not Be Moved" and Mavis's recollection of a '60s protest rally in which she and her fellow marchers were arrested for trying to integrate a Southern diner.

The album closes with Mavis performing a snippet of "I'll Take You There," the song that pumped through the loudspeakers to cap many of Obama's campaign rallies that year. *Live: Hope at the Hideout* was released on November 4, 2008, the same day that Obama won the election.

That night, the president-elect addressed a huge rally in Grant Park, on the unseasonably balmy Chicago lakefront. "Even as we stand here tonight, we know there are brave Americans waking up in the deserts of Iraq and the mountains of Afghanistan to risk their lives for us," he said. "There are mothers and fathers who will lie awake after the children fall asleep and wonder how they'll make the mortgage or pay their doctors' bills or save enough for their child's college education. There's new energy to harness, new jobs to be created, new schools to build, and threats to meet, alliances to repair. The road ahead will be long. Our climb will be steep. We may not get there in one year or even in one term. But, America, I have never been more hopeful than I am tonight that we will get there."

It was an appeal that could've been made in 1965, the same year that the Staple Singers' "Freedom Highway" was written. Mavis reprised the song at the Hideout: "March up freedom's highway / March, each and every day." Now a black man stood ready to accept the oath of office as president of the United States, a huge task ahead of him. Who could have imagined this day back in 1965?

"I think I voted for the right man, said we shall overcome," Mavis sings, and then lets out a shattering howl. "Made up my mind / And I won't turn around." She hadn't yet arrived. But there was no letup from the drums, bass, guitar, and voices. She'd come too far to stop now.

"My mind is made up," a breathless Mavis says as the song ends, as if addressing the congregation at a Sunday church service. "And my heart is fixed. And I just refuse to turn around."

42

"You Are Not Alone"

Jeff Tweedy was among the fans who squeezed into the Hideout on that claustrophobic June evening in 2008 to see Mavis Staples perform. Andy Kaulkin and Dave Bartlett had approached him about producing the next Mavis album. The Wilco singer didn't have to be sold on Mavis; he was in awe of her voice and legacy. But he was there to check out the band and mull over ideas about how he might approach the music before he agreed to do the job.

"We were just meeting Tweedy before the show," Holmstrom recalls. "He was saying 'hi,' but I kinda blew him off because I was more concerned about the gig than recording a hypothetical album and hobnobbing with the guy who might produce it."

But the performance by Holmstrom and the band impressed Tweedy. He had briefly flirted with the idea of having Wilco back Mavis on the record, but the Hideout show changed his mind. Afterward he told Mavis, "That band is good for you. They leave you space." Now they needed some get-acquainted time. After their schedules cleared, Tweedy and Mavis agreed to meet in a Hyde Park restaurant not far from her home. On his way to the South Side, Tweedy had a flat tire and showed up late looking sheepish and apologizing profusely. Mostly he was doing a fine impersonation of a scraggly drifter wearing a hardware-store cap.

Mavis was amused and a little skeptical. "Is he shy or scared that he's on the South Side?" she thought. He ordered sweet tea and called Mavis "Ms. Staples." They talked for nearly three hours about their families and music, and Mavis felt relieved, then exulted. "He was so open," she says. "I felt like I knew this kid and could do something good with him."

Holmstrom was summoned from California to the Wilco Loft, the band's recording studio and clubhouse on Chicago's North Side, in October 2009 to brainstorm. Tweedy wanted to keep the record uncluttered, steeped in Staples tradition. He had about sixty of the family's vintage tracks loaded on his iPod and was listening to them in a continuous loop. After hearing Holmstrom play at the Hideout, Tweedy knew the guitarist would be a valuable studio ally.

"Mavis and I would talk about gigs at the hotel afterward while we were on the road together," the guitarist says. "We had been doing the freedom songs for a couple years, and it was a powerful show and a really smart record to make—timely. But she started to tire of doing that stuff over and over, and she wanted to sing something more uplifting."

Among the songs Tweedy wanted to track were a pair of old Vee-Jay-era Staple Singers songs that Mavis had begun to perform with backing vocalist Donny Gerrard: a minimedley of "Too Close" and "On My Way to Heaven." "Too Close" had been one of Pop Staples's signature performances, a gospel tune dipped in sultry Mississippi blues. Now it would help bring Mavis's new Tweedy-produced album into focus: Holmstrom's guitar kicks it off, Gerrard sing-speaks, Mavis joins him. Then come sixty of the most sublime seconds on the album, a little moment that tells you everything you need to know about the band and the chemistry they had developed with Mavis. Turmes's bass repeats four notes, tumbles into Hodges's drumroll and a Pops-like wash of echo from Holmstrom. Mavis enters steadfast in her determination to reach higher ground despite those who "scandalize—scandalize!—my name." She is supported by the backing vocalists—Gerrard, Kelly Hogan, and Nora O'Connor—who subtly ratchet things up from gentle encouragement to a more strident, but not overpowering, insistence.

Tweedy lit up as he watched, and nodded at Holmstrom. "That's it!" He went home for the holidays after the two-week December recording session with that epiphany on rewind in his head. It would be the benchmark for how the album should sound. "I Belong to the Band—Hallelujah" and "Creep Along Moses," two more vintage gospel tracks, had a similar feel, with the vocals cut live on the floor of the studio. "Everybody in the same room, leaning into each other, going for it," Holmstrom says.

"Mavis had to take these older songs from the world they were in and take them into now. Jeff recorded everything on tape, kept the sound really organic. He didn't want to get all modern and slick with Mavis, which matches the way we play: the grungy, gritty tones of Hodges, the dark midrangy bass tone."

At the same time, Tweedy encouraged Mavis to sing in a more conversational voice, instead of pushing her to the outer edges of her range the way Cooder had. "This was more the way I was singing with my family in the early days," Mavis says. "I was tired of bustin' down like I had with Ry. This took me back to the days when I was a teenager, and Pops would tell me to sing the song and not oversing it. He didn't like all those gimmicks. Sing from the heart. Tell a story. That's what Tweedy wanted."

Another gospel standard, "Wonderful Savior," was recorded a cappella with Mavis and the backing singers in the stairwell outside the studio huddled around a single microphone in the midst of a freezing Chicago winter, their breath creating vapor so thick it nearly obscured their faces. Mavis refused to venture out until everyone in the studio loaned her an article of winter clothing. Beneath piles of secondhand scarves and hats, and with Kelly Hogan's bear-paw mittens on her hands, she tried to pretend she was back on the living room floor with her family on the South Side.

"Usually when they call me to do backup vocals, everything is done," says Hogan, a versatile singer who has been working in bands since the '80s. "Nora and I didn't know we'd be singing with the band and Mavis.

Yvonne was on the couch in the kitchen watching the Food Network. We wanted her to sing with us, but she was like, 'Oh, no, it's okay, you go on ahead.' But she listened to everything. On some of the older gospel songs, we would be trying to get the phrasing right, and she'd say, 'You're singing that wrong.' We'd have the emphasis on the wrong syllable and she'd show us how to do it.

"Nora and I sing a certain way, and it took awhile to figure out how to attack the vocals and blend. First we had to get over being scared shitless, and we had to get over it without the help of pinot grigio. It's not a session where you drink wine. The band doesn't even cuss around Mavis. Mavis cussed one time, and the band just lost it. She came in too soon on a line instead of pausing, and she was like, 'Oh, shit!' And the band fell out. 'Yeah! Yeah!' Everybody laughing. It's hard to take yourself too seriously when there are puppies running around."

The Loft bustled with Wilco band members and their families popping in to glimpse the towering musical icon in their midst, all five feet of her. Children and pet dogs milled about. Homemade goodies like banana pudding complemented the catering that Tweedy had brought in every day. "Did Ry Cooder get catering?" Tweedy teased Mavis. Mavis walked around in her reading glasses, chewing on pickles and asking if "Tweedy Bird" approved of a take. While waiting to do a vocal, she might break into a few bars of a song that suddenly floated in from her subconscious. "Please, Mr. Custer, I don't want to go," she blurted out one day, suddenly channeling a 1960 novelty pop hit.

The conversational singing tone that Tweedy encouraged also led to a couple of performances that showcased a less celebrated side of Mavis's singing. On Randy Newman's "Losing You," the muted backing suited a vocal that rises barely above a whisper, as if she's talking to Pops. Numerous takes were attempted, but none topped the subtle drama and deep feeling of the first. Tweedy also tailored an original song for Mavis to sing, after asking her permission. "I have this title in my head—'You Are Not Alone'—and I want to write this song for you," Tweedy told Mavis as the recording session got under way.

When he finished the song, "the lyrics just melted me," Mavis says. The song is delivered with stately patience, piano and acoustic guitar providing a foundation, a celesta adding a twilight glimmer. Mavis doesn't oversell or oversing; she sounds like she's bending down to kiss a loved one's forehead.

"A broken home, a broken heart / Isolated and afraid / Open up, this is a raid / I want to get through to you / You're not alone."

In a few lines, Tweedy summed up what Mavis's life in music had been about.

"It's like you dream about her singing that song to you, and there I was standing next to her as she was doing it," Hogan says. "I always felt Chicago was too separated, unlike Atlanta, where I'm from, which is more mixed up. 'You are not alone'—everybody needs that song. I want to go door-to-door and say, 'Here you go.' That's a miracle song. I can't believe I got to be on that record."

43

"When the gates swing open, let me in"

As she had with *Have a Little Faith* and *We'll Never Turn Back*, Mavis took the *You Are Not Alone* album on the road and immediately made the new songs a key part of her set list. She was not a nostalgia or oldies act relying on decades-old hits like many of her '60s and '70s peers were; she was an artist with new stories to tell. In 2011–12, she was busier than she had been in decades, performing 169 concerts.

Mavis was playing the new songs before *You Are Not Alone* was even released in 2010. Three weeks after her seventy-first birthday, she performed at the Lollapalooza festival in Grant Park, a few dozen blocks up the lakefront from her Chicago home. It was a steamy August afternoon, but Mavis looked radiant in a white blouse. She opened with an a cappella "Wonderful Savior," a daring move at a festival headlined by Lady Gaga and drawing seventy-five thousand nongospel fans a day.

"I saw a few jaws dropping, a few eyes getting big out in the audience, like, 'What is happening?'" Mavis says. "I thought, 'Oh, Lord, maybe I made a mistake.'"

But pretty soon a raucous outdoor church service broke out in the middle of the rock festival. The enthusiasm escalated when Tweedy joined her band on acoustic guitar, but he stayed in the background as

Mavis went about her work, touching hands and taking charge. Her version of "The Weight" hit with anvil force, as she slapped her chest with her palms while roaring, "And put the load, put the load, put the load right on me." She'd turned the song from something a little mysterious and mystical, as originally performed by The Band, into a personal manifesto of resilience in the face of hard times. As Mavis finished, the son of her old Muscle Shoals friend David Hood, Patterson, was getting ready to start a set with his Alabama band, the Drive-By Truckers, across the field. But before he played a note, Patterson waved and shouted tribute "to the great, great, great Mavis Staples." Forty years earlier, Mavis had immortalized Hood's father and his bass solo in "I'll Take You There": "David, little David, I need you here, help me now." Now Patterson was returning the favor at Mavis's Lollapalooza inaugural.

The National Academy of Recording Arts and Sciences concurred with Hood's assessment. In February 2011, it presented Mavis with her first Grammy Award in Los Angeles. When *You Are Not Alone* was announced as the winner of best Americana album, Mavis had a hard time believing it. Though visibly shaken and with eyes glistening, she spoke with eloquence about carrying on her father's legacy. "You laid the foundation," she said of Pops, "and I am still working on the building." When she returned to her seat, all she could think about as she clutched her award was that she had forgotten to mention Yvonne, Cleedi, and Pervis in her remarks. A few days later in her living room at home, Mavis was still shaking her head about the oversight.

"Yvonne is the main one," she said. "She's the one that got me up. When Pops passed, I didn't think I could sing. And Yvonne came over here one day and she said, 'Mavis, you know Pops would want you up there singing.' She told me off. And that was all I needed. And then I got up and I did 'Have a Little Faith' and I've been going ever since. And when I went back to her at the Grammys she was smiling and she was happy for me. I apologized to her, but she said not to worry about it— she let me off the hook. But I felt that Grammy was as much about her and the family as it was me."

Yvonne accompanied Mavis when she traveled to Woodstock, New York, to visit her old friend Levon Helm at his home in June 2011. The Band's founding drummer had survived throat cancer and the loss of his voice in the late '90s, and was now singing again. His late-career renaissance included back-to-back Grammy Awards for the acclaimed albums *Dirt Farmer* (2007) and *Electric Dirt* (2010).

In lieu of extensive touring while he recovered his health, Helm had begun hosting regular "Midnight Rambles" at his barn, informal concerts modeled after the traveling medicine shows he had seen as a youth growing up in Arkansas. Local musicians and various guests—including Elvis Costello, Emmylou Harris, Dr. John, and Gillian Welch—turned the Rambles into events. But for Helm, the biggest event of all was having Mavis on the premises.

"In the early days of the Ramble, it was just a house concert for twenty people," says his daughter, Amy Helm, a member of the group Ollabelle and a frequent performer at her father's shows. "The first name we talked about was Mavis. It was her and [bluegrass musician] Ralph Stanley that he most wanted to play the Ramble."

Levon's property had an idyllic, backwoods vibe perfect for getting lost in music making. There was a pond, frequently visited by Levon's two beloved dogs, behind the barn. Mavis rehearsed with her band and Levon's group, which included guitarist Larry Campbell, who had played with Bob Dylan frequently for the previous couple of decades. During breaks, Mavis, Yvonne, and Amy Helm would break off and have long, animated discussions in the kitchen over tea. When the night of the Ramble arrived, Levon was beaming as he slammed the drums and sang harmonies off Mavis's left shoulder. Less than a year later, Helm was dead, leaving his old friend to carry "The Weight" alone.

"For him, Mavis represented something essential about American music," Amy Helm says. "It's not just her singing. She and my father were of a similar fabric as artists and people. What they're doing is on such another level than most people, and yet instead of making you wonder how you're ever going to make anything that powerful come out of your body, their talent never asks to be worshipped. Her singing is one of the heaviest things you'll hear, but it's completely inclusive. It lights everybody up. It makes people feel they're a part of something, like they're inside of a song with her."

The next summer, after Bonnie Raitt released her first studio album in seven years, she took Mavis and her band on tour. Mavis opened, and as was Raitt's custom, she homed in on a song that the two could perform together: "Will the Circle Be Unbroken," the Staple Singers standard. It became a centerpiece of their 2012 concerts. In an appearance on the *Austin City Limits* public-television program, the two singers dueted on the Randy Newman song "Losing You," from Mavis's *You Are Not Alone* album. Mavis had sung it in tribute to Pops Staples, and it resonated with Bonnie because her father, Broadway singer John Raitt, had died in 2005. The duet solidified a family bond that had been forged over the previous twenty years.

"I grew up in the world of R&B and blues artists, people like Sippie Wallace and Katie Webster, and through getting to know Mavis and Pops and their family personally I got to see another side," Raitt says. "The tenets of what gospel music represents, the idea of being inspirational, uplifting, political, encouraging people to do the right thing—'Keep your eyes on the prize,' as Mavis sings. There's not a lot of trash talking, cheating, drinking, or smoking in that world. There is a lot of lively conversation, playfulness, and friskiness, framed in a way that has no salacious side to it. There is no disparity between who they are onstage and who they are as people."

It was that integrity that translated when Mavis performed at Lollapalooza to an audience that barely knew who she was, that was there at least initially to see Jeff Tweedy strum his guitar in the shadows. They left talking about the singer who demanded "put the load on me" with a conviction that was unshakable, a purpose that moved through her and embraced the audience as she stretched her arms wide.

In 2012, singer-guitarist Alan Sparhawk and his band Low started spending time in Wilco's Loft studio while recording a new album with

Tweedy as producer. Tweedy was also working on his next album with Mavis, *One True Vine,* a sparse collection of mostly acoustic songs that included Low's beautiful hymn "Holy Ghost."

"I had been listening to them for years—Pops's guitar playing was so rickety and wobbly, like he was trying to play organ chords," Sparhawk says. "As a guitar player, his style is very engaging. But I can feel my frame shake and start crying when I hear Mavis sing. She's one of the masters, and yet so human, so accessible, you can hear her whole body coming at you. It's a precious, precious thing when a voice has been making those sounds for that long."

On a cold, gray day in March 2013, Mavis, Yvonne, and Pervis buried their sister Cleotha, her long battle with Alzheimer's finally over. As usual, the voices at Trinity United Church of Christ—Staple Singers HQ for decades—were raising the rafters in celebration of a life well lived, seventy-eight years with music and family at the center.

Dorothy Tillman, who had marched with Martin Luther King before moving to Chicago and serving as a South Side alderman for twenty-two years, spoke of first seeing the Staple Singers touring the treacherous chitlin circuit "when I was a little girl in Alabama."

"As we fought for the justice of black people, I saw a family—mother, brother, father, and sisters—take a stand," she said, wearing her trademark wide-brimmed black hat. "They gave a voice to the movement. Dr. King loved the Staple Singers." And then Tillman paused to look at Mavis, Yvonne, and Pervis, seated in the pew directly in front of her pulpit. "A lot of people don't understand the role you played in changing this country."

The congregation, hundreds strong, stood and cheered. During a time of lynchings, cross burnings, and intimidation, "Mavis and her family were there. Some were scared, but the Staple Singers came to Alabama and sang," Tillman said, her voice rising. "The Staple Singers told our story through song and music."

The family's old friend, the great soul singer Otis Clay, paid homage to his fallen soul sister. "I am coming, Lord, trusting in your word," he declared, "When the gates swing open, let me in."

Cleedi Staples's life in public ended as it began: in a South Side church with the sound of gospel music bringing people out of their seats. The choir sang "I'll Take You There" in final tribute. Mavis walked slowly out of Holy Trinity arm in arm with Yvonne and Pervis, greeting well-wishers. Their sister was gone, but their work was not yet done.

Acknowledgments

This book wouldn't have been written without the cooperation of the Staples family, and I am grateful that Mavis, Yvonne, and Pervis opened their homes, archives, and memories to me.

I've been given the opportunity to write about the Staple Singers many times in the *Chicago Tribune* over the last two decades, and to follow my heart in illuminating music that matters. A writer couldn't ask for a better set of editors and colleagues, including Geoff Brown, Scott Powers, Kevin Williams, Carmel Carrillo, and Leo Ebersole. They're pros who make me better at my job.

Jason Saldanha, Robin Linn, and Annie Minoff of *Sound Opinions* are not only talented producers, they are wonderful people who make "work" fun. Besides being a good friend, my cohost, Jim DeRogatis, also happens to be an inspiring journalist.

Joe Ward and Ashley Carman provided countless hours of research assistance, interview transcriptions, and patience. WTTW Chicago and the Rock and Roll Hall of Fame in Cleveland generously shared material from their archives.

I couldn't ask for a better agent, sounding board, and ally than David Dunton. Every writer should be so fortunate. Brant Rumble published one of my books for Scribner previously and immediately signed up this one. I can't thank him enough for his faith in my abilities and his acute eye as an editor.

My parents-in-law, Dan and Pat Lyons, have always let me use their beautiful home in Georgia as a writing sanctuary. My wife's aunt and uncle, Cathy and Denny Coll, delight in planning book-signing parties for me, which gives me incentive to write something worth celebrating. My parents, Len and June, have my books piled up on their coffee table at home, for all visitors to see. I'm proud that they're proud.

My daughters, Katie and Marissa, took interest in my writing when they were kids. Now that they're young women, they're writing themselves for their student publications. I swear I had nothing to do with it. Deb is not only my wife and best friend, she's the one holding it together with patience and love when the long hours threaten to get the best of me. Thanks again, Deb. We did it, together.

Discography

The best of the Staple Singers on record, arranged chronologically

The Best of the Vee-Jay Years. Shout! Factory, 2007. Just about everything the Staples recorded during their tenure at Vee-Jay Records in Chicago, 1956–61, is worth owning. These recordings hold the essence of the Staples' "down-home" sound, with its roots in Mississippi Delta blues and early gospel-quartet harmonizing: Pops Staples's skeletal, reverb-drenched guitar lines; the high harmonies of Cleotha; Mavis's earth-shaking contralto lead vocals. The album skims the surface. From "Uncloudy Day" to "This May Be the Last Time," it touches on many of the high points but it omits too many essentials to be definitive, including Mavis's virtuoso turn on "On My Way to Heaven."

This Little Light. Riverside, 1964. Out of print but well worth seeking out. The Staples' final album for Riverside is their hardest-hitting protest album, with the title song—a freedom-march anthem—and two terrific Dylan covers (Pops's withering scorn in "Masters of War" and Pervis's poignant take on "A Hard Rain's A-Gonna Fall").

Great Day. Milestone, 1989. This double-album anthology documents the Staples' transition into folk and protest music with the Riverside label in the early to mid-'60s.

Freedom Highway. Epic, 1965. The Staples mix gospel fervor with fierce protest music on their home turf, a concert at New Nazareth Church on Chicago's South Side. One of the best live albums ever made (though sadly out of print).

Freedom Highway. Columbia/Legacy, 1991. This compilation from the Staples' years at Epic Records, 1965–68, confusingly shares a title with their must-own live album from the same period. A few tracks from the live album mix with songs from the group's five out-of-print Epic studio releases, including Pops's classic "Why? (Am I Treated So Bad)" and their pop-charting cover of Buffalo Springfield's "For What It's Worth."

Be Altitude: Respect Yourself. Stax, 1972. The peak moment in the Staples' successful run at Stax Records, with the Muscle Shoals rhythm section putting the Southern groove in the classics "Respect Yourself" and "I'll Take You There."

The Best of the Staple Singers. Stax, 1986. All the hits and a handful of deeper cuts from the group's half dozen albums for Stax, 1968–74.

The Ultimate Staple Singers: 1953–1984. Kent Records, 2004. A two-CD overview of the family's evolution from gospel and folk to protest music and soul. Besides the masterpieces ("Uncloudy Day," "Respect Yourself") and megahits ("I'll Take You There," "Let's Do It Again"), the compilation presents music from the group's first recording session for United Records in 1953, deep gems ("Long Walk to D.C.") and idiosyncratic ones ("Solon Bushi," a traditional Japanese folk song), rarities (Pops's take on the folk standard "John Henry"), and strong latter-day cuts (a cover of Talking Heads' "Slippery People").

Pops Staples solo

Father Father. Point Blank, 1994. The family's patriarch won a well-deserved Grammy for his second Point Blank solo album in the '90s. The stripped-down production suits Pops's slow-burn style, especially "Jesus Is Going to Make Up (My Dying Bed)," "The Downward Road," and a remake of "Why Am I Treated So Bad."

Mavis Staples solo

Mavis Staples and *Only for the Lonely*. Stax, 1986. Mavis's two solo albums for Stax weren't huge commercial successes, but they rank with the best soul releases of the era. Mavis's devastating take on the Bacharach-David perennial "A House Is Not a Home" is definitive, and she vows to rise above on "I Have Learned to Do Without You."

The Voice. Paisley Park, 1993. Prince produced two albums for Mavis, and the second ranks with her most enduring work—personal songs delivered with Paisley Park funk.

We'll Never Turn Back. Anti-, 2007. Ry Cooder's no-frills arrangements and Pops-like guitar playing bring out some of Mavis's most spontaneous and richly evocative performances as she reinterprets the freedom songs that provided the sound track for the civil rights movement.

Live: Hope at the Hideout. Anti-, 2008. An extraordinary politically charged concert. The recording captures a visceral musical conversation involving Mavis, her excellent band, and a revved-up audience against the backdrop of a historic presidential election.

You Are Not Alone. Anti-, 2010. Producer Jeff Tweedy encourages a more conversational vocal approach, and it's a revelation, particularly on a cover of Randy Newman's "Losing You" and the Tweedy-written title song.

One True Vine. Anti-, 2013. Once again Tweedy produces, in addition to playing most of the instruments with his son, Spencer, on drums. The collaboration peaks with a simmering reinterpretation of Pops's civil rights anthem "I Like the Things About Me," with Mavis shaping "a brand-new image of the same old me."

Notes on the source material

T he story traced in *I'll Take You There* is largely based on interviews in 2011–13 with Mavis Staples, Yvonne Staples, and Pervis Staples. Mavis covered her family's history in multiple interviews that stretched past thirty hours. She also responded to follow-up inquiries via e-mail, and Mavis, Pervis, and Yvonne opened up their personal archives to me and provided numerous out-of-print albums that filled in the gaps in the Staples' extensive discography. In addition, I used material from three in-depth interviews with Mavis between 2004 and 2010, and several interviews with her father, Pops Staples, in the 1990s. Cleotha Staples, who died in 2013, was unavailable for interviews in recent years, but she was the family's most enthusiastic archivist, and her trove of photographs and newspaper and magazine clippings underpinned my research.

Mavis also gave me a rare copy of her father's 180-page unpublished memoir, *The Man, Message, Music,* written in the late '90s with Leah Ousley. In the memoir, Pops provides the most extensive information available on his life growing up in Mississippi and his first years in Chicago, before the Staple Singers became famous.

Dozens of interviews were conducted with family friends, band members, critics, producers, collaborators, and music industry figures, including Dave Bartlett, Al Bell, Jerry Butler, David Byrne, Bill Carpenter, Ry Cooder, Steve Cropper, Leroy Crume, Donny Gerrard, Amy Helm, Levon Helm, Kelly Hogan, Rick Holmstrom, David Hood, Jimmy Johnson, Terry Manning, Prince, Bonnie Raitt, Robbie Robertson, Jon Shields, Alan Sparhawk, Marty Stuart, Jeff Tweedy, Jim Tullio, and Phil

Upchurch. Critic and author Anthony Heilbut was particularly generous with his insights not only into the early career of the Staple Singers but also in providing context on the Staples' gospel influences. His book *The Gospel Sound* remains the definitive overview of gospel music.

The work of two journalists in particular proved invaluable. Rob Bowman's book *Soulsville U.S.A.: The Story of Stax Records* and his liner notes for the three-volume *The Complete Stax/Volt Soul Singles* boxed set remain the go-to source on all things associated with the label where the Staple Singers had their greatest commercial success. Dave Hoekstra has covered the family extensively in the *Chicago Sun-Times* over the last three decades, and he produced and cowrote a 2002 documentary, *The Staple Singers,* for WTTW, the Chicago Public Broadcasting Service outlet. The quotes from Bob Dylan and Jesse Jackson in this book are from that documentary.

Index

MAVIS STAPLES
IN CONVERSATION WITH GREG KOT

The following is an edited transcript of a live onstage interview on June 7, 2014, at the Printers Row Lit Fest, sponsored by the Chicago Tribune.

Greg Kot: Let's go back to the beginning with you. You're eight years old and your father is gathering you around and saying, "We're going to sing, children." And within a year and a half, your aunt Katie comes and says, "Let's go to church." How were your nerves going in front of that first congregation and singing in public, because you'd never really sung in public. You're this little girl, eight years old. How did you feel when that happened?

Mavis Staples: I wasn't nervous, I guess, because I was with Pops, with my family. I was very shy. I couldn't look out at the audience. I'd always look up at the ceiling when I was singing. But I felt good about it. I felt that people liked us and that made me happy. I never thought we would sing as long as we have, or we'd be famous, per se. But I just felt good. I felt happy. There were times when I was confused, because I would sing and they'd have to stand me on a chair or something so people could see where the voice was coming from. And I'd get confused because people would start crying and they'd walk around the stage and put money in my hand. I got home one day, and I asked Mama, "What did I do to hurt those people? People were crying." And she said, "Oh, baby, they're happy. You're making them happy. Those are happy tears that they're crying." And I said, "Oh, well they give me money." She said, "They want to give you something because they're so happy, they just want to put something in your hand." I used to put my money on the piano, and, when I got ready to leave, my money would be gone. So I told Mama, "The money that people gave me, it was gone."

GK: In the church?

MS: In the church. Right there in the church.

GK: Thieves in the temple!

MS: Thieves in the temple, I tell you, they're everywhere. So Mama started sewing little pockets on my dresses. She would sew these pockets on the side of my little dress, and I'd put my money in my pocket. So I was a happy child. Even at that age. You know how they say poor little Michael Jackson didn't have any childhood? I had my childhood. I would go to play. I didn't like to rehearse. Pops would tell us, "Okay, now, we're going to rehearse," and I would always be the last one coming to rehearsal. At one point he told us—my brother—I've got to back up. My brother, Pervis, he would sing the lead because his voice was very high, and I sang baritone. So one day Pops told me, "Now, Mavis, you're going to have to sing lead because Pervis can't get up there no more." For some reason the Lord blessed me, where I could sing high and low. I said, "Daddy, I don't want to sing that lead." I said I like background, I like the baritone. That's the prettiest voice in the background to me. And he kept saying, "Mavis, you have to sing lead. Pervis's voice is changing." It was puberty, you know, and Pervis couldn't sing up there. I kept saying no, no, no. But he had a little piece of a belt. He had cut it to about the size of a ruler, and he'd say, "Mavis, you have to sing." "No, Dad, no." He started reaching for that little . . . I said, "Okay, Daddy, I'll sing the lead." And from that time on, I sang the lead. I'd sing high and I'd sing low.

Pops had us on the floor. We would sing on the floor. Let me tell you how it always started. Pops used to sing with an all-male group, the Trumpet Jubilees. There were six of them, and these guys wouldn't come to rehearsal. Pops would go to rehearsal, there might be two of them there, might be three. One night he came home, and he was so disgusted, he went straight to the closet where he had a little guitar that he'd bought from the pawn shop. He called us children into the living room, sat us on the floor in a circle, and began to give us voices to sing that he and his sisters and brothers would sing when they were in Mississippi—fourteen of them, seven boys and seven girls. They had so many children, they ran out of names. When they got down to the last two, which was Uncle Sears and Pops, they named Uncle Sears, Sears, and Pops, Roebuck. They had 'em a Sears Roebuck in the family. So we would be singing these voices, and Pops would be teaching us. When we first started singing, people thought we were old. Because we would sing these old sounds and the old songs, and one night, my aunt Katie—she lived with us—she came through the living room and said, "Shucks, y'all sound pretty good. I believe I want y'all to sing at my church." And, Lord, we were so happy. We were going to sing someplace else than on the floor. We went to

Aunt Katie's church that Sunday. We sang this song, the very first song Pops taught us. We sang it, and people kept clapping us back. Well, we had sat down. We didn't know what clapping us back was. We didn't know what that meant, and somebody had to tell us, "They want y'all to sing again, baby." We had to sing that same song three times. It was the only song Pops had taught us all the way through. So Pops said, "Shucks, these people like us. I think we're going to go home and learn some more songs." The rest is history.

GK: You probably weren't even aware of this at the time because it was so natural. Pops brought together those four-part harmonies that he'd learned in the gallery, singing in Mississippi, and the guitar playing that he'd learned from Charley Patton. He was combining two styles of music that weren't supposed to go together. Duke Ellington saw you at a jazz festival in the early '60s, and he pulled Pops aside and said, "Pops, what you guys are doing is incredible. It's gospel in a blues key." And Pops said, "I think you're right, Duke. You got that right." Being in the middle of that, I guess it's hard to look at it from the outside, but did you know that you were unique, not sounding like any other gospel group at the time? Were you aware of that?

MS: No, Greg. We didn't know nothing. We were just singing. We liked what we were doing. We liked the sound that we had. But we didn't realize that our sound was unique from anybody else's. We were singing what our father taught us. Our very first record happened because this lady, [DJ and future Vee-Jay Records founder] Vivian Carter, was at church that Sunday when we sang—I didn't tell you that very first song he taught us was "Will the Circle Be Unbroken." She heard us, she called Pops, and said y'all need to be on record. Pops said, "Well, no, Vivian, I don't want my children to make no record. I don't know nothing about them records, and that business." So he waited, I guess it was maybe three years later. Pops had gotten books. He got Yvonne to read books, and she helped Pops learn about the business of music. People like Sister Mahalia Jackson, the Soul Stirrers, they would tell him different things. He learned it. And he called Vivian and said, "Okay, Vivian, my children can sing on your record now." We made this record, "Uncloudy Day." I was singing bass on this record. Everyone was singing down in harmony, "Oh, they tell of a home where no storm clouds will rise . . ." All of us singing down in harmony, and my part would be, "Well, well, well, oh, Lord, they tell me now . . ." And, man, that record. Vivian called Pops one day and she said,

"Staples, this record is selling like an R&B. I hadn't never seen nothing like this."

We started getting letters from everywhere, all over. Daddy said these people want us to come sing in Atlanta, Georgia; in Memphis, Tennessee; Durham, North Carolina. All right, well, we would go on weekends. Pops would go up to the school and tell the teacher, "Give Mavis some homework because she won't be back on Monday." All the concerts were on Sundays and we'd drive, then Sunday night we'd start driving back home. So we'd get to these places and the disc jockey had announced, "This is little [teenage] Mavis. This little girl is singing this part." Well, people didn't believe that I was a little girl. They would actually bet that that is not a little girl. That's got to be a man or a big fat lady. So people would tell us about it when we'd get to town, "People are betting, they're actually betting that she's not a little girl." I was a little skinny girl. What we would do, after we found that out, we'd fool them. We'd sing the song in harmony and just as my part would come, they'd be so busy watching to see and talking, and my brother would step up to the mic like he was going to sing it, and people would say I told you that wasn't no little girl. While they're going through all of that, I'm singing, "Well, well, well, oh . . . ," and, boy, we would have so much fun. One man came and told me, "Little girl," he was mad at me, "I bet my whole paycheck on you." Pops said, "You shouldn't bet." But, yeah, we had fun with that. I loved going on those trips on the weekend. I loved staying in the hotel. I could call downstairs and order me some breakfast, you know, room service.

GK: You were still going to high school at the time at Parker on the South Side. There's two Parkers, one on the North Side and one on the South Side.

MS: Mine was on the South Side, 69th Street.

GK: The South Side gets some criticism these days. It's obviously a violent area, a lot of parts of the South Side. The North Side, too, for that matter. But back then, when you were growing up on the South Side, born and bred on the South Side of Chicago . . .

MS: I still live on the South Side.

GK: That was a remarkable area. Remarkable talent. You mentioned Vivian

Carter. She ran a black-owned label, Vee-Jay Records. There were businesses, cultural institutions, bars, tons of artists, right in your neighborhood. You were around all these people. Do you ever look back and say, man, I was friends with Sam Cooke and Lou Rawls and Johnnie Taylor? Mahalia Jackson was basically your second mom. Tell us a little bit about what it was like growing up in the, what did you call it? What was the name you called it?

MS: We lived then on 33rd Street, and we called it the Dirty Thirties. I went to Doolittle Grammar School on 35th Street. Sam [Cooke] was at Doolittle, Lou Rawls, all of us, all of Sam's brothers. I was the baby. I was the youngest. Sam and my older sister Cleotha were the same age. But my brother, Pervis, and the doo-woppers, they were just like you read about sometimes. They would stand under that lamp pole in the summertime and just doo-wop, doo-wop, doo-wop. After a while, they started singing gospel. Sam had his group. Pervis had his group. Spencer Taylor had his group. And on Sundays this church, Hopewell Baptist Church on 35th Street, would let them sing. They named it the battle of the gospel singers. Pervis and Sam had these bangs, hair sticking straight up. Pops told them, "You don't get that hair back, I'm going to cut 'em off." That's when they started using Murray's hair pomade. They'd slick those bangs back, put a stocking cap on. My sister would be looking for her other stocking.

GK: So your father influenced fashion on the South Side, too? He did everything.

MS: That's right. But they would sing and they would be battling it out up in the pulpit, and nobody would be in this church but us children, and we'd be eating french fries and potato chips. Pervis and Sam, after a while they started yelling for the watermelon man. See back then . . . I'm telling you, Greg, I have been so blessed for what I have seen. I've seen the horse and wagon. I've seen stores leave a crate of eggs and chickens out in front of the store all night. Nobody would bother them. Sam and Pervis, they got on the watermelon man. The horse would be pulling the rag man, the coal man, the ice man, and the watermelon man, and I lived all of this. To have seen, from my day—like we always say, back in the day—Pervis and Sam would be yelling for this watermelon man, and all the ladies would come to the window. All of us kids would be running behind the wagon, because he would give us a plug of watermelon. And that was their job. The watermelon man paid them. Then Pervis had a snowball wagon and he would give credit to all the ladies. He would give their children snowballs, and he would have a little book, and he'd count it up.

GK: That's how he got their phone numbers? Pervis knew how to work the traffic.

MS: He turned out to be a pretty good player.

GK: I'd go to interview Pervis at his house, and every time he'd open the door, he'd say, "Here comes the man with all the questions." Pervis would say, "You know, I got some stories to tell. I'm not so sure I want to tell you." But the neighborhood, the talent that came out of there, it's just mind-blowing, the fact that you were in the middle of all this.

I want to take us a step forward, because the '60s were a remarkable decade for the family and for you. A lot of people don't realize, when Martin Luther King Jr. gave his speech on the March on Washington, the "I Have a Dream" speech, music was such a huge part of that day. Mahalia Jackson was there and Bob Dylan was there, Joan Baez. This melding of the folk and gospel movements symbolized that day. You were close family friends with Martin Luther King. What's your fondest memory of meeting Dr. King, and what was it about his personality that maybe people don't know about? They heard him in public and he was always so authoritative and passionate, but what about the King that you knew?

MS: You could feel Dr. King. You could feel his humbleness. He wouldn't talk to us girls a lot. He and Pops would talk all the time, but he would mostly say, "How you girls doing this morning?" We'd come down for breakfast. "How y'all doing?" We'd say, "Oh, fine, Dr. King." He'd always want to shake your hand. But what I've kept, what I hang on to, is Dr. King's laughter. Because most of the time I'd look at him, he would either seem sad or serious, the look on his face a lot of the times. We'd be leaving the motel. All the men would be down in the parking lot in a huddle, and all of the sudden they'd break out laughing, and I'd hear Dr. King. His laughter. That'd make me feel so happy because I felt like Dr. King was happy. He was a man that you just marveled over. I would just look at him.

When we first met him, Pops knew Dr. King from the radio. We happened to be in Montgomery, Alabama, one Sunday, and Pops called us girls to his room. He said, "Listen, y'all, this man Martin is here and he has a church here. I would like to go to his eleven o'clock service. Do you all want to go?" We said, "Yeah, Dad, we want to go." So we went on down to Dexter Avenue Baptist Church. We were ushered in and seated, and someone let Dr. King know that we were at the service, and he acknowledged us. He said, "We're glad to have Pops Staples and his daughters here this morning, and we hope you enjoy the service." Well, we enjoyed the service. Dr. King would stand at the front door as the worshippers filed out, and he would shake everybody's hand. Us girls shook his hand first, and Pops, when his turn came, he stood there and talked to Dr. King for a little while. We get back to the hotel and Pops called us to his room again. He said, "Listen, y'all, I like this man's message. I really like his message, and I think that if he can preach it, we can sing it." And we began writing freedom songs: "Freedom Highway" and "Why? (Am I Treated So Bad)." "Why? (Am I Treated So Bad)" was Dr. King's favorite, and he'd always tell Pops, "Stape"—he called Pops, Stape— "you're going to sing my song tonight, right?" And Pops said, "Oh, yeah, Doctor, we're going to sing your song." Dr. King was just a great man.

The last time we saw him, he was in Chicago and he wanted Pops to meet him at a South Side restaurant. He wanted to talk to Pops about something. So Pops took me and Yvonne and my mother, all of us went up there. Coretta was there and we talked for a while, and then Dr. King started telling Pops what he wanted. He said, "You and the girls, people in Chicago know you all. Now Jesse Jackson is about to move to Chicago, and I want him to have a Saturday morning show, a meeting every Saturday morning, and I want him to call it Operation Breadbasket. I want him to have big baskets where people can bring food and drop it in these baskets. Now I want you and your girls to go. I want you to sing because, if they announce on the radio that you all will be there, the people will come out. They don't know Jesse Jackson." Pops said, "Yeah, Doctor, we'll do that," and we did, for many Saturday mornings until it got to where people were coming on Jesse's name. We had to get back to our world. And Jesse Jackson, he changed it from Operation Breadbasket to Operation Push. I didn't like that. I felt like Dr. King named it Operation Breadbasket for a reason. All of that had changed. There were no more baskets. It was just Operation Push. I don't know what Operation Push is about today, but they still have it. But I didn't like that. I didn't like that he changed it from Operation Breadbasket to Operation Push.

GK: Well, I think a lot changed when King died in '68. The ship was kind of rudderless at that point. But I was interested in how important King's influence was to your family. You mentioned writing the freedom songs, and, for a family that came up through gospel, that wasn't necessarily an easy thing to do. I think Pops had a real vision. He was able to write those kinds of songs even though he was a strict gospel man, and there were a lot of gospel people who were saying, "This isn't pure gospel music anymore. Pops, what are you doing?" Do you remember some of that conflict or tension, and how did your father handle that sort of pressure?

MS: Yeah, Pops was going to do what he was going to do. He felt like we needed to be in this movement, and we were doing what we were supposed to be doing. We were singing songs. It wasn't that we were singing garbage. Pops used to tell the songwriters, "If you want to write for the Staples, read the headlines. We want to sing about what's happening in the world today, and if it's something wrong, we want to try to sing a song to fix it." He was steadfast in what he wanted to do. Some of the people wanted to put us out of the church. "The Staple Singers are singing the devil's music!" We did so many interviews. I would tell the people, the devil ain't got no music. All music is God's music, and we're singing songs to help with this movement. It turned out that the songs that we sang were the soundtrack of the civil rights movement. Congressman John Lewis told me, "Baby, you're family . . ."—I was so glad he remembered me. I went to his office to ask him to write the liner notes for the freedom CD [*We'll Never Turn Back* in 2007] that I made, and he told me, "Yes, I'll write your liner notes. Your family kept us motivated. Your songs that you always sang kept us going." He said, "You just let me know when you need these liner notes." I saw Congressman Lewis when I went to the Civil Rights Summit back a couple of months ago, and everybody was there. Andrew Young, Vernon Jordan, and . . .

GK: A lot of people in the original movement who were there from the ground floor.

MS: Dr. King's baby daughter was there, Bernice, and Bubba Clinton.

GK: Bubba Clinton? You refer to him as Bubba? Well, you're on a first-name basis with Bill because you sang at the White House, so why not, right?

MS: Right, we sang for his inauguration. We sang for Kennedy's inauguration. That's how old we are.

GK: That's a beautiful sentiment, and I want to amplify some of what you just said, because when you talk about being on the front lines of the civil rights movement, people don't realize . . . It was really brought home for me when your older sister Cleotha died. They had a beautiful funeral for her on the South Side, at the church [Trinity United Church of Christ] that you've been at forever. Former Chicago alderman Dorothy Tillman gave an incredible eulogy. She was in Alabama as a part of the movement. She was working for King in the early '60s and she was looking at Mavis and Yvonne and Pervis right there in the front row and saying thank you for what you did for us, because you were the only group that didn't just play the big cities, Memphis and Jackson, and get out of the South. You were playing the churches and the little town that nobody else wanted to go to. She said you gave us hope in the middle of this. You would come in and sing. And it was treacherous. It was just Pops driving. You would drive a little bit once you got old enough. It was just the family. No security, nothing, and it was amazing, in some ways, that you got out alive.

MS: Now that's right. That's the truth. Because Pops was bold and brave. Pops would tell us stories about when he was a boy. He conditioned us before we started going in the South. Our records were hot in the South first, and Pops, he'd be driving, and he'd say, "I'm going to tell y'all, everybody don't like you. Everybody is not going to be friends with you in the South. So, you all be careful." One time Daddy told us, and I was so glad he told us . . . Yvonne and Cleedi [Cleotha] and I were going shopping in Jackson, Mississippi, and Pops said, "All right now, you all go on, go down there shopping, but don't start nothing." But then in the next breath, he said, "Don't take nothing, either." And lo and behold, it happened. We went in this store. We saw these shoes in the window that we wanted for the stage. We go in and Cleedi, she was the oldest, so she was our leader. We let Cleedi do all the talking. She said, "We like that shoe, do you have . . . ?" She gave them all three sizes, and the lady came out with all three sizes. Cleedi said, "Well, we better try them on." When she said that, the lady said, "Well, hon, if you want to try them on, you have to go behind that curtain over there." The curtain was an old raggedy sack hanging there, and Cleedi said, "Well, we can't take these." The lady said, "Y'all don't live here, do ya?" And Cleedi said,

"Yeah, we live here. We've been living here all our lives." She said, "We live on Church Street." She wasn't going to say, "Oh, no, we're from Chicago."

I'm telling you, Greg, I was so glad to see those "colored only" signs come down. Bathrooms, water fountains—man, we got stuck out on the road one Thanksgiving. Normally people invite you to dinner, but this particular time nobody invited us to dinner. That's when Pops said, we'll never be away from home again on Thanksgiving. We went in a store and got us some cold cuts and bread, and made us some sandwiches, and we parked on the side of the road. Well, it just happened, this cow was staring me down. I said, "Daddy, the cow don't like it 'cause we're sitting here." The cow wouldn't stop looking at me. I looked at the cow, and I said, "Daddy, we got to move, that cow, he's going to charge in a minute." And the killer was the cow was black and white. I said, the cow's already integrated.

GK: The cow was mad he wasn't invited to Thanksgiving dinner anywhere, either.

MS: He was mad, too. So, yeah, we had some times. We had some times that were pretty frightening, but we weathered the storm. We went on. We were determined we were going to sing our songs, we were going to go on down in the South and march. One day, us youngsters, we took off marching. We didn't have any of the older people with us. We were just marching and singing, marching and singing, and somebody yelled out, "Let's get something to eat." So we stopped in this restaurant. The waitress, when we went in, she went in the back. And we sat there and waited until she came out again. When she finally came out, she told us, "Y'all get out, we don't serve your kind." We just sat there, and we sat so long, looking at each other and talking. And she finally came out again. She said, "Y'all get out. I'm going to call the police." And, lo and behold, we heard the police coming. When we heard the police coming, we locked arms like we do, and we started singing this song: "We shall not, we shall not be moved." And the police got us on out of there. I told them, we better not try this no more, without the grown-ups. We almost got put in jail. We couldn't sit in restaurants. We couldn't stay in hotels. A lot of the families that had big homes would have tourist homes, and we would stay in tourist homes. The Lorraine Motel, that was the first black hotel where we could stay. We couldn't stay anywhere else in Memphis. We couldn't go to the movies unless we sat in the balcony. And Pops, we went all the way to South Africa. Johannesburg.

GK: This was in the '70s?

MS: In the '70s. Pops went over to the theater and he found out that they wanted the blacks to sit up in the balcony, and Pops told the promoter, he said no. He said, "No, I'm not gonna let my children sing like that." He said Dr. King had just gotten all that mess straightened up in the States, so we're not gonna come over here and sing like that. So you send us home, do what you gotta do, but we're not singing with the blacks sitting in the balcony. They moved our show to Soweto, the soccer stadium, and, Greg, that was the very first time blacks and whites sat side by side in South Africa. You saw police walking around with German shepherds, thinking there was gonna be some trouble. It was peaceful.

GK: Forty thousand people were in the big outdoor concert. And it was because Pops put his foot down and said we're gonna go home. We're not gonna play. There probably would have been a riot if he hadn't played.

MS: So many people were happy to see us. Black and white. And, Greg, what killed me in South Africa, every other lady you walked into, her name was Mavis. I don't know one other Mavis over here.

GK: They must've been making babies listening to Staple Singers songs. You didn't know that you had these great uses for your music.

MS: Men would come up to me, "My daughter is Mavees. My wife is Maveeees." Only other Mavis I know is Jay Leno's wife, Mavis.

GK: We have a few other things we want to talk about. One, your biggest fan, Bobby Dylan. Yvonne loves to refer to him as Bobby, my friend Bobby. We mentioned this whole thing about folk and gospel coming together in the '60s. I think it was very symbolic. You saw it at the Newport Folk Festival in '63. You saw it at King's "I Have a Dream" speech in DC. Dylan was a huge gospel fan, particularly of the Staple Singers, before he even saw them in person. Growing up in northern Minnesota, he would listen to the gospel stations and he would hear Mavis's voice. He would hear Pops's guitar. And it was the most powerful sound he'd heard. So Bob knew about you guys well before you knew about his existence, and the Staples—again showing Pops's visionary approach to music—were the first group outside of the folk community to cover Dylan's songs. Very early on you were on Bob's mind. And obviously Bob not only liked your music. He really liked you, Mavis.

Jeff Tweedy, who has produced the last couple of Mavis records, was on tour with Dylan a year ago. And Tweedy was a little intimidated. So to break the ice he says to Dylan, "By the way, Mavis says hi," because he knew that Pops knew Dylan. And Dylan turned to him and said, "Tell Mavis she shoulda married me back then." I still think he's holding a torch for ya. How about you, does it go both ways?

MS: Well, I often wonder, had we gotten married and had kids, would they be Dylan-Staples, or Staples-Dylans.

GK: You would've made some beautiful music together.

MS: Yes.

GK: The other thing I wanted to get into, because we're covering a lot of ground in a short amount of time: You basically reinvented yourself in the past ten years. I can't think of a musical career that has had what you've incorporated, basically being a part of three or four musical movements in different decades. And that was tough, a huge step, to become a solo artist after Pops died. Now tell me, when Pops died in 2000, that was an end for you in some ways. It was very difficult for you to even think about playing music at that time, right? How did you get yourself out of that?

MS: Yvonne did it. My sister. I was just pitiful. I'd sit down on the couch and couldn't get up. I didn't know what to do. I was just empty. You know, my father is gone. I had been with my father every day for the last fifty years, singing together, always together, and I didn't know what to do. Pops left me, and I still don't know what key I sing in. He would just start hitting the guitar and I'd start singing. I never knew any of the keys. So Yvonne, she came by my house one day and she looked at me and she said, "Mavis, what are you doing? What are you doing? You get up. You know Dad would want you to keep singing. Pops would want you to keep singing.

You can't do this." She said some words to me that I can't repeat. She told me off. And I looked at Yvonne and I knew she was right. When she said, "You know Pops would want you to keep on singing, Mavis," I got started. I started calling record companies. All these record companies we had been on. We had been on Warner Brothers, Epic, Columbia, and Universal. Everybody turned me down. Everybody said no.

So I said, well, if they don't want to record me now, I'm gonna make my own record. I went to the bank, got money out of the bank, and I met up with this guy, Jim Tullio. He had a song that he wanted me to sing for two of his friends that he lost in this tragedy in New York. And the song was called "In Times Like These." He called Yvonne, and she said, "Mavis, this man said that Levon Helm told him that you're the only person who could sing this song." So I said, "Tell him to fax the lyrics over," and I started reading the lyrics, and the lyrics fit me like a glove. I said, "I want to sing this song for him." After we finished that, that's when he asked me what was I gonna do. I said, well, I'm trying to make me a record. I said, I've been putting some songs together, but all of the record companies are gone. Curtis Mayfield, his record studio is gone. So Tullio told me, "I have a little makeshift studio at my home in my basement." He said, "I can help you." He lived in Winnetka. And so Yvonne and I started driving there every day. And I started enjoying it. It started coming together. I started getting more money out of the bank, for different musicians and different background singers and whatnot, so now I got it together, this record, and I'm gonna shop it now. Now I can let the record companies hear what I got. Well, they still turned me down. And just as I was about to start selling the new record out the trunk of my car . . .

GK: Which is where the family started.

MS: Sure did.

GK: Back in the '50s.

MS: Pops had a label, you know. Pops was smart.

Bruce Iglauer came through. I said, well, that's a blues label. But I'm going with Bruce Iglauer. And he took the record. The name of the record was *Have a Little Faith*. Which I had. I had a lot of faith. I knew that if the people could hear this record, and, lo and behold, Bruce Iglauer got that record going and another record company picked me up, Anti- Records. And that's when I got with Jeff Tweedy, I won a Grammy—the first one I won—and even the second record we made with Jeff Tweedy was nominated for a Grammy. And I said, "Shucks, ain't no stopping me now." I was so glad to get that Grammy. Pops had told us with "I'll Take You There," we were supposed to get that Grammy [in 1973]. We had these long faces, and he said, "Listen, I don't want y'all worrying about not getting a Grammy. A Grammy, that's an award. You're all singing for your just reward. And you'll get that one day. So don't be feeling bad." So I always remember what Pops said. I never cared about a Grammy. But for some reason I wanted to win this Grammy. I think it was because of all the work that I had done to get myself going again. And I talked to Pops, I said, "Daddy, I know what you told us. I haven't forgotten what you told us about this Grammy. But, Daddy, don't pay me no mind. I wanna win this Grammy this time."

GK: Well, your speech that day was beautiful at the Grammys. You basically talked about Pops instead of yourself. And your family. It's interesting, a few years ago, we did an interview around the time of *We'll Never Turn Back*, the record that you did with Ry Cooder, which, by the way [to the audience], if you don't have that record you should have that record. It's an amazing record that Mavis released in 2007.

You were basically going back to an era when these songs were in the air, and recontextualizing them and bringing them forward and talking about today. Those same songs still resonate today. And I was saying, Mavis, it's amazing. You're performing these songs to an audience that probably wasn't even born when these incidents were happening, and I said, "What about the history?" And you said, "I'll be the history." And that's what you're doing right now. You're carrying forward that Pops legacy. And that seems to be the motivating force here. Martin Luther King's message and Pops's message still need to be heard.

MS: I'm still here. And, yes, I get so surprised when I look in the audience and see all these young people, whole new generations, and they want to hear what I have to say. And it feels so good, Greg, because I'm sitting there, and they're waiting to see what I'm gonna do, where I'm coming from, and it makes me feel so good. I'm just about the happiest old girl in the world.

About the Author

Greg Kot is the music critic at the *Chicago Tribune* and the cohost of the nationally syndicated public-radio show *Sound Opinions*—"the world's only rock 'n' roll talk show." His books include *Ripped: How the Wired Generation Revolutionized Music* and *Wilco: Learning How to Die.* He lives in Chicago with his wife and two daughters.